POTPOURRI OF
POULTRY
& SEAFOOD
FAVORITES

BENGALI CHICKEN WITH BLACK-EYED PEAS, recipe on page 37.

Favorite Recipes® of Home Economics Teachers

©Great American Opportunities Inc. MCMLXXXV
P. O. Box 77, Nashville, Tennessee 37202
Library of Congress Cataloging in Publication Data on page 126.

Dear Homemaker,

"**Poultry & Seafood Favorites**" seems almost too small a title for a cookbook that includes such a large selection of foods and an even greater collection of truly delectable recipes.

If you depend on chicken dishes for menu planning, love to cook turkey, and are always on the lookout for a new way to prepare your favorite freshwater fish or seafood, this is a cookbook you will use again and again. There are also recipes for game birds and waterfowl! Plus, you'll find informative introductory reading and charts to further ensure your poultry and seafood cooking success and enjoyment.

If you're already familiar with Home Economics Teachers' cookbooks, you know you are in for a treat. In any case, you'll quickly find you have a cookbook filled with dependable, home-tested, family-favorite recipes. Enjoy!

Mary Jane Blount
Managing Editor

Advisory Board

Favorite Recipes Press wants to recognize the following who graciously serve on our Home Economics Advisory Board:

CHARLOTTE BOYETTE
Past President, New York State
   HET Association
Fairport, New York

SANDRA CROUCH
Home Economics Teacher
Sparta, Tennessee

PAULA HARTSFIELD
Director, Home Economics Education
Missouri Department of Elementary
   and Secondary Education

MARILYN BUTLER
Vocational Home Economics Teacher
Midwest City, Oklahoma

KATHERINE JENSEN
Home Economics Teacher
Brigham City, Utah

FRANCES KING
Supervisor, Home Economics Education
Georgia Department of Education

CAROLYN KRATZ
Supervisor, Home Economics Education
Pennsylvania Department of
   Education

SUE SMITH
State Specialist, Home Economics
   Education
Alabama Department of Education

Contents

Poultry & Seafood, Versatile, Creative —
  Perfect for all Occasions! 4
Seafood Availability Chart 8
Fish Cooking Guide 10
Seasonings for Seafood 11
Poultry 12
Game Birds 52
Seafood 66
Herb and Spice Chart 116
Cheese Chart 118
Equivalent Chart 120
Index 121
Order Information 127
Order Form 128

CANARD CONCORDE, recipe on page 57. FRIED SHRIMP WITH CURRIED CONCORD DIP,
recipe on page 111.

⚜ Poultry & Seafood ⚜

Versatile, Creative – Perfect for all Occasions!

Light, lean, versatile and delectable – these are the qualities that make poultry and seafood today's choice foods. They're perfect for the creative gourmet and for the practical weight watcher, as well as for the budget-minded homemaker!

Poultry and seafood are nutritious, too. High in protein, low in calories, and full of flavor, both represent a wide selection of different foods. That's good news for the meal planner, because it means that both can be served often, but in a host of different ways! Baked, broiled, grilled, chilled in salads and more, poultry and seafood in the menu mean variety and good taste that all ages will enjoy.

You can make the most of poultry and seafood when you know when to buy, which cuts or types are best for the recipes you like, and how to cook your choice to perfection.

POULTRY & GAME BIRDS

Poultry is a perfect entree for any occasion, including elegant dinners, casual buffets, family meals or friendly picnics. The many varieties of poultry offer a wide array of flavors to choose from, all delicious!

Chicken is the most versatile of the poultry family. Its adaptable flavor makes the cook's job both easier and more rewarding. Turkey is another popular poultry because it is bred to provide lots of succulent white meat, is economical, and is full of flavor.

When buying chicken or turkey, choose one with a good fatty layer for tenderness. It should have short legs, plump body and unbruised skin. Whole birds and cut-up parts are both available ready to cook and are equally economical. Specialty cuts, such as deboned breasts, are naturally more expensive. However, they're all meat and perfect for certain recipes, such as "Chicken and Artichoke Hearts" and "Crab-Stuffed Chicken," which makes them worth the extra cost for special occasions.

Poultry stores well both in the refrigerator and the freezer. Before storing, however, poultry should be removed from the store packaging, washed (remove the giblets), and patted dry. For **refrigerator storage**, cover the chicken well to prevent moisture loss. Store giblets only for up to 24 hours and whole poultry for two to three days.

For **freezer storage**, wrap the poultry in vapor moisture-proof paper. Whole chickens may be frozen for up to one year; and chicken pieces for up to six months. Never freeze poultry with stuffing inside.

To freeze cooked poultry, remove the stuffing first. Then, remove the meat from the bones. Never freeze a whole cooked and stuffed bird. Cooked poultry meat keeps up to two months in a home freezer or two to three weeks in the refrigerator's freezer compartment. Chicken will thaw overnight in the refrigerator, while a whole turkey may take one to three days, depending on its size.

Game birds include land birds such as quail, grouse, dove, squab, wild turkey, pheasant, and waterfowl, such as ducks and geese. Before storing, most game birds must be cured in a cool, dry place for the aging and tenderizing of the meat. As a general rule, younger birds are hung for a few days and older birds for a week or more.

Once cured, game birds can also be frozen before cooking, following the same procedures as for poultry. Freezing also helps to age and tenderize wild fowl. When ready to cook, thaw the bird slowly to preserve moisture, preferably in the refrigerator. Allow five to six hours per pound in the refrigerator or two to three hours at room temperature. Cook immediately, and do not refreeze.

STUFFINGS FOR POULTRY

Typically well seasoned and starch based, stuffings (or dressings) are flavorful accompaniments to both poultry and fish, as well as to a host of other foods. The dressing can be baked in a separate pan, in alternating layers with the food being cooked, or used to fill a food pocket or cavity.

Stuffing poultry and game birds is economical, improves their appearance and flavor, and prevents natural food juices from escaping. Dress richly flavored poultry, wild fowl or fish with a simple fruit stuffing. Orange, apple, or prune stuffings are best for ducks and geese, while wild rice is a good base for stuffing smaller wild birds. If you don't prefer a dressing, placing an apple, celery or onion in the cavity helps to absorb fat and cut down on gamy flavor.

When using a dressing, allow one cup per pound of meat or fish. Use dressings soon after preparation. They can be prepared one day in advance and stored in the refrigerator, but no longer. Fill food pockets and cavities lightly, as stuffing absorbs juices and expands as it cooks. Onions, shallots, or garlic should be sauteed before being combined with the bread and liquid. Favorite dressing additions include precooked sausage or pork, clams, oysters, and mushrooms, plus herbs, raisins, chestnuts, olives and more.

Cooked dressings may be stored for two to three days in the refrigerator and should be removed from the food cavity before storing. Dressings do not freeze well.

CUTTING UP A CHICKEN

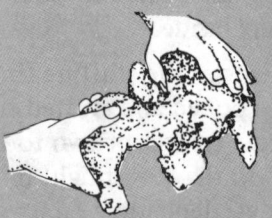

To separate drumstick from thigh, hold leg in both hands and bend to crack joint. Cut through joint.

Place chicken, breast side up, on cutting board. Pull one leg away from body and slice through skin between leg and breast.

Lift chicken and bend back leg until hip joint cracks. Remove leg from body by cutting close to body through hip joint. Repeat with other leg.

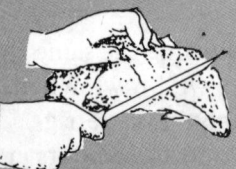

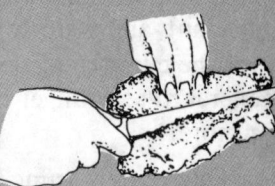

Divide breast lengthwise in two by holding it, skin side down, and bending it back to snap the breastbone.

Remove each wing by bending it back and cutting through joint.

Place carcass on one side. Cutting from leg joint with poultry shears or kitchen shears, cut to backbone and along backbone to neck. Turn carcass and cut along other side to remove breast. Backbone will remain intact.

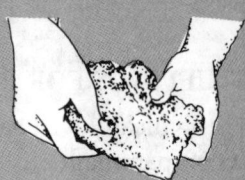

With knife, cut breast in half along breastbone, leaving breastbone on one half of breast.

BONING A CHICKEN OR TURKEY BREAST

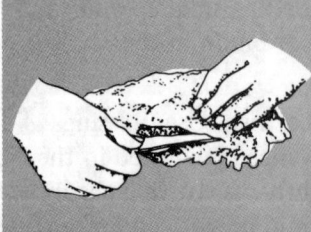

With sharp knife, working with one side of breast, starting parallel and close to large end of rib bone, cut and scrape meat away from bone and rib cage, gently pulling back meat in one piece as you cut. Repeat with remaining side of breast; discard bones.

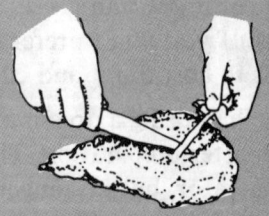

Remove skin; then cut out white tendon.

Seafood

Today's shopper will usually find seafood in convenient ready-to-eat form, whether fresh, frozen or canned. Canned, frozen, and dried fish are typically available in almost any store. A fresh fish, on the other hand, is quite perishable and must be kept very cold from the time it is caught until it is cooked. For that reason, the fish market has long been the traditional place to purchase fresh fish and shellfish. Today, however, more and more supermarkets are offering a wide choice of popular varieties in fresh, ready-to-cook form. Whenever you purchase a fresh fish, it should smell clean and fresh, although like a fish. Gills should be pink to red, with bright, bulging eyes and firm, elastic flesh. Fresh shrimp should have a mild odor and firm meat. Purchase only live crab and lobsters. (Hint: Tails will curl under when picked up.) Fresh scallops should have a sweet odor, firm white flesh, and be free of liquid when bought in packages. Shells of live clams, mussels, and oysters should be tightly closed; or, if slightly opened, should close immediately when tapped lightly. Gapping shells indicate the shellfish is dead and shouldn't be eaten. Shucked oysters should be plump, naturally creamy in color, and in a small amount of clear liquid.

At home, fresh fish should only be stored briefly in the refrigerator, or every other food will also smell like fish! For longer periods, the fish or shellfish should be wrapped tightly in aluminum foil and kept in a container with a tight-fitting cover. Store in the coldest part of the refrigerator for up to two days. Wash before cooking.

Cook whole, dressed fish as is, or cut into steaks or fillets. To cut steaks, slice a large dressed fish crosswise into sections approximately one inch thick. To cut fillets, use a sharp knife to slit the dressed fish along the back from the tail to the head. Then, cut down to the backbone just above the collarbone. Turn the knife flat and cut the flesh lengthwise along the backbone. Cut the flesh away from the rib bones, then lift the entire side of the fish in one piece. Repeat the process on the other side. To skin fillets, lay them flat on a working surface, skin side down, hold the tail end with your fingers and cut through the flesh to the skin about ½ inch from the end of the fillets. Flatten the knife forward while holding the free end of the skin firmly between the fingers.

As a general rule, most fish should be cooked 10 minutes per inch, whatever the cooking method chosen. For example, if a salmon measures 4 inches at its thickest point, poach it for 40 minutes. Saute a ½-inch thick salmon fillet for 5 minutes. Broil a 1½-inch fish steak for 7½ minutes on each side, and so forth. For suggested temperatures, methods, and approximate times, use the following cooking guide.

America's waters have always teemed with an abundance of delectable seafood: oysters, clams, shrimp, and lobster from the seas; bass, trout, catfish, and salmon from the rivers and lakes. And, like poultry, seafood is an extremely popular choice for the way Americans eat today. Most varieties are low in calories and saturated fat. And, because there are so many types available, the choices of interesting seafood recipes are virtually limitless!

Seafood Availability Chart

Saltwater Fish	Season	Market Form	Recommended Cooking Method
Bass	Year-round	Fresh: Whole, Steaks, Fillets; Frozen Fillets	Fry, saute, bake, broil, poach
Cod	Year-round, especially from September to December	Fresh: Whole, Steaks, Fillets; Frozen: Steaks, Fillets; Salted; Canned	Fry, saute, bake, broil, grill, poach, steam
Flounder	Year-round	Fresh and Frozen Whole, Fillets	Fry, saute, bake, broil, grill
Haddock	Year-round	Fresh: Whole, Fillets, Steaks; Frozen Fillets; Smoked (as finnan haddie); Canned	Fry, saute, bake, broil, poach, steam, chowder
Halibut	Year-round	Fresh: Whole (by the pound), Steak, Fillets; Smoked Fillets	Fry, saute, bake, broil, grill, poach, steam
Mackerel	Spring to fall	Fresh: Whole, Steaks, Fillets; Frozen Fillets; Pickled; Salted; Smoked	Fry, saute, bake, broil, grill, poach, steam
Mullet	Year-round	Fresh: Whole, Fillets; Smoked	Fry, saute, bake, broil, grill, poach
Ocean Perch	Year-round	Frozen: Fillets, Steaks	Fry, saute, bake, broil, poach
Pompano	Year-round	Fresh: Whole, Fillets	Saute, bake, broil, poach
Red Snapper	Year-round, especially summer and winter	Fresh: Whole, Fillets, Steaks	Fry, saute, bake, broil, poach
Salmon	Year-round, especially summer and fall	Fresh and Frozen: Steaks, Fillets; Smoked; Kippered; Salted; Canned	Fry, saute, bake, broil, poach, steam
Shad	January to July	Fresh and Frozen Boned; Fresh and Canned Roes	Fry, saute, bake, broil, grill
Sole	Year-round	Fresh: Whole, Fillets; Genuine Dover Sole only frozen	Fry, saute, bake, broil, grill, poach
Swordfish	June to October	Fresh and Frozen: Steaks, Fillets	Bake, broil, grill, steam

Saltwater Fish	Season	Market Form	Recommended Cooking Method
Tuna	Year-round	Fresh: Whole, Fillets, Steaks; Smoked; Canned	Bake, broil, grill, steam
Whiting	Year-round, especially summer and fall	Fresh and Frozen: Whole, Fillets; Smoked	Saute, bake, broil, poach

Freshwater Fish	Season	Market Form	Recommended Cooking Method
Bass	Year-round	Fresh whole	Fry, saute, bake, broil
Brook Trout	Year-round	Fresh and Frozen: Whole, Fillets; Smoked	Fry, bake, broil, poach
Catfish	Year-round	Fresh: Whole, Fillets	Fry, bake, broil, poach
Perch	Year-round	Fresh: Whole, Fillets; Frozen fillets	Fry, saute, bake, broil
Pike	Year-round	Fresh: Whole, Fillets; Frozen whole	Fry, bake, broil, poach
Whitefish	April to December	Fresh: Whole, Fillets; Smoked	Saute, bake, broil, poach, steam

Shellfish	Season	Market Form	Recommended Cooking Method
Clams – hard and soft	Year-round	Fresh; Canned; Shucked; Pickled	Raw, steam, fry, chowder
Crab – hard soft	Year-round May to September	Fresh; Cooked in shell; Canned; Iced; Smoked	Boil, steam, saute
King Crab	Year-round	Frozen legs; Canned	Broil, bake
Lobster: Northern	Year-round	Fresh, Canned, and Cooked in shell; Lobster Meat	Broil, boil
Rock	Year-round	Frozen tails in shell	Broil
Mussels	Spring and summer	Fresh; Canned; Pickled; Smoked	Raw, boil, steam, broil
Oysters	September to April	Fresh in shell; Shelled in liquid; Frozen; Smoked	Raw, steam, fry, bake
Scallops: Sea	Year-round, especially spring, fall, winter	Fresh; Frozen; Canned	Fry, saute, broil, bake
Bay		Fresh; Frozen; Canned	
Shrimp	Year-round, especially spring and summer	Fresh in shell, Shelled; Frozen in shell, Shelled; Canned	Boil, fry, saute, broil, bake

Fish Cooking Guide

COOKING METHOD	MARKET FORM	RECOMMENDED TEMPERATURE (in degrees)	APPROXIMATE TIME
Baking	Whole	400	20-25 minutes
	Fillets	400	15-20 minutes
	Frozen fried	425	15-20 minutes
Broiling	Whole		10-16 minutes (turning once)
	Fillets, steaks		10-15 minutes
	Frozen fried		10-15 minutes
Charcoal grilling	Whole	Moderate	12-18 minutes (turning once)
	Fillets, steaks	Moderate	10-12 minutes (turning once)
Deep-fat frying	Whole	350	3-5 minutes
	Fillets, steaks	350	3-5 minutes
	Frozen breaded	350	3-5 minutes
Pan-frying	Whole	Moderate	12-15 minutes (turning once)
	Fillets, steaks	Moderate	8-10 minutes (turning once)
	Frozen breaded	Moderate	8-10 minutes (turning once)
Poaching	Fillets or Steaks	Simmer	5-10 minutes
Steaming	Fillets or steaks	Boil	5-10 minutes

TO CUT A FILLET

With a sharp knife, cut through the fish along the back from the tail to head end. Then cut down to the backbone just above the collarbone.

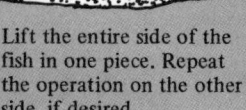

Turn the knife flat and cut the flesh along the backbone to the tail. Cut the flesh away from the rib bones.

Lift the entire side of the fish in one piece. Repeat the operation on the other side, if desired.

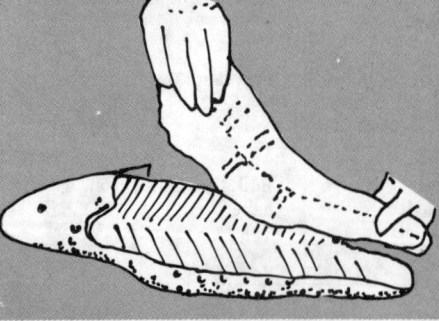

To skin fillets, lay them flat on a working surface, skin side down. Holding the tail end with your fingers, cut through the flesh to the skin about one-half inch from the fillet's end. Flatten knife on skin and cut the flesh away from skin by pushing knife forward while holding free end of skin firmly between fingers.

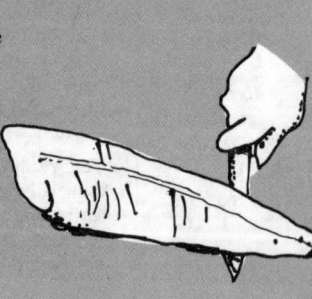

Seasonings for Seafood

SEASONING	DESCRIPTION	USES
Allspice	Small, dried berry whose flavor resembles that of cloves, cinnamon, and nutmeg.	Add to poaching or steaming liquid for both fish and shellfish.
Barbecue seasoning	Blend of many zesty spices such as chili, cumin, garlic, cloves, etc.	Sprinkle over broiling or grilling fish and shellfish.
Basil	Bright green herb with a gently pungent flavor.	Combine with lemon juice for a simple sauce to pour over cooked fish.
Bay leaf	Fragrant dried laurel leaves.	Add to poaching or steaming liquid.
Celery (seed, salt, and flakes)	The flavorful fruit of wild celery.	Add to poaching or steaming liquid; sprinkle on baking fish.
Cloves (ground)	Dried, dark brown, nail-shaped flowerbuds with an exotic flavor.	Sprinkle on fish before baking.
Crab boil or shrimp spice	Includes whole peppercorns, bay leaves, red peppers, mustard seed, ginger, allspice, savory.	Use with crab, lobster and shrimp when boiling, baking, or grilling.
Dillseed	Small, sharply flavored, oval-shaped seed.	Add to poaching or steaming liquid.
Ginger (ground)	Light buff root-spice with an unmistakable pungency.	Sprinkle sparingly on cooking fish.
Mace	Exotic red spice with a gentle flavor.	Add to fish sauces or stews and scalloped dishes.
Marjoram	Grayish green herb with a slightly bitter flavor.	Sprinkle on broiling or baking fish; use in sauces.
Mustard (dry)	Yellow or black aromatic seed with a distinctively tangy flavor.	Add to fish sauces, croquettes, and scalloped dishes.
Nutmeg	Warm and sweet spice that is tan in color.	Add to fish cakes and casseroles.
Oregano	Agreeably flavorful and aromatic herb.	Combine with melted butter for use with shellfish.
Paprika	Mild, brilliant red spice related to pepper.	Add to oil or butter for basting fish; use as a garnish.
Parsley (fresh and dried)	Brilliant green, strong-flavored herb.	Sprinkle generously on cooking fish for a dash of color.
Pickling spice	Blend of mustard, cassia, allspice, dillseed, cloves, tumeric, cardamom, mace.	Sprinkle on broiled fish; add to poaching or steaming liquid.
Rosemary	Grayish-green herb with a pleasant pine flavor.	Flavors fish stocks; sprinkle on broiling or baking fish.
Savory	Small, brownish-green herb with a pungent taste.	Sprinkle on broiling or baking fish; add to fish sauces.
Thyme	Fresh, aromatic herb that is similar in taste to savory.	Combine with stuffings; use in chowders; add to fish before cooking.

Poultry

Versatile taste appeal — that's the hallmark of poultry, in all its varieties. Chicken, once reserved only for Sunday dinner and other special occasions, is now the one poultry homemakers depend upon for economy and flavor. It's as good grilled, fried, or roasted as it is mixed in a creamy casserole, a tangy tomato sauce or in a chilled salad. And, its adaptable flavor pleases finicky family members as easily as it does the discriminating palate. All that, and it's economical, too!

Turkey runs a popular second choice to chicken, and for good reason. Tender and baked to a golden brown, turkey takes the featured spot on many holiday tables, year after year. Versatile and full of flavor, it fills the house with a wonderful aroma as it bakes and can serve a crowd without ruining the budget. Then, after all is said and done, the leftovers work wonderfully in casseroles, sandwiches, hash, soup and more.

Poultry, from its most economical form to its most elegant, is always one of the best choices to prepare for mealtime. It's as much at home at a picnic or tailgate party as it is for Wednesday night supper or an anniversary brunch. For most cooks, poultry means variety, and they depend on it to make any mealtime special.

◂SPAGHETTI WITH CHICKEN BREASTS, recipe on page 24.

Poultry

Chicken

DUTCH CHICKEN-CORN SOUP

1 lg. chicken, cut up
Salt and pepper to taste
2 stalks celery, chopped
1 med. onion, chopped
4 c. fresh corn
2 med. potatoes, chopped
3 hard-boiled eggs, chopped
2 c. flour
1 egg

Cook chicken in water to cover in saucepan until tender. Bone and chop chicken; reserve stock. Bring stock to a boil; season to taste. Add vegetables. Cook until vegetables are tender. Add chicken and hard-boiled eggs. Mix flour and egg in bowl until crumbly. Drop by teaspoonfuls into soup. Simmer, covered, for 10 to 15 minutes. Yield: 8 servings.

Sharon Reddell
Austin, Texas

CHUNKY CHICKEN GIZZARD SOUP

3 lb. chicken gizzards and hearts
1 onion, chopped
1 c. chopped celery
1/2 tsp. pepper
1 tbsp. salt
4 potatoes, chopped
8 oz. egg noodles
1/2 tsp. (or more) brown gravy sauce (opt.)

Cut gizzards into bite-sized pieces. Combine gizzards, hearts, onion, celery, pepper and salt with water to cover in 6-quart saucepan. Simmer, covered, for 1 1/2 hours. Add potatoes and water to cover. Cook for 15 minutes. Add enough water to bring soup level to 5 quarts. Bring to a boil; add noodles. Cook for 15 minutes. Stir in gravy sauce.

Diane Brown
Grayville, Illinois

SOUTHWESTERN CHICKEN CHILI

1 oz. dry red chili pods
3 lb. chicken, coarsely ground
1 or 2 cloves of garlic, finely chopped
Cumin to taste
2 tsp. chili powder

1/4 c. butter
1 c. chopped onion
1 13-oz. can tomato juice
2 tbsp. cornmeal
1 tbsp. flour
1 tsp. salt

Combine chili pods and 2 cups water. Simmer, covered, for 15 minutes; drain, reserving liquid. Peel, seed and chop chili. Saute chicken with garlic, cumin and chili powder in butter in 9-inch skillet until tender. Add onion. Cook for 10 minutes longer. Combine tomato juice, cornmeal, flour, salt and chili in bowl. Add to chicken mixture. Cook for 5 minutes, stirring constantly. Add enough water to reserved chili liquid to measure 3 cups. Stir into chicken mixture. Simmer for 45 minutes. Adjust seasonings.

Judy Compton
Albany, Texas

INDONESIAN CHICKEN SOUP

1 3 1/2-lb. chicken, cut up
2 tsp. salt
4 green onions, sliced
2 stalks celery, chopped
1/2 bay leaf
2 tbsp. chopped green onion
1/2 clove of garlic, crushed
2 tbsp. oil
1/2 tsp. turmeric
1/4 tsp. ginger
1 c. cooked vermicelli
1/2 c. coarsely chopped celery leaves
1/2 c. coarsely chopped green onion tops
3 hard-boiled eggs, sliced
1 c. finely shredded cabbage
1 c. parboiled bean sprouts
1 c. shoestring potatoes

Combine chicken, salt, sliced green onions, chopped celery, bay leaf and 7 cups cold water in stock pot. Simmer until chicken is tender. Bone chicken; cut into julienne strips. Skim broth. Saute 2 tablespoons chopped green onion and garlic in oil in skillet until golden. Add to broth with seasonings. Simmer for 30 minutes; strain. Layer vermicelli, celery leaves, green onion tops, eggs, cabbage, bean sprouts, chicken and potatoes in serving bowls. Fill with broth. Yield: 6 servings.

Roberta Gross
Clinton, Iowa

BRUNSWICK STEW

1 3 1/2-lb. chicken, cooked, boned
2 28-oz. cans tomatoes

Poultry

3 lg. onions, chopped
6 lg. carrots, sliced
1/2 bunch celery, sliced
1 can tomato sauce
3   16-oz. packages frozen baby lima beans
1 lg. potato, chopped
4   16-oz. packages frozen niblet corn
2 lb. beef, cooked, chopped
2 lb. pork, cooked, chopped
2 hot peppers, chopped
Tabasco sauce, salt and pepper to taste

Combine all ingredients in stock pot. Simmer for 8 hours, stirring occasionally. Yield: 30 servings.

Lynette Tart
Fairbanks, Alaska

QUICK CHICKEN STEW

1   3-lb. chicken
6 stalks celery, chopped
6 carrots, chopped
1 onion, chopped
6 med. potatoes, peeled, chopped
Pepper to taste
6 chicken bouillon cubes

Cook chicken in 2 quarts water in 5-quart stock pot for 1 hour, adding water if necessary. Remove chicken; bone and chop. Add remaining ingredients to broth. Cook for 45 minutes. Stir in chicken. Heat to serving temperature. Yield: 6 servings.

Tessa Phipps
Davenport, Iowa

CRUNCHY CHICKEN SALAD

6 c. chopped cooked chicken
4 c. sliced celery
1/4 c. chopped green pepper
1/4 c. chopped onion
1 cucumber, chopped
8 sweet pickles, chopped
1 c. mayonnaise
1 1/2 tsp. prepared mustard
2 tbsp. sweet pickle juice
Salt and pepper to taste

Combine first 6 ingredients in large bowl; mix well. Mix mayonnaise, mustard, pickle juice, salt and pepper in bowl. Pour over chicken mixture; toss to coat. Spoon into large lettuce-lined salad bowl. Garnish with olives, tomato slices and egg slices. Yield: 12 servings.

Lauren Lewis
Palo Alto, California

CHICKEN SALAD ROYALE

4 c. chopped cooked chicken
1 c. chopped celery
1 c. seedless grape halves
1 sm. package sliced almonds
1 tsp. salt
1/4 tsp. pepper
3/4 c. mayonnaise
1/4 c. sour cream

Combine chicken, celery, grapes and almonds in bowl. Sprinkle with salt and pepper. Add mayonnaise and sour cream; mix well. Chill in refrigerator. Spoon onto lettuce-lined serving plates. Yield: 4-5 servings.

Beverly Goodman
Marion, Virginia

CHICKEN CURRY SALAD

1/4 c. mango chutney
6 tbsp. sour cream
3/4 c. salad dressing
1 tsp. curry powder
1/4 tsp. each salt and white pepper
1/4 tsp. lemon juice
1 lb. chopped cooked chicken
1/2 c. chopped celery

Combine chutney, sour cream, salad dressing and seasonings in bowl; mix well. Add chicken and celery; mix well. Spoon onto lettuce-lined plates. Garnish with peanuts and sliced peaches.

Rose Verret
Metairie, Louisiana

FLYING FARMER CHICKEN SALAD

5 c. chopped cooked chicken
2 tbsp. oil
2 tbsp. orange juice
2 tbsp. vinegar
1 tsp. salt
3 c. cooked rice
1 1/2 c. green grapes
1 1/2 c. sliced celery
1   13 1/2-oz. can pineapple tidbits, drained
1   11-oz. can mandarin oranges, drained
1 c. slivered almonds, toasted
1 1/2 c. mayonnaise

Combine chicken, oil, orange juice, vinegar and salt in bowl. Marinate in refrigerator overnight. Add remaining ingredients; toss to mix. Yield: 12 servings.

Lorene Arent
Wausa, Nebraska

Poultry

LUNCHEON CHICKEN SALAD

1 lb. chopped cooked chicken
2 hard-boiled eggs, sliced
20 grapes, sliced
1/2 c. chopped pecans
2 or 3 stalks celery, chopped
1/2 c. mayonnaise

Combine all ingredients in bowl; mix well. Chill until serving time. Yield: 4 servings.

Carol Dupont
Garretsville, Ohio

CHICKEN AND ARTICHOKE HEARTS

6 chicken breasts
1 1/2 tsp. each paprika, salt and pepper
1/4 c. butter
1 12-oz. jar marinated
   artichokes, drained
1/2 lb. mushrooms
2 tbsp. butter
2 tbsp. flour
2/3 c. chicken consomme
3 tbsp. Sherry

Sprinkle chicken breasts with seasonings. Brown in 1/4 cup butter in skillet. Arrange chicken breasts and artichokes in greased casserole. Saute mushrooms in 2 tablespoons butter in skillet for 5 minutes. Add flour; mix well. Stir in consomme and Sherry. Cook until thickened, stirring constantly. Pour over chicken breasts. Bake, covered, at 325 degrees for 1 1/2 hours or until chicken is tender. Yield: 6 servings.

Dean Dark
Calaveras, California

CHICKEN BREASTS A LA RUSSE

1 c. butter, softened
1 clove of garlic, crushed
1 tbsp. chopped chives
2 tbsp. chopped parsley
1 tsp. salt
6 whole chicken breasts, boned
1/4 c. milk
1 2 3/8-oz. package seasoned
   coating mix
1 c. heavy cream
1 c. sour cream
1 c. cottage cheese
6 lg. Idaho baking potatoes, baked
1 sm. can sliced beets, drained

Combine butter, garlic, chives, parsley and salt in bowl; mix well. Pat into long roll on waxed paper. Chill until firm. Pound chicken breasts to flatten, keeping skins intact. Divide butter into 6 portions. Place on chicken breasts. Roll chicken tightly around butter; secure with toothpicks. Dip each piece in milk; coat heavily with coating mix. Arrange in greased shallow baking pan. Bake at 400 degrees for 45 minutes. Combine cream, sour cream and cottage cheese in blender container. Process until smooth. Season to taste. Knead and split potatoes; scoop pulp onto platter. Arrange chicken breasts over potatoes. Spoon sour cream mixture over chicken breasts. Garnish with beet slices. Yield: 6 servings.

Photograph for this recipe on this page.

CHICKEN CHALUPAS

4 whole chicken breasts, baked
1 can cream of chicken soup
1 can cream of mushroom soup
1 c. milk
1 8-oz. carton sour cream
1/2 c. finely chopped onion
1 sm. can chopped green chilies
1 tbsp. butter
12 corn tortillas, cut into strips
1/2 lb. grated sharp cheese

Cut chicken into bite-sized pieces. Blend soups, milk and sour cream in bowl. Stir in onion and chilies. Melt butter in 9 x 13-inch baking dish. Layer half the tortillas, chicken, soup mixture and cheese in prepared baking dish. Repeat layers. Chill for 24 hours. Bake at 350 degrees until heated through. Yield: 10 servings.

Robby Lalum
San Luis Obispo, California

Poultry

COMPANY CHICKEN

1   3-oz. jar sliced dried beef
8 chicken breasts, boned, skinned
8 slices bacon
1 can cream of mushroom soup
1 c. sour cream
1 tsp. Worcestershire sauce
1/2 tsp. pepper
1 tsp. Tabasco sauce
1 tsp. parsley flakes

Pour boiling water over dried beef in dish. Let stand for 5 minutes; drain. Arrange over bottom of greased 9 x 13-inch baking dish. Wrap chicken with bacon; arrange over dried beef. Combine remaining ingredients in bowl; mix well. Spoon over chicken. Bake at 375 degrees for 1 hour. Yield: 8 servings.

Effie Free
Ormonda Beach, Florida

CHICKEN LITTLE FINGERS

1 1/2 c. buttermilk
2 tbsp. lemon juice
2 tsp. Worcestershire sauce
1 tsp. soy sauce
1 tsp. paprika
1 tbsp. Greek seasoning
1 tsp. salt
1 tsp. pepper
2 cloves of garlic, chopped
6 whole boneless chicken breasts, cut
    into 1/2-in. strips
4 c. bread crumbs
1/2 c. sesame seed
1/4 c. melted butter
1/4 c. melted shortening

Combine first 9 ingredients in large bowl; mix well. Add chicken; stir to coat. Marinate, covered, overnight Drain well. Combine bread crumbs and sesame seed in bowl; mix well. Coat chicken with bread crumb mixture. Arrange in 2 greased 9 x 13-inch baking dishes. Mix butter and shortening in bowl. Brush over chicken. Bake at 350 degrees for 35 minutes or until tender.

Kim Cogdill
Sylva, North Carolina

MOZZARELLA CHICKEN

1 c. bread crumbs
3 tbsp. Parmesan cheese
2 tbsp. chopped parsley
4 chicken breasts, boned
1 c. flour
1 tsp. salt
1/2 tsp. pepper
1 egg, beaten
1/4 c. margarine
1/2 c. Italian cooking sauce
4 slices mozzarella cheese

Combine bread crumbs, Parmesan cheese and parsley in bowl; mix well. Coat chicken with flour seasoned with salt and pepper. Dip into egg; coat with crumb mixture. Brown in margarine in skillet. Place in greased 8 x 8-inch baking dish. Pour cooking sauce over chicken. Top with cheese. Bake at 350 degrees for 15 minutes or until cheese melts and chicken is tender.

Karen Gattis
Friendswood, Texas

CHICKEN MILANO

1 med. onion, chopped
2 tbsp. butter
1 can tomato soup
2/3 c. beer
1 tsp. curry powder
1/2 tsp. oregano
Pepper to taste
6 chicken breasts
1/4 c. Parmesan cheese

Saute onion in butter in saucepan until tender. Stir in soup, beer, curry powder, oregano and pepper. Simmer for 10 minutes. Arrange chicken breasts in greased 7 x 12-inch baking dish. Pour tomato mixture over chicken. Bake at 350 degrees for 50 minutes. Sprinkle with cheese. Serve over egg noodles or rice.

Melissa Smithwick
Prescott, Arizona

QUICK-STEP CHICKEN

6 chicken breasts
Salt and pepper to taste
1 tsp. Italian seasoning
1/2 c. chopped onion
1/2 c. chopped celery
1 jar spaghetti sauce

Arrange chicken in greased baking dish. Sprinkle with salt, pepper and Italian seasoning. Layer onion and celery over chicken. Pour spaghetti sauce over chicken. Bake at 350 degrees for 1 hour or until chicken is tender, turning frequently. Serve over spaghetti.

Sandy Smithwick
Fresno, California

17

Poultry

BAKED CHICKEN REUBEN

4 chicken breasts
1 can sauerkraut, drained
4 slices Swiss cheese
1 c. Thousand Island salad dressing

Place chicken breasts in greased 9 x 13-inch baking dish. Layer sauerkraut and Swiss cheese over chicken. Top with dressing. Bake, covered with foil, at 325 degrees for 1 hour.
Yield: 4 servings.

Lillie Paul
Winter Haven, Florida

CHICKEN SALTIMBOCCA

12 boneless chicken breasts
1/2 c. flour
1/3 c. clarified butter
12 thin slices prosciutto
12   1/2-oz. slices Monterey Jack cheese
1/4 c. chopped shallots
3 lg. cloves of garlic, minced
1/2 lb. mushrooms, sliced
1/2 c. dry white wine
1 c. chicken broth
1 tsp. each fresh thyme, oregano
1 tbsp. flour
1/2 c. Sherry
1/2 c. cream
Salt and pepper to taste

Coat chicken with flour. Brown in butter in skillet. Arrange in buttered 9 x 13-inch baking dish. Top each piece with prosciutto and cheese. Saute shallots and garlic in pan drippings until tender. Add mushrooms, wine, broth and herbs. Bring to a boil. Cook for 10 minutes. Stir in 1 tablespoon flour and a small amount of Sherry. Stir in remaining Sherry and cream; season with salt and pepper. Cook until thickened, stirring constantly. Pour sauce over chicken. Bake at 375 degrees for 20 minutes.
Yield: 6 servings.

Vera Webb
Elizabethtown, Pennsylvania

SUPER CHICKEN

6 chicken breasts
1 tbsp. seasoned salt
1/4 c. dry white wine
1 c. chicken bouillon
1/2 tsp. instant onion
1/2 tsp. curry powder
2 tbsp. flour
1 c. canned sliced mushrooms

Sprinkle chicken with seasoned salt. Place in greased baking dish. Mix wine, bouillon, onion and curry powder in bowl. Pour over chicken. Cover with foil. Bake at 350 degrees for 30 minutes. Bake, uncovered, for 30 minutes longer or until tender. Place chicken on heated serving plate. Strain pan juices. Blend flour with 1/4 cup water and pan juices in saucepan. Cook over low heat until thickened, stirring constantly. Add mushrooms. Heat to serving temperature. Spoon over chicken. Yield: 6 servings.

Katy Cloud
Concord, New Hampshire

LEMONADE CHICKEN BREASTS

6 chicken breasts, skinned
1 stick margarine, melted
Salt and pepper to taste
1 can frozen lemonade concentrate, thawed

Brown chicken in margarine in skillet; season with salt and pepper. Place in greased 7 x 10-inch baking dish; pour lemonade concentrate over chicken. Bake at 300 degrees for 15 minutes, basting several times. Bake, covered, for 30 minutes or until tender.

Janine Cook
Junction, Utah

CHICKEN ELEGANTE

8 chicken breasts
Salt and pepper to taste
1 stick margarine, melted
1/4 c. white wine
2 cans cream of chicken soup
1/2 c. mayonnaise
1 c. sour cream
1 tbsp. parsley flakes
1 tsp. paprika
6 c. cooked rice

Season chicken breasts with salt and pepper. Coat with margarine. Place in baking dish. Sprinkle wine over chicken. Bake at 350 degrees for 1 hour. Combine pan drippings and remaining ingredients except rice with 1 cup water in saucepan. Heat until blended. Stir half the soup mixture into rice; spoon into greased baking dish. Arrange chicken over rice; top with remaining soup mixture. Bake at 350 degrees for 45 minutes.

Paula Stansfield
Mt. Sterling, Kentucky

Poultry

CHICKEN WITH WILD RICE

1 stick margarine, melted
1 pkg. long grain and wild rice mix
1 pkg. dry onion soup mix
4 lg. chicken breasts

Layer margarine, rice, rice seasonings and half the soup mix in 9 x 13-inch casserole. Pour 2 cups hot water over layers. Arrange chicken breasts over rice. Sprinkle remaining soup mix on top. Bake, covered, at 325 degrees for 1 1/4 hours. Bake, uncovered, for 15 minutes longer. Yield: 4 servings.

Tracy Leigh Levan
Columbia, Pennsylvania

BOMBAY CHICKEN

3 lb. chicken breasts
1/3 c. flour
1 1/2 tsp. salt
Pepper to taste
1/4 c. butter
1/2 c. thinly sliced onion
1/2 c. golden raisins
4 c. cooked rice
1/2 c. flaked coconut
1/4 c. salted peanuts
1 1/2 tsp. curry powder

Coat chicken with mixture of flour, salt and pepper. Brown in butter in skillet; remove chicken. Saute onion in pan drippings until tender. Stir in raisins. Cook until plump. Add rice, coconut, peanuts and curry powder; mix well. Spoon into greased 7 x 11-inch baking dish. Arrange chicken on top. Bake at 350 degrees for 1 hour. Yield: 4 servings.

Sonja Hargrave
Kansas City, Missouri

SUNDAY CHICKEN

1 tsp. curry powder
1 apple, finely chopped
1 onion, finely chopped
2 tbsp. melted butter
1 can mushroom soup
1 c. cream
Salt and pepper to taste
6 chicken breasts
1/4 c. thinly sliced onion
1/4 c. slivered almonds
2 tbsp. butter
1/4 c. seedless raisins
1 1/3 c. rice, cooked

Saute first 3 ingredients in 2 tablespoons butter in skillet until onion is tender. Add soup, cream and seasonings; mix well. Place chicken in single layer in greased baking dish. Pour sauce over chicken. Bake at 350 degrees for 1 1/2 hours. Saute sliced onion and almonds in 2 tablespoons butter in skillet until golden brown. Stir in raisins and rice. Heat through. Serve chicken over rice. Yield: 6 servings.

Marilyn Tisdale
Wilmington, North Carolina

TAHITIAN CHICKEN

3 lb. chicken breasts
3 tbsp. flour
Salt and pepper to taste
1 tbsp. margarine
1/2 c. pineapple chunks
1 10-oz. bottle of maraschino cherries
1 8-oz. bottle of sweet and sour salad dressing

Coat chicken with mixture of flour, salt and pepper. Brown in margarine in skillet. Place in greased baking dish. Add remaining ingredients and 1/2 cup water. Bake at 350 degrees for 1 hour. Serve over rice or noodles. Yield: 4 servings.

Provi Monroe
Macon, Georgia

CURRIED CHICKEN

1 green pepper, chopped
2 lg. onions, sliced
2 cloves of garlic, crushed
1 tbsp. oil
4 bouillon cubes
2 lg. tomatoes, sliced
6 chicken breasts
1 tbsp. allspice
1 tsp. ginger
1 tbsp. curry powder
1 tsp. salt
1/4 tsp. pepper

Saute green pepper, onions and garlic in oil in skillet. Add bouillon cubes, tomatoes and 2 cups water; stir until bouillon dissolves. Coat chicken with mixture of seasonings. Place in greased baking dish; pour sauce over chicken. Bake at 350 degrees for 1 1/2 hours or until chicken is tender. Serve with rice.

Vicki Cummings
Bowling Green, Ohio

Poultry

CHICKEN WAIKIKI BEACH

4 chicken breasts
1/2 c. flour
1/3 c. oil
1 tsp. salt
1/4 tsp. pepper
1 20-oz. can sliced pineapple
1 c. sugar
3/4 c. cider vinegar
1 tbsp. ginger
1 chicken bouillon cube
2 tbsp. cornstarch
1 lg. green pepper, sliced into rings

Coat chicken with flour. Brown in oil in skillet. Place skin side up in baking dish. Season with salt and pepper. Drain pineapple, reserving syrup. Add enough water to syrup to measure 1 1/4 cups. Combine with next 5 ingredients in saucepan. Boil for 2 minutes, stirring constantly. Pour over chicken. Bake at 350 degrees for 30 minutes. Top with pineapple and green pepper. Bake for 30 minutes longer or until chicken is tender. Serve with rice.
Yield: 4 servings.

Catherine Sterling
Carbon, Pennsylvania

SOUR CREAM CHICKEN CORDON BLEU

8 whole chicken breasts, boned, skinned
8 1-oz. slices cooked ham
8 1-oz. slices Swiss cheese
3 tbsp. minced parsley
1/4 tsp. pepper
1 egg, beaten
1/2 c. Italian bread crumbs
1/4 c. butter
1 can mushroom soup
1 8-oz. carton sour cream
1/3 c. dry Sherry
1 4-oz. can sliced mushrooms, drained

Pound chicken breasts to 1/4-inch thickness with meat mallet. Place ham and cheese slices in center of each. Sprinkle with parsley and pepper. Roll to enclose filling; secure with toothpicks. Dip into egg; coat with crumbs. Brown in butter in skillet. Place in greased 8 x 12-inch baking pan. Add remaining ingredients to pan drippings; mix well. Pour over chicken. Bake at 350 degrees for 40 minutes or until chicken is tender. Yield: 8 servings.

Pam Reardon
Salisbury, North Carolina

CHICKEN CORDON BLEU SUPREME

4 chicken breasts, skinned, boned
1/2 tsp. salt
Pepper to taste
4 thin slices boiled ham
2 oz. Swiss cheese, cut into 4 sticks
1/4 c. flour
2 tbsp. butter
1/4 lb. fresh mushrooms, sliced
1 med. yellow onion, chopped
1 tbsp. butter
1 tsp. instant chicken bouillon
1 tbsp. chopped parsley
1 tsp. chopped chives
1/4 c. heavy cream

Flatten chicken breasts with meat mallet. Sprinkle with salt and pepper; top with ham and cheese. Roll to enclose filling; secure with toothpicks. Coat with flour. Brown in 2 tablespoons butter in large skillet. Place in greased baking dish. Saute mushrooms and onion in 1 tablespoon butter in skillet until tender. Add 3/4 cup water, bouillon, parsley and chives. Pour over chicken. Bake, covered, at 350 degrees for 20 minutes or until tender. Remove chicken to serving platter; keep warm. Stir cream into drippings in saucepan. Simmer until slightly thickened. Spoon sauce over chicken. Serve with rice pilaf.

Nancy Herrin
Vega, Texas

ROLLED CHICKEN BREASTS WITH COUNTRY HAM AND RICE

1 box wild rice mix
1 bouillon cube
1 onion, chopped
1 green pepper, chopped
1/2 c. chopped celery
1/3 c. margarine
2 tbsp. flour
Salt and pepper to taste
1 c. cooked white rice
1 3-oz. can sliced mushrooms, drained
6 sm. slices country ham
6 oz. sharp Cheddar cheese, cut
    into 6 sticks
6 chicken breasts, boned, skinned
1/3 c. flour
2 eggs, slightly beaten
3/4 c. fine dry bread crumbs

Prepare wild rice using package directions. Dissolve bouillon cube in 1 cup water. Saute onion, green pepper and celery in margarine in skillet until tender. Add 2 tablespoons flour, seasonings and bouillon. Cook until thickened, stirring constantly. Add cooked rices and mushrooms. Pour into greased 8 x 10-inch baking dish. Saute ham slices lightly in skillet. Place 1 slice ham and 1 stick cheese on each chicken breast. Roll as for jelly roll, folding in edges; secure with toothpicks. Coat with flour; dip into beaten eggs. Roll in bread crumbs seasoned with salt and pepper. Arrange over rice mixture. Bake at 325 degrees for 30 minutes or until chicken is brown and tender. Yield: 6 servings.

Kendra Jones
Pierre, South Dakota

CHICKEN KIEV

    1 stick butter, softened
    1 tbsp. chopped chives
    8 chicken breasts, boned, skinned
    Salt and pepper to taste
    2 eggs, beaten
    1/3 c. fine dry bread crumbs
    1/3 c. grated Parmesan cheese
    1/4 c. melted butter

Combine softened butter and chives in bowl; mix well. Shape into balls. Freeze until firm. Flatten chicken with meat mallet. Season with salt and pepper. Place butter ball on each chicken piece. Fold to enclose filling; secure with toothpicks. Dip into eggs; coat with mixture of bread crumbs and cheese. Place in greased shallow baking dish. Drizzle melted butter over all. Bake at 450 degrees for 25 minutes, basting once.

Debra Stephens
Yanceyville, North Carolina

CRAB-STUFFED CHICKEN

    4 lg. chicken breasts, boned
    3 tbsp. melted butter
    1/4 c. flour
    3/4 c. milk
    3/4 c. chicken broth
    1/3 c. dry white wine
    1/2 c. chopped onion
    1 tbsp. butter
    2 7 1/2-oz. cans crab meat, drained
    1 6-oz. can mushrooms, drained
    2 tbsp. parsley
    1/2 tsp. each salt and pepper
    1/2 c. coarsely crumbled saltine crackers
    1 c. shredded Swiss cheese
    1/2 tsp. paprika

Flatten chicken with meat mallet. Blend 3 tablespoons butter and flour in saucepan. Add milk, chicken broth and wine. Cook until thickened, stirring constantly. Saute onion in 1 tablespoon butter in saucepan until tender. Stir in crab meat, mushrooms, parsley, salt, pepper,

cracker crumbs and 2 tablespoons sauce. Top each chicken piece with 1/4 cup crab mixture. Fold in sides; roll to enclose filling. Place seam side down in greased baking dish. Pour remaining sauce over top. Bake, covered, at 350 degrees for 1 hour. Sprinkle with cheese and paprika. Bake until cheese is melted.

Susan Godwin
Pensacola, Florida

APPLE-SPICED CHICKEN

    3 lb. chicken breasts
    1/4 c. oil
    1 tsp. salt
    Pepper to taste
    1/4 c. apple jelly
    1 tbsp. lemon juice
    1/2 tsp. allspice

Brush chicken with oil; season with salt and pepper. Place skin side down in broiler pan. Broil 5 to 6 inches from heat source for 20 minutes or until lightly browned; turn chicken. Broil for 15 to 20 minutes longer or until tender. Melt apple jelly in saucepan. Stir in lemon juice and allspice. Brush chicken with half the jelly mixture. Broil for 1 to 2 minutes longer. Transfer to serving dish; brush with remaining glaze. Serve with honeyed apple rings.

Cheryl Frampton
Canutillo, Texas

BARBECUED CHICKEN BREASTS

    1/2 c. vinegar
    1 c. catsup
    2 tbsp. prepared mustard
    1 tsp. crushed red pepper
    1 lg. onion
    1/4 c. packed brown sugar
    2 tsp. salt
    1 tsp. pepper
    1 stick butter
    1/4 c. lemon juice
    1/4 c. Worcestershire sauce
    12 chicken breasts, skinned

Combine first 8 ingredients in food processor; puree. Pour into saucepan. Add 1 cup water, butter, lemon juice and Worcestershire sauce. Bring to a boil. Simmer for 10 minutes. Pour over chicken breasts in shallow dish. Marinate for 2 hours. Drain chicken, reserving marinade. Grill over hot coals for 45 minutes or until tender, basting with reserved marinade and turning frequently.

Barbara Brown
Brownwood, Texas

Poultry

CHEESY CHICKEN BREASTS

1 1/2 c. bread crumbs
1 1/2 c. grated Swiss cheese
1 c. flour
1/2 tsp. poultry seasoning
1/4 tsp. each salt and pepper
1/2 tsp. paprika
4 chicken breasts
2 eggs, beaten
1/2 c. margarine, melted

Combine bread crumbs and cheese in bowl; mix well. Mix flour and seasonings in bowl. Dip chicken breasts in seasoned flour, eggs and bread crumb mixture in order listed. Cook in margarine in electric skillet at 300 degrees for 45 minutes or until brown and crispy, turning occasionally. Yield: 4 servings.

Mandy Tisdale
Covington, West Virginia

ISLAND-STYLE CHICKEN

1   8-oz. can pineapple chunks
2 lb. chicken breasts
2 tbsp. shortening
1 can chicken broth
1/4 c. vinegar
2 tbsp. brown sugar
2 tsp. soy sauce
1 clove of garlic, minced
1 med. green pepper, coarsely chopped
3 tbsp. cornstarch

Drain pineapple, reserving juice. Brown chicken in shortening in skillet; drain. Add reserved juice, broth, vinegar, brown sugar, soy sauce and garlic. Cook, covered, over low heat for 40 minutes. Add green pepper and pineapple. Cook for 5 minutes longer. Stir in mixture of cornstarch and 1/4 cup cold water. Cook until thickened, stirring constantly. Serve with rice.

Margaret Simpson
Decatur, Illinois

CHICKEN BREASTS WITH ALMOND-OLIVE SAUCE

2 eggs, beaten
Salt and pepper
4 chicken breasts, boned
1/2 c. fine dry bread crumbs
3 tbsp. olive oil
2 tbsp. butter
1/2 c. sliced almonds
2 tbsp. flour
1 1/2 c. milk
1/3 c. sliced pimento-stuffed olives
2 tbsp. chopped parsley
Dash of garlic powder
4 med. potatoes, peeled, sliced, boiled

Combine eggs, 3/4 teaspoon salt and 1/4 teaspoon pepper in bowl. Dip chicken in egg mixture; coat with bread crumbs. Cook chicken in olive oil in skillet over low heat for 20 minutes. Place chicken on heated serving platter; keep warm. Add butter to skillet. Saute almonds for 2 minutes or until golden, stirring constantly. Stir in flour. Cook over low heat until smooth and bubbly, stirring constantly. Stir in milk gradually. Add olives, parsley and garlic powder. Cook over low heat until thickened, stirring constantly. Add salt and pepper to taste. Arrange hot cooked potatoes on platter with chicken. Spoon a small amount of almond-olive sauce over chicken and potatoes. Serve remaining sauce with chicken and potatoes. Garnish with parsley and whole stuffed olives.

Photograph for this recipe on opposite page.

CHICKEN PAELLA

1/4 lb. Italian sausage, sliced
2 chicken breasts, split
Salt and pepper to taste
1 sm. green pepper, chopped
1 med. onion, chopped
1 clove of garlic, minced
3/4 c. brown rice
1 1/4 tsp. turmeric
4 sm. carrots, sliced
1   10-oz. package frozen peas
1   10-oz. package frozen artichokes
1/4 c. pitted ripe olives
12 cherry tomato halves

Saute sausage in skillet for 10 minutes; remove sausage and drain. Season chicken with salt and pepper. Brown in pan drippings. Remove chicken. Add green pepper, onion and garlic. Cook until tender. Add rice, turmeric and 3 cups hot water. Bring to a boil. Add sausage, carrots and chicken. Simmer, covered, for 20 minutes. Rinse peas and artichokes in hot water to separate. Arrange with olives around chicken. Cook, covered, for 15 to 20 minutes or until chicken and rice are tender. Add tomatoes; toss to mix. Heat to serving temperature.

Frances Wadsworth
Palm Coast, Florida

Poultry

PATIO CHICKEN

4 chicken breasts
1/4 c. butter
2 tsp. seasoned salt
1/4 tsp. crushed thyme
Pepper to taste
1 med. green pepper, chopped
1 sm. onion, chopped
1/4 tsp. Tabasco sauce
2 tsp. seasoned salt
1 8-oz. package wide egg noodles
1 can cream of celery soup
1/2 c. ripe olives, sliced

Brown chicken in butter in large skillet. Sprinkle with 2 teaspoons seasoned salt, thyme and pepper to taste. Cook, covered, for 30 minutes or until tender. Remove chicken. Combine next 3 ingredients with 2 teaspoons seasoned salt, pepper and 4 cups water in bowl. Add to pan drippings. Bring to a boil. Add noodles gradually. Cook, covered, over low heat for 20 minutes, stirring occasionally. Add soup, olives and chicken. Heat to serving temperature. Yield: 4 servings.

Hope Dietz
Mt. Vernon, New York

CHICKEN PICCATA

1 egg
1 tbsp. lemon juice
1/4 c. flour
1/8 tsp. garlic powder
1/8 tsp. paprika
4 chicken breasts, skinned, boned
1/4 c. butter
2 chicken bouillon cubes
2 tbsp. lemon juice

Beat egg with 1 tablespoon lemon juice in small bowl. Combine flour, garlic powder and paprika in bowl; mix well. Dip chicken pieces in egg mixture; coat with flour mixture. Brown chicken in butter in skillet. Dissolve bouillon cubes in 1/2 cup boiling water. Add to chicken with 2 tablespoons lemon juice. Simmer, covered, for 20 minutes or until tender. Yield: 4 servings.

Kim Leissler
Plano, Texas

CHICKEN ROSE

2 chicken breasts, skinned, boned
3 tbsp. flour
6 tbsp. corn oil margarine
Rose wine

3/4 c. sliced mushrooms
2 tbsp. chopped parsley

Coat chicken with flour; shake off excess. Brown chicken on both sides in margarine in large skillet. Pour in enough wine to cover bottom of skillet. Add mushrooms and parsley. Simmer over medium heat for 5 minutes, stirring occasionally. Yield: 4 servings.

Carol Kendrick
Montgomery, Alabama

PLUM-GLAZED CHICKEN AND RICE

6 chicken breasts
Salt and pepper to taste
1/2 c. plum preserves
Juice and grated rind of 1 lg. orange
2 tbsp. light corn syrup
3 c. cooked rice

Place chicken in baking pan. Sprinkle with salt and pepper. Bake, covered, at 350 degrees for 1 hour or until tender. Combine preserves, 1/4 cup orange juice and corn syrup in saucepan; mix well. Bring to a boil. Pour over chicken. Bake for 10 minutes or until chicken is glazed. Combine remaining orange juice, orange rind and hot rice; mix well. Spoon onto serving plate. Arrange chicken over rice.

Carolyn Simpson
Burns, Nevada

Poultry

SAUCY CHICKEN

4 chicken breasts
2 tbsp. butter
Salt and pepper to taste
1 env. chicken gravy mix
1 tbsp. minced onion
1 c. apple juice
1 to 2 tbsp. lemon juice
1/2 c. half and half

Brown chicken breasts in butter in large skillet; drain. Season with salt and pepper. Move chicken to one side of pan. Add gravy mix, onion, apple juice and lemon juice; mix well. Arrange chicken in sauce. Simmer, covered, for 30 minutes or until tender, stirring occasionally. Stir in cream. Cook until heated through. Yield: 4 servings.

Francine Woods
Scottsbluff, Nebraska

SPAGHETTI WITH CHICKEN BREASTS

1 tbsp. butter
1/2 c. chicken broth
4 boned chicken breasts
Pepper to taste
Paprika to taste
8 oz. spaghetti, cooked
1 15-oz. jar homestyle spaghetti
   sauce, heated

Melt butter in skillet. Add chicken broth and breasts. Sprinkle with pepper. Cook, covered, over medium heat for 10 minutes. Turn breasts. Sprinkle with paprika. Cook, covered, for 15 minutes. Serve hot over spaghetti with sauce. Yield: 4 servings.

Photograph for this recipe on page 12.

SWEET AND SOUR CHICKEN STIR FRY

1/2 c. Smucker's Low Sugar Apricot Spread
1 tbsp. vinegar
1 tsp. garlic salt
1 tsp. ginger
1 tsp. soy sauce
1/8 tsp. crushed red pepper
2 med. zucchini, cut in half
   lengthwise, sliced
1/2 lb. small mushrooms
1/2 tsp. salt
1/4 c. oil
2 whole chicken breasts, skinned, boned,
   cut into 1-in. cubes
1 6-oz. package frozen pea pods, thawed

Combine apricot spread, vinegar, garlic salt, ginger, soy sauce and crushed red pepper in bowl; mix well. Stir-fry zucchini and mushrooms with salt in 2 tablespoons oil in wok until zucchini is tender-crisp. Transfer mixture to platter. Add remaining 2 tablespoons oil in wok. Stir-fry chicken until tender. Add zucchini mixture and pea pods. Cook until heated through. Add apricot mixture; toss gently to mix well. Cook until heated through. Serve with rice.

Photograph for this recipe on this page.

CHICKEN CASHEW

1/4 c. soy sauce
2 tbsp. cornstarch
4 lg. chicken breasts, boned, sliced
1/2 c. slivered cashews
1/3 c. oil
1 lg. onion, chopped
2 carrots, sliced diagonally
2 stalks celery, sliced diagonally
2 cloves of garlic, chopped
1 head cauliflower, cut into flowerets
1 lb. mushrooms, sliced
1 c. bouillon

Blend soy sauce and cornstarch in shallow dish. Add chicken, turning to coat. Marinate for several minutes. Saute cashews in a small amount of oil in electric skillet at 375 degrees until golden brown; drain. Brown slightly drained chicken in oil in skillet; set aside. Add vegetables. Cook, covered, for 2 minutes. Add bouillon. Cook, uncovered, for 4 minutes. Stir in chicken and cashews. Serve with wild rice.

Anne Linwood
Bedford, Indiana

Poultry

CHICKEN CHOW MEIN

3 to 4 c. shredded cabbage
5 tbsp. oil
6 green onions, sliced diagonally
1 sm. can sliced mushrooms
1 can sliced water chestnuts
4 chicken breasts, boned, sliced
1 c. chicken broth
6 tbsp. soy sauce
1 tbsp. cornstarch

Stir-fry cabbage in 2 tablespoons oil in wok on high for 2 minutes; remove cabbage. Add 1 tablespoon oil and green onions. Stir-fry for 1 minute. Add mushrooms and water chestnuts. Cook for 1 minute longer; remove vegetables. Stir-fry chicken in remaining 2 tablespoons oil for 5 minutes or until tender. Blend broth, soy sauce and cornstarch in bowl. Add to chicken. Cook until thick, stirring constantly. Return stir-fried vegetables to wok. Cook for 1 minute. Serve over rice. Yield: 4 servings.
Note: May use shrimp with or in place of chicken. Snow peas, bean sprouts, bamboo shoots, broccoli, carrots and peas may be added with vegetables, stir-frying for 1 to 2 minutes after each addition.

Lynn C. Smith
Hudson, North Carolina

CHICKEN GINGER

1/2 c. black jelly mushrooms
3 tbsp. shredded gingerroot
1 tbsp. sliced onion
3 tbsp. oil
2 cloves of garlic, minced
4 whole chicken breasts, boned, sliced
1 tbsp. soy sauce
4 spring onions, finely chopped
1/2 c. sliced bamboo shoots
Sugar to taste
Lemon juice to taste
1 pkg. frozen snow peas

Soak mushrooms in hot water to soften; trim and rinse. Soak gingerroot in a small amount of hot salted water for several minutes; drain and pat dry. Saute sliced onion in oil in skillet for several minutes. Add garlic, chicken, ginger and 1 tablespoon soy sauce. Stir-fry for 5 minutes. Add chopped onions, bamboo shoots, sugar, lemon juice and mushrooms. Stir-fry for 5 minutes. Add snow peas. Cook until tender-crisp.

Sonja Gerdes
Waterloo, Iowa

SKILLET CHICKEN AND PEPPERS

4 chicken breasts, boned, sliced
3 tbsp. soy sauce
1 tbsp. Sherry
2 tsp. cornstarch
1/8 tsp. each sugar, garlic powder
2 med. green peppers, cut into
    1/4-in. strips
1/2 lb. mushrooms, thinly sliced
5 tbsp. oil
2 pita bread rounds, split (opt.)

Combine first 6 ingredients in bowl. Stir-fry green peppers and mushrooms in 2 tablespoons oil in skillet for 2 minutes or until tender-crisp; remove vegetables. Stir-fry chicken mixture in 3 tablespoons oil in skillet for 5 minutes or until tender. Return vegetables to skillet. Add 1/2 cup water. Bring to a boil, stirring to deglaze skillet. Serve with pita rounds.
Yield: 4 servings.

Veta Sampson
Midland, Texas

COQ AU VIN

4 slices bacon, chopped
2 tbsp. chopped onion
1   3-lb. chicken, cut up
8 shallots, chopped
1/2 c. chopped carrot
1 clove of garlic, minced
2 tbsp. Brandy
2 c. sliced mushrooms
2 tbsp. butter
3 or 4 sprigs of parsley
1 med. bay leaf
1/4 tsp. thyme
1 stalk celery, chopped
2 c. Burgundy

Saute bacon and onion in skillet until brown; remove. Brown chicken in bacon drippings; remove. Add shallots, carrot, garlic and Brandy. Cook for 3 minutes. Saute mushrooms in butter in skillet. Tie parsley, bay leaf, thyme and celery in cheesecloth to make bouquet garni. Place bouquet garni in 2-quart casserole. Layer chicken, vegetables, mushrooms, bacon and onion in casserole. Deglaze skillet with Burgundy. Pour over layers. Bake, covered, at 350 degrees for 2 hours. Remove bouquet garni.
Yield: 4 servings.

Cheryl Frampton
Canutillo, Texas

Poultry

OVEN-BARBECUED CHICKEN

1   3-lb. chicken, cut up
1/4 c. oil
1/2 c. chopped onion
1/4 c. chopped celery
1/2 c. catsup
2 tbsp. lemon juice
1 tbsp. brown sugar
1 tbsp. Worcestershire sauce
1 tbsp. vinegar
1 tbsp. prepared mustard
1/2 tsp. salt
Pepper to taste

Brown chicken in oil in skillet. Arrange in 8 x 12-inch baking dish. Saute onion and celery in pan drippings until tender. Stir in remaining ingredients and 3 cups water. Simmer for 15 minutes; skim. Spoon sauce over chicken. Bake at 325 degrees for 1 1/4 hours or until tender, basting several times. Yield: 4 servings.

Nancy Vinklarek
Flatonia, Texas

CHICKEN AND GARDEN VEGETABLES CASSEROLE

1   3-lb. chicken, cut up
3 tbsp. butter
1 c. chopped onion
3 med. carrots, cut into 1 1/2-in. strips
1 med. zucchini, sliced
1 med. green pepper, cut into 1-in. pieces
1 lg. clove of garlic, crushed
1 1/2 c. corn
3/4 tsp. thyme
1 1/2 tsp. salt
1/8 tsp. pepper
8 oz. medium egg noodles, cooked, drained
2 chicken bouillon cubes
3 med. tomatoes, cut into wedges (opt.)

Brown chicken in butter in large skillet. Remove chicken. Add onion, carrots, zucchini, green pepper, garlic and corn. Cook over medium-high heat for 2 minutes, stirring constantly. Stir in thyme, salt and pepper. Combine noodles and corn mixture. Pour into 9 x 13-inch baking dish. Arrange chicken over top. Dissolve bouillon cubes in 3/4 cup boiling water. Pour over chicken and noodle mixture. Bake, tightly covered, at 350 degrees for 45 minutes. Arrange tomatoes around edges of dish. Broil until tomatoes are heated through. Yield: 6 servings.

Photograph for this recipe on this page.

GOURMET CHICKEN

1   3-lb. chicken
1/8 tsp. each parsley, oregano
3 bay leaves
3 cloves of garlic
Salt and pepper to taste
1 head cauliflower, chopped
1 bunch broccoli, chopped
7 or 8 carrots, coarsely chopped
1 lb. mushrooms
1 can cream of chicken soup
1 can cream of mushroom soup
3/4 c. chicken broth
2 c. shredded mozzarella cheese

Combine chicken, seasonings and water to cover in saucepan. Simmer for 1 hour. Remove chicken, garlic and bay leaves. Add vegetables. Cook for 8 to 10 minutes. Remove vegetables; place in large casserole. Bone chicken; add to casserole. Add soups and chicken broth; mix well. Sprinkle with cheese. Bake at 325 degrees for 30 minutes. Yield: 8-10 servings.

Maurine Taylor
Gilmer, Ohio

ORANGE DELIGHT CHICKEN

1/4 c. melted butter
Juice and grated rind of 1 orange
2 tbsp. lemon juice
2 tbsp. grated onion
2 tbsp. chopped celery tops
1 tsp. salt
1/8 tsp. cinnamon

Dash each of cayenne pepper, cloves
1 fryer, cut up
1/2 c. orange marmalade, melted

Combine butter, orange juice, orange rind, lemon juice, onion, celery tops and seasonings in greased baking pan; mix well. Place chicken in sauce, turning to coat well. Bake at 400 degrees for 20 minutes; turn chicken. Bake for 40 minutes longer, basting occasionally. Brush with marmalade. Broil for 1 to 2 minutes or until browned.

Effie Gish
Winston, North Dakota

GOLDEN PEACHY CHICKEN

2 1/2 lb. chicken pieces
1/4 c. peach syrup
3 tbsp. lemon juice
1 1/2 tbsp. soy sauce
1 lg. can peach halves, drained
1/4 to 1/2 c. margarine

Arrange chicken pieces in single layer in greased shallow baking dish. Combine peach syrup with lemon juice, soy sauce and 2 mashed peach halves in bowl; mix well. Pour over chicken. Dot chicken with margarine. Bake at 375 degrees for 1 1/2 hours, basting frequently. Arrange remaining peach halves in pan. Bake for 15 minutes longer or until chicken is tender.

Marjorie Little
Pembroke, Massachusetts

QUICK CHICKEN POTPIE

1 chicken
2 onions
2 cans cream of chicken soup
2 cans cream of mushroom soup
Salt and pepper to taste
1 stalk celery, chopped
1 can peas and carrots
1 stick margarine
2 cans refrigerator biscuits

Cook chicken and onions in 2 quarts water in saucepan until chicken is tender. Bone and chop chicken. Add soups and seasonings to broth; mix well. Cook over medium heat for 10 minutes. Add celery, peas and carrots and chicken. Bring to a boil. Melt margarine in 9 x 13-inch baking dish. Dip biscuits in margarine. Add hot chicken mixture to casserole. Arrange biscuits over top. Bake at 450 degrees until biscuits are golden brown. Yield: 8-10 servings.

Marilyn Pergerson
Reidsville, North Carolina

CRUNCHY BAKED CHICKEN

1 egg
1/3 c. milk
2 c. oats
1/2 c. melted butter
1/3 c. Parmesan cheese
1/3 c. chopped nuts
1/4 tsp. garlic salt
1 3-lb. chicken, cut up

Mix egg and milk in bowl. Combine oats, butter, cheese, nuts and garlic salt in bowl; mix well. Dip chicken in milk mixture. Coat with oat mixture. Place in foil-lined baking dish. Bake at 375 degrees for 45 minutes or until tender. Yield: 4 servings.

Hollie Watson
Batavia, New York

MOIST AND CRISPY CHICKEN

3 c. crisp rice cereal, finely crushed
1 tsp. paprika
1/2 tsp. salt
1/4 tsp. pepper
1 broiler-fryer, cut up
1/2 c. mayonnaise

Combine cereal, paprika, salt and pepper in large plastic food bag; shake to mix. Brush chicken with mayonnaise. Shake 1 piece at a time in cereal mixture until well coated. Place on rack in broiler pan. Bake at 425 degrees for 40 minutes or until golden brown and tender. Yield: 4 servings.

Angela Young
Omaha, Texas

SOUR CREAM
OVEN-FRIED CHICKEN

1 c. sour cream
2 cloves of garlic, mashed
2 tbsp. lemon juice
2 tsp. Worcestershire sauce
2 tsp. seasoned salt
1 tsp. each paprika, salt
Pepper to taste
2 1/2 lb. chicken pieces, skinned
2 c. Ritz cracker crumbs

Combine sour cream and seasonings in bowl; mix well. Dip chicken pieces into sour cream mixture; coat with crumbs. Place on baking sheet. Bake at 350 degrees for 1 hour.

Selma Sailors
Diller, Nebraska

Poultry

EASY BAKED PARMESAN CHICKEN

1   3-lb. chicken, cut up
1/2 c. melted margarine
1 c. cornflake crumbs
1/2 c. Parmesan cheese
1 1/2 tsp. salt
1/4 tsp. pepper
1 tsp. garlic powder

Rinse chicken; pat dry. Brush with margarine. Roll in mixture of cornflake crumbs, cheese and seasonings. Place on greased foil-lined baking sheet. Bake at 375 degrees for 1 hour. Yield: 4 servings.

Chris Smith
Stanislaus, California

SESAME-FRIED CHICKEN

1 stick margarine
1 egg, beaten
1/2 c. milk
1 c. flour
1 tsp. baking powder
2 tsp. salt
2 tbsp. sesame seed
2 tsp. paprika
1/4 tsp. pepper
1   2 1/2-lb. chicken, cut up, skinned

Melt margarine in shallow 10 x 16-inch baking dish. Mix egg and milk in shallow dish. Combine flour with next 5 ingredients. Dip chicken pieces in egg mixture; coat with seasoned flour. Place in baking dish, turning to coat with margarine. Bake at 400 degrees for 30 minutes. Turn chicken. Bake for 30 minutes longer or until tender.

Audra Smallwood
Irvine, Kentucky

SPICY OVEN-FRIED CHICKEN

1/2 c. yellow cornmeal
1/2 c. flour
1 1/2 tsp. each salt, chili powder
1/2 tsp. each oregano, pepper
1 fryer, cut up
1/2 c. milk
1/3 c. melted butter

Combine cornmeal, flour and seasonings; mix well. Dip chicken pieces in milk; coat with cornmeal mixture. Place skin side up in large shallow baking dish. Drizzle with butter. Bake at 375 degrees for 50 to 55 minutes or until golden brown and tender. Yield: 4 servings.

Ricardo Contreras
Fabens, Texas

JAMBALAYA CHICKEN

1   3-lb. chicken, cut up
1/4 c. olive oil
1/4 c. butter
1 lg. onion, chopped
1/2 c. chopped green onions
2 stalks celery, sliced
1/2 green pepper, chopped
2 cloves of garlic, minced
1 1/2 c. chopped boiled ham
1   16-oz. can tomatoes
1/4 c. tomato paste
1 c. chicken broth
1 tsp. salt
1/2 tsp. pepper
1 3/4 tsp. thyme
1 1/4 tsp. basil
Dash of cayenne pepper
1 tbsp. minced parsley
1 1/2 c. rice
1/2 lb. shrimp

Brown chicken in olive oil and butter in Dutch oven over medium heat. Remove to drain. Add onion, green onions, celery, green pepper and garlic. Saute until tender. Stir in remaining ingredients except rice and shrimp. Add chicken. Simmer, covered, for about 30 minutes. Stir in rice and shrimp. Bake at 350 degrees for 25 minutes. Stir gently. Bake, uncovered, for 15 minutes longer. Toss to fluff rice. Yield: 8 servings.

Eleanor Weatherhead
Dayton, Ohio

SAFFRON CHICKEN PILAF

2 lg. onions, sliced
1 1/2 c. oil
2 sticks cinnamon
3 lb. chicken thighs
1 1/2 tsp. garlic powder
1 1/2 tsp. ginger
1 1/2 tsp. coriander
2 tsp. salt
1/4 tsp. turmeric
1 lg. tomato, quartered
1 c. yogurt
3 lb. long grain rice, cooked
1/4 tsp. saffron
1/2 c. milk

Saute onions in oil in skillet until golden. Add cinnamon and chicken. Saute until chicken is lightly browned. Stir in next 5 seasonings and tomato. Simmer for 15 minutes or until chicken is tender. Stir in yogurt. Layer half the rice, chicken mixture and remaining rice in casserole. Stir saffron into milk. Pour over layers. Bake, covered, at 350 degrees for 35 minutes.

Madeline Merrill
Houston, Texas

ORANGE CHICKEN

1 chicken, cut up
Salt and pepper to taste
Flour
1/4 c. oil
1 lg. onion, sliced
1 sm. can frozen orange juice
    concentrate, thawed

Season chicken with salt and pepper. Coat with flour. Brown chicken in hot oil in skillet. Arrange in greased 9 x 13-inch baking dish. Saute onion in pan drippings until tender. Spread onion over chicken. Spread orange juice concentrate over top. Bake at 350 degrees for 1 hour. Serve with rice. Yield: 4 servings.

Claire Beckler
Naples, Florida

SPANISH CHICKEN

1   2 1/2-lb. chicken, cut up
1/2 c. chopped onion
1 clove of garlic, minced
2 tbsp. minced parsley
1 1/2 tsp. salt
3 tbsp. oil
2 tbsp. margarine
1 clove of garlic
2 onions, thinly sliced
2 green peppers, sliced
6 pieces of celery
2   15-oz. cans tomatoes
1 3/4 c. rice
1 tbsp. oil
2 1/2 c. chicken broth
1 tsp. saffron

Brown chicken with chopped onion, 1 clove of garlic, parsley and salt in 3 tablespoons oil in skillet. Remove chicken. Add margarine, 1 clove of garlic, sliced onions, green peppers and celery. Saute until lightly browned. Add tomatoes. Simmer for 30 minutes. Saute rice in 1 tablespoon oil in saucepan for 2 minutes or until golden, stirring constantly. Add chicken broth. Simmer, covered, for 20 minutes. Add saffron. Layer rice, chicken and tomato sauce in casserole. Bake, covered, at 350 degrees for 25 minutes or until rice is fluffy. Garnish with green peas, pimentos and hard-boiled egg slices.

Mildred Wood
Gaffney, South Carolina

ARROZ CON POLLO

2 cloves of garlic
1 onion, minced
1 fryer, cut up
1/2 c. olive oil
3 c. chicken broth
3 ripe tomatoes, quartered
1 bay leaf
1/2 tsp. saffron
2 tbsp. salt
1 1/4 c. long grain rice
2 green peppers, chopped

Saute garlic, onion and chicken in olive oil in Dutch oven until golden brown. Add remaining ingredients. Bring to a boil. Boil for 5 minutes. Bake, covered, at 350 degrees for 45 minutes or until chicken and rice are tender. Garnish with green peas. Yield: 8 servings.

Lenora Hudson
Sulphur, Oklahoma

GOLDEN CHICKEN
WITH APRICOT SAUCE

1/2 c. chopped celery
1/4 c. chopped onion
1 1/2 tbsp. butter
1/2 c. rice, cooked
1/4 tsp. salt
1/2 c. drained chopped apricot halves
8 chicken thighs, boned
Apricot Sauce

Saute celery and onion in butter in skillet until tender-crisp. Add rice, salt and apricots; mix well. Place 2 tablespoons rice mixture on each chicken thigh. Fold to enclose filling; secure with toothpick. Arrange skin side up in 2-quart baking dish. Bake at 375 degrees for 40 minutes. Pour Apricot Sauce over chicken. Bake for 30 minutes longer, basting occasionally. Remove toothpicks before serving.

APRICOT SAUCE

1/2 c. apricot jam
1/2 c. apricot nectar
1/2 c. catsup
2 tsp. mustard
1 tbsp. red wine vinegar
1 clove of garlic, minced
2 tbsp. chopped chives
1/2 tsp. salt

Combine all ingredients in saucepan. Simmer for 10 minutes. Yield: 6 servings.

Eleanor Weatherhead
Dayton, Ohio

Poultry

EASY CHICKEN CASSEROLE

1 6-oz. box long grain and wild rice mix
1 can cream of mushroom soup
1 can cream of celery soup
1 tbsp. chopped parsley
1/2 tsp. salt
1/4 tsp. pepper
Pinch of curry powder
10 chicken pieces
3/4 pkg. dry onion soup mix
1/2 c. slivered almonds

Combine first 7 ingredients and 1 soup can water in greased 9 x 13-inch baking dish; mix well. Arrange chicken skin side up in prepared dish. Top with soup mix and almonds. Bake, covered, at 350 degrees for 1 1/4 hours or until chicken is tender. Yield: 10 servings.

Nina Lonchar
Allegheny, Pennsylvania

GREEK CHICKEN ROLL

1 4 1/2-lb. chicken, cut up
4 c. chicken broth
3 tbsp. chopped parsley
3 tbsp. pimento
2 tbsp. dry mustard
2 tbsp. lemon juice
2 tbsp. chopped mint
1 tsp. salt
1 to 2 tsp. ground aniseed (opt.)

Simmer chicken in broth in saucepan for 45 minutes or until tender. Remove chicken; cool. Bone and chop chicken. Cool broth slightly; skim. Boil until reduced to 3 cups. Cool in bowl until slightly thickened. Add chicken and remaining ingredients; mix well. Mold into 2 1/2 x 9-inch roll on 12 x 16-inch foil. Fold in sides of foil; roll tightly from narrow end. Secure with string; place on tray. Refrigerate overnight. Slice chicken roll; arrange on platter. Garnish with parsley and cucumber slices.

Virginia Lund
Cedar Falls, Iowa

BLUE RIBBON BARBECUED CHICKEN

1 med. onion, sliced
2 stalks celery, cut in lg. chunks
2 bay leaves
1 tbsp. salt
1/8 tsp. Tabasco sauce
1 tbsp. parsley flakes
2 12-oz. cans beer
1 3-lb. chicken, cut up

Combine all ingredients except chicken in bowl; mix well. Place chicken in single layer in baking dish. Pour marinade over chicken. Marinate, covered, for several hours, turning chicken twice. Place on grill over hot coals. Cook for 1 hour or until tender and crisp, turning frequently and basting with sauce every 5 minutes.

Lucille Johnston
Litchfield, Illinois

BARBECUE SAUCE FOR CHICKEN

1 1/2 c. oil
3/4 c. soy sauce
1/4 c. Worcestershire sauce
1/2 c. red wine vinegar
1/3 c. lemon juice
2 tbsp. dry mustard
2 1/4 tsp. salt
1 tsp. pepper
1 1/2 tsp. parsley
2 cloves of garlic, crushed

Combine all ingredients in order listed in bowl; mix well. Marinate chicken in sauce. Use marinade for basting while cooking.

Mary Lu Buckman
Contra Costa, California

GRILLED HAWAIIAN CHICKEN

1 c. orange juice
1 to 2 tbsp. grated orange rind
1/4 c. honey
2 tsp. ginger
1 1/2 tsp. thyme
1 tsp. seasoned salt
1 tsp. seasoned pepper
1 bay leaf, crumbled
8 chicken quarters

Combine all ingredients except chicken in large plastic bag. Add chicken. Place bag in bowl. Marinate in refrigerator for several hours to overnight, turning occasionally. Drain, reserving marinade. Grill over hot coals for 45 minutes, basting with reserved marinade and turning chicken frequently. Yield: 8 servings.

Cynthia Berend
Mt. Vernon, Texas

LEMON-GRILLED CHICKEN

2 tsp. each salt, pepper, tarragon
and paprika
1/4 c. lemon juice
3 broiler-fryers, split

Mix seasonings and lemon juice in bowl. Brush all sides of chicken. Place skin side up on grill. Cook over medium coals for 20 minutes. Turn; brush with lemon mixture. Cook for 30 to 45 minutes longer or until chicken is tender.

Henrietta Thomas
Hopkinsville, Kentucky

RUBY-GLAZED CHICKEN

1 chicken, cut up
Salt and pepper
1/4 c. butter
1/4 c. currant jelly
1 tbsp. each Worcestershire sauce,
lemon juice

Grill chicken over hot coals for 30 minutes, turning occasionally. Season with salt and pepper. Heat remaining ingredients in saucepan, stirring until smooth. Brush glaze on chicken. Grill for 15 to 20 minutes longer or until tender, turning and brushing frequently with remaining glaze.

Martha Ann Johnson
Manton, Michigan

GRILLED PEANUT BUTTER CHICKEN

1 tbsp. oil
1/4 tsp. pepper
1/3 c. chunky peanut butter
2 tbsp. soy sauce
1 tbsp. wine vinegar
1 sm. clove of garlic
1/4 tsp. cardamom
1/4 tsp. cinnamon
10 chicken breast halves, skinned, boned

Combine first 8 ingredients and 1/4 cup water in bowl; mix well. Pour over chicken in shallow dish. Marinate in refrigerator overnight. Grill over hot coals for 5 minutes on each side.

Karen Sparkman
Orlando, Florida

CHICKEN CACCIATORE

1 3-lb. chicken, cut up
2 tbsp. olive oil
2 tbsp. butter
1/2 lb. mushrooms, sliced
1 med. onion, chopped
2 green peppers, chopped
2 cloves of garlic, minced
2 tbsp. chopped parsley
1/2 c. dry white wine
1 can tomato paste
1 1/2 tsp. salt
1/4 tsp. each oregano, thyme
1 tsp. basil
1 8-oz. package vermicelli, cooked
2 tbsp. butter

Brown chicken in olive oil and 2 tablespoons butter in skillet. Drain chicken, reserving 3 tablespoons pan drippings. Saute mushrooms, onion, green peppers and garlic in reserved drippings in skillet until onion is tender. Add parsley, wine, tomato paste, seasonings, 1/2 cup water and chicken. Simmer for 45 minutes, stirring occasionally. Toss vermicelli with 2 tablespoons butter; place in deep serving dish. Arrange chicken over vermicelli; top with sauce. Yield: 4-5 servings.

Virginia Savedge
Eastville, Virginia

CHICKEN CONFETTI

1 4-lb. chicken, cut up
1 tsp. salt
1/8 tsp. pepper
1/4 c. oil
1/2 c. chopped onion
1 clove of garlic, minced
2 tsp. salt
1/4 tsp. pepper
2 16-oz. cans tomatoes
1 16-oz. can tomato sauce
1 6-oz. can tomato paste
2 tbsp. chopped parsley
2 tsp. basil
1 8-oz. package spaghetti, cooked

Sprinkle chicken with 1 teaspoon salt and 1/8 teaspoon pepper. Brown in oil in skillet. Drain, reserving 3 tablespoons oil. Saute onion and garlic in reserved oil in skillet. Add chicken, 2 teaspoons salt, 1/4 teaspoon pepper and remaining ingredients except spaghetti. Simmer, tightly covered, for 1 to 1 1/2 hours or until tender, stirring occasionally and adding water if necessary; skim. Serve over spaghetti. Top with Parmesan cheese. Yield: 4 servings.

Michelle Thomas
Mt. Vernon, New York

Poultry

CHICKEN CHOW MEIN

1 lb. chicken, slivered
2 tbsp. butter
6 onions, sliced lengthwise
5 beef bouillon cubes
2 bunches celery, sliced diagonally
1 can bean sprouts
1/4 c. flour
2 tbsp. sugar
Soy sauce to taste

Saute chicken in butter in skillet. Add onions, bouillon cubes dissolved in 1 cup boiling water and celery. Cook for 15 to 20 minutes. Stir in bean sprouts and flour blended with 1/2 cup water. Cook until thickened, stirring constantly. Add sugar and soy sauce. Serve over crisp chow mein noodles. Yield: 4-6 servings.

Martha Dawson
Dover, Delaware

EASY CHICKEN CURRY

1/2 lb. onions, sliced
1 stick margarine
1/2 lb. onions, finely chopped
4 cloves of garlic, minced
1/4 tsp. turmeric
1 tsp. each cumin, ginger, paprika
2 tsp. each chili powder, coriander
2 lb. chicken pieces
1/2 c. yogurt
2 bay leaves

Saute sliced onions in margarine in skillet until golden brown. Combine chopped onions, garlic, seasonings and 1 tablespoon water in bowl; mix well. Stir into sauteed onions. Cook over low heat for 3 to 4 minutes, stirring constantly. Add chicken. Cook over medium heat until chicken is brown. Stir in yogurt and bay leaves. Simmer, covered, for 1 hour or until chicken is tender. Remove bay leaf; serve with peanuts, coconut, chutney, crumbled bacon and pickled watermelon rind. Yield: 6 servings.

Beverly Abbott
Libson Falls, Maine

CROCK•POT CHICKEN

1 3-lb. chicken, cut up
1 tsp. salt
1/2 tsp. pepper
1/2 c. milk
1 can cream of chicken soup
1 pkg. chicken gravy mix

Sprinkle chicken with salt and pepper. Combine milk, soup and gravy mix in medium bowl. Coat chicken with soup mixture. Place chicken in Crock·Pot. Pour remaining soup mixture over chicken. Cook on High for 4 hours. Cook on Low for 4 hours, stirring occasionally.

Betty Lou Horton
Tanner, Alabama

SAUCY FRIED CHICKEN

1 sm. onion, minced
1 scallion, minced
1 sprig of thyme, minced
1 clove of garlic, minced
2 tsp. salt
1/4 c. flour
1 3-lb. chicken, cut up
1 egg
1/4 c. bread crumbs
1/2 c. oil
1 tsp. grated orange rind
2 tsp. cornstarch
1/4 c. sugar
2 tsp. margarine
1 med. carrot, chopped
1 sprig of parsley, finely chopped
4 tsp. orange juice

Combine onion, scallion, thyme, garlic, salt and flour. Coat chicken with flour mixture. Dip in egg beaten with 1 teaspoon water; coat with crumbs. Fry in oil in skillet until golden brown and tender. Drain. Place on heated serving plate. Boil orange rind in 1 cup water in saucepan for 2 minutes. Add cornstarch dissolved in 1 tablespoon water, sugar, margarine, carrot and parsley; mix well. Simmer until thickened, stirring constantly. Remove from heat; add orange juice. Serve with chicken.
Yield: 4 servings.

Laura Hill
Spartanburg, South Carolina

DIFFERENT FRIED CHICKEN

1 egg, beaten
1/2 c. milk
1 c. flour
1/4 c. cornmeal
1/2 tsp. baking powder
1/4 tsp. each garlic powder, paprika
   and basil
Pepper to taste
1/2 tsp. salt

1 chicken, cut up
Oil for deep frying

Mix egg and milk in bowl. Combine next 3 ingredients and seasonings in shallow bowl. Dip chicken in egg mixture; coat with flour mixture. Deep-fry for 20 to 30 minutes or until brown. Arrange on rack in roasting pan filled with boiling water. Steam at 225 degrees for 10 to 15 minutes. Yield: 4 servings.

Ruth Robare
Albany, Oregon

CURRIED FRIED CHICKEN

2 or 3 cloves of garlic, chopped
1 med. onion, chopped
3/4 tsp. salt
Pepper to taste
1 tbsp. curry powder
2 to 3 lb. chicken pieces
2 tbsp. oil
1 tbsp. curry powder

Combine garlic, onion, salt, pepper and 1 tablespoon curry powder in bowl; mix well. Roll chicken in garlic mixture. Brown chicken in oil in skillet over medium heat. Sprinkle with 1 tablespoon curry powder. Fry for several minutes longer. Add a small amount of water if necessary. Simmer, covered, for 20 minutes or until tender. Serve with rice and Oriental vegetables.

Doris Hahn
Des Moines, Iowa

CHICKEN MARENGO

1 2 1/2-lb. chicken, cut up
1/4 c. oil
1/2 c. chopped onion
1 clove of garlic, minced
1/4 tsp. marjoram
1 3-oz. can sliced mushrooms
1/2 c. dry white wine
1 tsp. salt
1/8 tsp. pepper
2 8-oz. cans tomato sauce
1 5-oz. package yellow rice, cooked

Brown chicken in oil in skillet over low heat. Add onion, garlic and marjoram. Cook until onion is tender. Drain mushrooms, reserving liquid. Add mushroom liquid, wine, salt and pepper to skillet. Simmer, covered, for 35 minutes or until chicken is tender. Stir in tomato sauce

and mushrooms. Simmer, covered, for 5 minutes. Serve over rice. Garnish with parsley. Yield: 5 servings.

Karin Bargar
Lansing, Michigan

PRUNE-CHICKEN SAUTE

2 tbsp. butter
2 tbsp. olive oil
1 clove of garlic
1 3-lb. chicken, cut up
Salt and pepper
1/2 onion, thinly sliced
1/4 c. chopped celery
1/4 tsp. tarragon
1/2 c. California prunes
1 c. dry white wine

Melt butter in skillet. Add oil and garlic. Cook until garlic is golden. Remove and discard garlic. Sprinkle chicken with salt and pepper. Brown in garlic oil. Layer onion, celery, tarragon and prunes over chicken. Pour wine over all. Cook, covered, for 45 minutes to 1 hour or until chicken is tender. Yield: 4 servings.

Photograph for this recipe below.

Poultry

CHICKEN MOSAIC

1 lb. chicken cutlets
1/4 c. flour
3 tbsp. butter
1/4 lb. Swiss cheese, cut into strips
1/4 lb. prosciutto, cut into strips
12 black Greek olives, sliced
1/4 c. white wine

Coat chicken with flour. Saute on both sides in butter in skillet. Arrange cheese and prosciutto strips to form grid on each cutlet. Place olives in center of each square formed by grid. Add wine. Cook for 4 minutes longer or until cheese is melted. Serve immediately. Yield: 4 servings.

Patricia Edwards
Wilson, North Carolina

ONE-POT COUNTRY CHICKEN

1   3-lb. fryer, cut up
3 tbsp. oil
Salt and pepper
1/2 tsp. paprika
1 lg. onion, thickly sliced
2/3 c. slivered green pepper
4 med. potatoes, peeled, thickly sliced
4 tsp. parsley flakes
1 beef bouillon cube
1/2 c. frozen green peas

Brown chicken in oil in large skillet. Season with salt and pepper. Sprinkle with paprika. Let stand in skillet for several minutes; remove chicken. Saute onion and green pepper in pan drippings until onion is tender. Arrange potatoes in single layer over sauteed vegetables. Sprinkle with 1/4 teaspoon salt, 1/8 teaspoon pepper and parsley flakes. Arrange chicken pieces over potatoes. Dissolve bouillon cube in 3/4 cup hot water. Add to skillet. Cook, covered, over low heat for 20 minutes. Sprinkle peas around chicken. Cook, covered, until peas and chicken are tender. Yield: 4 servings.

Evangline Maxwell
Spencer, Iowa

MICROWAVE PARMESAN CHICKEN

1 egg, beaten
1 tbsp. milk
1/4 c. flour
1/2 c. Parmesan cheese
1 tsp. paprika
1/2 tsp. salt
Dash of pepper

1   3-lb. fryer, cut up, skinned
1/4 c. melted butter

Mix egg and milk in bowl. Combine flour, Parmesan cheese, paprika, salt and pepper in bowl; mix well. Dip chicken in egg mixture. Coat with seasoned flour. Place in greased 9 x 13-inch glass baking dish. Drizzle with butter. Microwave, covered, on High for 15 minutes. Let stand for 5 minutes. Yield: 4 servings.

Violet Mosley
Avon Park, Florida

PEPSI CHICKEN

1 stick margarine
1 chicken, cut up
1   12-oz. can Pepsi Cola
1   20-oz. bottle of catsup

Melt margarine in electric skillet. Arrange chicken in skillet. Add remaining ingredients. Cook at 250 degrees for 2 hours or until chicken is brown and tender. Yield: 4 servings.

Dawn Haney
Monroe, Pennsylvania

SINGAPORE CHICKEN

3 tbsp. cornstarch
Juice of 1 lemon
1 1/2 tsp. salt
2 tsp. soy sauce
1 1/2 tsp. sesame oil
1 1/2 tsp. grated gingerroot
2 tbsp. white wine
1/4 c. cream of coconut
1   3-lb. chicken, cut up
1 3/4 c. chopped onion
5 1/2 tbsp. peanut oil
1   16-oz. can tomatoes

Combine first 8 ingredients in bowl; mix well. Arrange chicken pieces in single layer in shallow dish; pour marinade over chicken. Chill, tightly covered, overnight. Drain, reserving marinade. Saute onion in peanut oil in Dutch oven until golden. Remove onion; add chicken. Brown chicken on all sides. Add reserved marinade, sauteed onion and tomatoes. Bring to a boil. Simmer until chicken is tender, stirring frequently. Serve over rice. Yield: 4-6 servings.

Alice Applegate
Knoxville, Iowa

TARRAGON CHICKEN

1 c. dry white wine
1/4 c. lemon juice

2 tbsp. red wine vinegar
2 tbsp. oil
1 lg. clove of garlic, crushed
1 1/2 tsp. tarragon
1 tsp. Beau Monde seasoning
1/2 tsp. salt
1 3-lb. chicken, cut up
3 c. small whole frozen onions, thawed
3 med. zucchini, cut into strips
1 clove of garlic, crushed
3 tbsp. oil
2 tbsp. butter
3/4 tsp. salt
1/8 tsp. white pepper
2 med. tomatoes, cut into wedges

Combine wine, lemon juice, vinegar, 2 tablespoons oil, 1 clove of garlic, tarragon, Beau Monde and 1/2 teaspoon salt. Add chicken; turn to coat well. Marinate, covered, in refrigerator for 6 hours or longer, turning chicken occasionally. Drain, reserving marinade. Grill chicken 4 to 5 inches from medium coals for 45 minutes or until chicken is tender, turning occasionally. Brush chicken frequently with reserved marinade. Saute onions, zucchini and 1 clove of garlic in 3 tablespoons oil in skillet for 5 minutes or until zucchini is tender-crisp, stirring constantly. Add butter, 3/4 teaspoon salt, white pepper and tomato wedges. Cook until tomatoes are heated through, stirring occasionally. Arrange chicken on large serving platter. Arrange vegetables around chicken.
Yield: 4 servings.

Photograph for this recipe on this page.

SLOW AND EASY CHICKEN

2 carrots, sliced
2 onions, sliced
2 stalks celery with leaves, chopped
1 3-lb. chicken
2 tsp. salt
1/2 tsp. pepper
1/2 c. chicken broth
1/2 to 1 tsp. basil

Place carrots, onions and celery in slow cooker. Add chicken, salt, pepper, broth and 1/2 cup water. Sprinkle with basil. Cook on Low for 8 to 10 hours. Yield: 4 servings.

Mattie Finney
Burton, Washington

SPICY BAKED CHICKEN

1 chicken
1/4 tsp. each onion powder, garlic powder
1/4 tsp. each paprika, salt and pepper

Place chicken in shallow baking pan. Sprinkle with half the spices. Bake at 350 degrees for 30 minutes. Sprinkle with remaining spices. Bake for 30 minutes longer or until tender.
Yield: 4 servings.

Brett Slusser
Merrill, Wisconsin

ROAST CHICKENS WITH HERBS

2 broiler-fryers
6 cloves of garlic
4 bay leaves
6 tbsp. butter, melted
1 tsp. each salt and pepper
1/2 tsp. each thyme, oregano and marjoram
1/2 tsp. each sage, basil

Rub skin of each chicken with clove of cut garlic. Stuff each chicken cavity with 2 bay leaves and 3 cloves of garlic. Blend butter and seasonings in small bowl. Spoon 1 tablespoon herb butter into each cavity; truss. Brush generously with remaining herb butter. Place chickens, breast side down, on rack in shallow roasting pan in cold oven. Turn on oven to 425 degrees. Roast for 45 minutes. Turn chickens breast side up. Bake for 40 minutes longer, basting occasionally with remaining butter mixture and pan drippings. Cool slightly; cover loosely with foil. Chill in refrigerator until ready to serve. Cut chickens into pieces; garnish with watercress.

Evelyn Fuller
Selma, Alabama

Poultry

ROAST CHICKENS WITH BUTTERNUT SQUASH

2 sm. chickens
Salt and pepper to taste
1 tsp. tarragon
2 tbsp. butter, melted
2 sm. butternut squash, peeled, quartered
3 tbsp. honey
3 tbsp. dry Sherry

Season chickens with salt and pepper inside and out. Sprinkle cavities with tarragon. Place in baking dish; brush with butter. Bake at 375 degrees for 20 minutes. Cook squash in boiling salted water in saucepan for 5 minutes; drain. Arrange around chickens. Bake for 15 minutes longer. Brush chickens and squash with mixture of honey and Sherry. Bake for 15 minutes longer or until tender, basting frequently with pan drippings.

Maxine Barber
Martinez, California

ROAST CHICKEN WITH DILLED STUFFING

1/2 c. chopped celery
1/2 c. chopped onion
1/2 c. melted butter
5 c. dry white bread cubes
1/2 tsp. dillweed, crushed
1/2 tsp. salt
Dash of pepper
2 tsp. chicken-seasoned stock base
1 4 to 5-lb. chicken
1/4 c. melted butter
1/4 c. flour
1 1/4 tsp. Beau Monde seasoning

Saute celery and onion in 1/2 cup butter in saucepan for 5 minutes, stirring occasionally. Remove from heat; stir in bread cubes, dillweed, salt and pepper. Add stock base dissolved in 1/2 cup boiling water; toss until well mixed. Stuff chicken; truss. Place breast side up on rack in shallow roasting pan. Brush with 1/4 cup melted butter. Roast at 375 degrees for 2 to 2 1/2 hours or until tender, brushing occasionally with melted butter. Remove to heated serving platter; keep warm. Drain drippings, reserving 1/2 cup. Stir in flour until smooth. Cook over low heat until bubbly, stirring constantly. Stir in 2 cups water gradually. Cook, until thickened, stirring constantly. Stir in Beau Monde seasoning. Serve with chicken.

Photograph for this recipe on page 42.

ROAST CHERRY-GLAZED CHICKEN

1/4 c. minced onion
1 tbsp. melted butter
1 1/2 tsp. curry powder
1 c. cherry preserves
1 tsp. grated orange rind
1/4 c. orange juice
1 5-oz. package brown and wild rice mix, cooked
1/3 c. cherry preserves
1/2 c. chopped celery
1 3-lb. chicken
1 tbsp. melted butter

Saute onion in 1 tablespoon melted butter in skillet until tender. Blend in curry powder, 1 cup preserves, orange rind and orange juice. Simmer for 2 minutes, stirring occasionally. Combine rice mix, 1/3 cup cherry preserves and celery in bowl; mix well. Stuff chicken with rice mixture; truss. Place breast side up on rack in shallow roasting pan. Brush with 1 tablespoon melted butter. Roast at 375 degrees for 1 hour. Brush with cherry sauce. Roast for 30 minutes longer, brushing several times with sauce. Serve with remaining sauce.
Yield: 4 servings.

Photograph for this recipe on opposite page.

CHICKEN STUFFED WITH SPINACH DRESSING

8 oz. chopped spinach, cooked
1/2 c. chopped mushrooms
2 tbsp. butter
2 slices bread, crumbled
2 tbsp. milk
1 tsp. each fresh chopped thyme, oregano, sage and savory
1 tbsp. fresh chopped rosemary
2 bay leaves, crumbled
2 tbsp. fresh chopped parsley
2 cloves of garlic, pressed
Salt and pepper to taste
8 oz. ricotta cheese
1 egg, beaten
1/2 c. grated Monterey Jack cheese
1 3-lb. chicken, boned
2 tbsp. olive oil
1/2 c. chicken stock
1/2 c. fresh lemon juice
1/2 c. white wine

Squeeze excess moisture from spinach. Saute mushrooms in butter in skillet. Mix bread and milk in bowl. Add spinach, seasonings, ricotta cheese, egg, Monterey Jack cheese and mushrooms; mix well. Spoon stuffing into chicken. Reshape; tie securely. Place in greased baking dish. Brush with olive oil. Bake at 350 degrees for 1 hour. Slice. Combine chicken stock, lemon juice and wine in saucepan. Cook until light golden brown. Serve with stuffed chicken. Yield: 4 servings.

Judith Jones
Richards, North Carolina

BENGALI CHICKEN WITH BLACK-EYED PEAS

    1   3-lb. roasting chicken
    1 c. yogurt
    3 tbsp. lemon juice
    1 clove of garlic, minced
    1 tsp. salt
    1 tsp. ginger
    1/4 tsp. cumin
    1/2 tsp. turmeric
    Dash of Tabasco sauce
    1   16-oz. package frozen black-eyed
        peas, cooked
    2 1/2 to 3 tbsp. lemon juice
    1 clove of garlic, minced
    1 c. chicken broth
    1 med. onion, finely chopped
    1 sm. carrot, minced
    Salt and pepper to taste
    1 c. yogurt
    2 to 3 tbsp. minced scallions
    Herb seasoning to taste

Truss chicken; place in glass bowl. Mix 1 cup yogurt with 3 tablespoons lemon juice, 1 clove of garlic and next 5 seasonings. Spread over chicken. Let stand, covered, in refrigerator for several hours. Combine peas, 2 1/2 to 3 tablespoons lemon juice, 1 clove of garlic, chicken broth, onion, carrot, salt and pepper in bowl; mix well. Turn into greased baking dish; place chicken on peas. Roast at 350 degrees for 1 1/4 hours or until chicken is tender, adding additional liquid as necessary. Blend 1 cup yogurt, scallions and herb seasoning in small bowl. Serve with chicken.

Photograph for this recipe on page 1.

CHICKEN LIVER CASSEROLE

    3/4 lb. chicken livers
    Salt and pepper to taste
    Flour

    1/4 c. butter
    1/4 c. chopped onion
    1/4 c. chopped celery
    1 c. rice
    2 c. chicken broth
    1 tsp. parsley

Season chicken livers with salt and pepper. Coat with flour. Brown in butter in skillet. Place livers in greased casserole. Saute onion, celery and rice in pan drippings. Stir in broth and parsley. Pour over livers. Bake at 350 degrees for 40 minutes or until rice is tender and liquid is absorbed.

Imogene Brashear
Palatka, Florida

CHICKEN LIVERS AND MUSHROOMS

    1 lb. chicken livers
    2 tbsp. flour
    1/4 c. olive oil
    1/2 c. chopped onion
    1/4 c. Sherry
    1 c. sliced mushrooms
    2 tbsp. chopped parsley
    1 tsp. each basil, rosemary
    1 1/2 c. chicken broth
    Salt and pepper to taste

Coat chicken livers with flour. Brown in olive oil in skillet. Add remaining ingredients. Simmer, covered, for 20 minutes. Serve over rice or spaghetti. Yield: 4 servings.

Leslie Cottrell
Bridgeville, California

Poultry

PARTY CHICKEN LIVERS

2 lb. chicken livers
1 1/2 tsp. salt
1/4 c. butter
1/4 c. finely chopped onion
1/4 c. Sherry
1/2 tsp. Tabasco sauce

Sprinkle chicken livers with salt. Brown several at a time in butter in skillet; remove to chafing dish. Saute onion in pan drippings until tender. Add Sherry and Tabasco sauce. Deglaze skillet. Pour over livers. Cook for 10 minutes, stirring frequently.

Photograph for this recipe above.

CRUSTY CHICKEN AMANDINE

1 can cream of chicken soup
1 c. mayonnaise
1/2 c. sour cream
1/2 c. chopped celery
1/2 c. chopped onions
1   4-oz. can mushroom pieces, drained
1   8-oz. can sliced water
    chestnuts, drained
Salt to taste
5 to 6 c. chopped cooked chicken
1/4 c. butter, melted
1/2 c. shredded cheese
1/2 c. slivered almonds
1 pkg. refrigerator crescent rolls

Combine soup with next 7 ingredients in large bowl; mix well. Stir in chicken. Pour into greased 9 x 13-inch baking dish. Bake at 375 degrees until bubbly. Combine butter, cheese and almonds in saucepan. Cook over medium heat until blended, stirring constantly. Cover hot chicken mixture with crescent rolls; spread with cheese mixture. Bake for 25 minutes longer. Yield: 10 servings.

Susan Sheffield
Richmond, Virginia

CHICKEN-ARTICHOKE CASSEROLE

1 c. butter, melted
1/2 c. flour
3 1/2 c. milk
3 oz. Swiss cheese, grated
2 oz. Cheddar cheese, grated
1 tsp. red pepper
Salt to taste
3 to 4 c. chopped cooked chicken
1   8-oz. jar button mushrooms, drained
2   14-oz. cans artichoke hearts, drained

Blend butter and flour in large saucepan over medium heat. Stir in milk gradually. Add cheeses and seasoning. Cook until cheese is melted and sauce is bubbly, stirring constantly. Stir in chicken, mushrooms and artichoke hearts. Pour into large greased casserole. Bake at 350 degrees for 30 minutes.

Leola Dawn
Lawrence, Kansas

CHICKEN-ASPARAGUS DINNER

1/4 c. flour
1/2 tsp. each salt and pepper
1 c. milk
1/4 c. butter
1 c. chicken broth
1/2 c. whipping cream, whipped
3 tbsp. dry onion soup mix
1 c. sour cream
2 c. cooked asparagus
2 c. chopped cooked chicken
1/2 c. grated sharp Cheddar cheese

Blend flour, salt and pepper with cold milk in saucepan. Add butter. Cook over low heat until thickened, stirring constantly. Blend in broth. Fold in whipped cream. Mix soup mix with sour cream in small bowl. Layer asparagus, chicken, sour cream mixture, white sauce and cheese in greased shallow baking dish. Bake at 350 degrees for 30 minutes. Yield: 6 servings.

Mary Sargent
Edmond, Oklahoma

CHEESY CHICKEN CASSEROLE

2   10-oz. packages frozen broccoli, cooked
2 c. milk
2   8-oz. packages cream cheese, softened
1 tsp. each salt, garlic salt
3/4 c. Parmesan cheese
4 to 5 c. chopped cooked chicken
3/4 c. Parmesan cheese

Cut broccoli into bite-sized pieces; arrange in greased 2-quart casserole. Combine milk, cream cheese, salt and garlic salt in double boiler. Cook until cheese is melted, stirring constantly. Stir in 3/4 cup Parmesan cheese. Pour 1 cup sauce over broccoli; arrange chicken over sauce. Top with remaining sauce. Sprinkle with 3/4 cup Parmesan cheese. Bake at 350 degrees for 30 minutes. Yield: 8-10 servings.

Verna Larson
Crawfordsville, Georgia

CURRIED CHICKEN CASSEROLE

    1 1/2 lb. broccoli, cooked, sliced
    8 to 10 slices cooked chicken
    1/2 c. mayonnaise
    2 tbsp. lemon juice
    2 to 3 tsp. curry powder
    1 1/2 tsp. Worcestershire sauce
    1 can cream of mushroom soup
    1 can cream of chicken soup
    1 4-oz. can sliced mushrooms
    2 c. buttered bread crumbs
    Paprika

Layer broccoli and chicken in greased 9 x 13-inch casserole. Blend next 6 ingredients in bowl. Stir in mushrooms. Pour over chicken. Top with buttered crumbs; sprinkle with paprika. Bake at 350 degrees for 30 minutes or until bubbly. Yield: 8 servings.

Jody Whittier
Santa Barbara, California

EASY CHICKEN DIVAN

    2 pkg. frozen broccoli, cooked
    6 chicken breasts, cooked, boned
    1 c. mayonnaise
    1 tsp. lemon juice
    1/2 tsp. curry powder
    1 can cream of chicken soup
    1 can cream of celery soup
    3/4 c. grated sharp Cheddar cheese
    1/2 c. bread crumbs
    1 tbsp. melted butter

Layer broccoli and chicken in buttered 9 x 13-inch casserole. Combine next 5 ingredients in bowl; mix well. Pour over chicken. Top with mixture of cheese, crumbs and melted butter. Bake at 350 degrees for 25 minutes or until browned. Garnish with pimento.

Cindy Warfield
Canton, Ohio

CHICKEN AND BISCUITS CASSEROLE

    1 3 1/2-lb. chicken, cut up
    3 c. chicken broth
    1 1/2 c. chopped celery
    1 c. chopped onion
    1 c. sliced carrots
    Salt and pepper to taste
    1/3 c. melted butter
    1/2 c. flour
    1/2 tsp. poultry seasoning
    1 1/2 c. milk
    1 c. flour
    1/2 c. shredded Cheddar cheese
    1 1/2 tsp. baking powder
    1/4 tsp. salt
    3 tbsp. butter, softened
    1/2 c. milk

Combine first 5 ingredients, salt and pepper in 4-quart saucepan. Simmer, covered, for 45 minutes or until chicken is tender; drain, reserving broth. Bone and cut chicken into bite-sized pieces. Combine melted butter, 1/2 cup flour and poultry seasoning in large saucepan; blend well. Cook until thickened, stirring constantly. Stir in 1 1/2 cups milk and 1 1/2 cups reserved broth gradually. Bring to a boil, stirring constantly. Cook for 1 minute, stirring constantly. Stir in vegetables and chicken. Spoon into greased 2-quart casserole. Combine 1 cup flour, cheese, baking powder and 1/4 teaspoon salt in bowl; mix well. Cut in softened butter until crumbly. Add 1/2 cup milk; mix just until moistened. Drop by rounded tablespoonfuls over chicken mixture. Bake at 425 degrees for 20 minutes or until biscuits are golden.

Barbara Bradford
Portland, Oregon

CHICKEN CASSEROLE WITH CASHEWS

    3 to 4 c. chopped cooked chicken
    1 can chicken with rice soup
    1 can cream of mushroom soup
    1 sm. can evaporated milk
    1 can chow mein noodles
    1 c. grated Swiss cheese
    1 sm. package cashews (opt.)

Combine chicken, soups and milk in bowl; mix lightly. Pour into greased 9 x 13-inch baking dish. Layer remaining ingredients over top. Bake at 350 degrees for 30 minutes or until golden. Yield: 6 servings.

Diane Centar
Billings, Montana

Poultry

CHICKEN-MACARONI OVERNIGHT CASSEROLE

2 c. milk
2 cans cream of mushroom soup
1 8-oz. package macaroni
1 can sliced water chestnuts, drained
2 c. chopped cooked chicken
1 c. chopped onion
1 1/2 c. grated Cheddar cheese
3 hard-boiled eggs, chopped
1/4 tsp. salt
1/3 c. chopped parsley
1 hard-boiled egg, thinly sliced
1 can pimento strips (opt.)

Combine milk and soup in large bowl; mix well. Add uncooked macaroni, water chestnuts, chicken,. onion, cheese, chopped hard-boiled eggs and salt; mix well. Refrigerate, tightly covered, overnight. Pour macaroni mixture into greased 9 x 13-inch baking dish. Bake at 325 degrees for 1 1/4 hours or until bubbly. Top with parsley, sliced hard-boiled egg and pimento strips. Yield: 8 servings.

Joan Newton
Mystic, Connecticut

CRAB AND CHICKEN DUET

1/2 c. sliced mushrooms
1/4 c. chopped onion
3 tbsp. butter
3 tbsp. flour
1/2 tsp. salt
1/8 tsp. white pepper
1 1/2 c. chicken broth
1/2 c. white wine
2 egg yolks, beaten

1 c. green peas
1 6-oz. package frozen crab meat, thawed, chopped
1/2 c. heavy cream, whipped
3 chicken breasts, cooked, sliced
1/4 c. Parmesan cheese
Paprika

Saute mushrooms and onion in butter in saucepan. Mix in flour, salt and pepper. Add broth and wine gradually. Cook until thickened, stirring constantly. Stir a small amount of hot mixture into egg yolks; stir egg yolks into hot mixture. Cook for 2 minutes, stirring constantly; remove from heat. Fold in peas, crab meat and whipped cream. Place chicken in greased shallow baking dish. Pour crab mixture over chicken. Sprinkle with cheese and paprika. Bake at 325 degrees for 15 minutes or until heated through and golden brown.
Yield: 6 servings.

Shirley Mayes
Macon, Georgia

SAVORY CHICKEN CASSEROLE

1 can cream of mushroom soup
1 can cream of chicken soup
1/2 soup can chicken broth
1 tsp. onion powder
4 c. cooked rice
3 c. chopped cooked chicken
1 c. grated Cheddar cheese
2 tbsp. chopped pimento

Mix soups and broth in saucepan. Heat until smooth, stirring constantly. Add remaining ingredients. Pour into greased 2 1/2-quart casserole. Bake at 375 degrees for 25 to 30 minutes or until bubbly. Yield: 8 servings.

Photograph for this recipe on this page.

SOUR CREAM-CHICKEN SQUARES

2 c. biscuit mix
1 c. chopped cooked chicken
1 4-oz. can mushroom pieces
1 2-oz. jar pimentos, chopped, drained
1/3 c. sliced green onions
1 c. shredded Cheddar cheese
1 8-oz. carton sour cream
1/3 c. mayonnaise
3 eggs, beaten
1 tsp. garlic salt
1/8 tsp. pepper

Combine biscuit mix and 1/2 cup cold water in bowl. Beat 20 strokes. Knead 5 times on floured surface. Roll into 10 x 14-inch rectangle. Press over bottom and 1/2 inch up sides of greased 9 x 13-inch baking pan. Mix remaining ingredients in bowl. Spoon over crust. Bake at 350 degrees for 25 minutes or until set. Yield: 6 servings.

Beulah Noland
Tehama, California

THREE-CHEESE CHICKEN BAKE

    1/2 c. chopped green pepper
    1/2 c. chopped onion
    3 tbsp. butter, melted
    1 can cream of chicken soup
    1/2 c. milk
    1 6-oz. can mushrooms, sliced, drained
    1 6-oz. package egg noodles, cooked
    3 c. chopped cooked chicken
    1 1/2 c. small curd cottage cheese
    10 oz. American cheese, shredded
    1/2 c. Parmesan cheese

Saute green pepper and onion in butter in skillet for 5 minutes; remove from heat. Add soup and milk; mix well. Fold in mushrooms. Alternate layers of noodles, chicken, soup mixture, cottage cheese and American cheese in greased 9 x 13-inch baking dish until all ingredients are used. Sprinkle with Parmesan cheese. Bake at 350 degrees for 45 minutes. Yield: 8 servings.

Janice Scott
Harlan, Kentucky

CHICKEN TARTS

    1 1/2 c. flour
    3/4 tsp. salt
    2/3 tsp. poultry seasoning
    1/2 c. shortening
    1/4 c. (about) chicken broth
    1 sm. can chopped mushrooms, drained
    3 tbsp. butter
    3 tbsp. flour
    1/4 tsp. each celery salt, onion powder
        and pepper
    1/2 c. sour cream
    4 to 5 c. chopped cooked chicken

Combine 1 1/2 cups flour, salt and poultry seasoning in bowl. Cut in shortening until crumbly. Add enough broth to make dough; mix well. Press over bottom and sides of 12 muffin cups. Saute mushrooms in butter in skillet. Blend in 3 tablespoons flour, celery salt, onion powder, pepper and sour cream. Stir in chicken; add a small amount of additional

broth if necessary. Spoon into prepared muffin cups. Bake at 450 degrees for 15 minutes. Garnish with sliced olives. Yield: 12 servings.

Betty Dishman
Marshall, West Virginia

CHICKEN-ALMOND CASSEROLE

    3 c. chopped cooked chicken
    2 c. cooked rice
    4 hard-boiled eggs, chopped
    2 cans cream of mushroom soup
    1 1/2 c. chopped celery
    1 sm. onion, chopped
    1 c. mayonnaise
    2 tbsp. lemon juice
    3/4 c. sliced almonds
    1 c. soft bread crumbs
    2 tbsp. melted butter

Combine first 9 ingredients in bowl; mix well. Spoon into lightly greased 2-quart casserole. Toss crumbs with butter in bowl; sprinkle over top. Chill, covered, overnight. Let stand at room temperature for 1 hour. Bake, uncovered, at 350 degrees for 40 minutes or until bubbly. Yield: 8-10 servings.

Cynthia Lansing
Bennington, Vermont

QUICK ORIENTAL
CHICKEN-RICE CASSEROLE

    1 pkg. herb-seasoned long grain and
        wild rice mix
    Chicken broth
    1 can French-style green beans, drained
    1 can cream of celery soup
    1/4 c. minced onion
    1 can sliced water chestnuts, drained
    1/2 c. slivered almonds (opt.)
    1/2 c. mayonnaise
    1 2-oz. jar chopped pimentos
    2 c. chopped cooked chicken
    Paprika

Prepare rice mix according to package directions using chicken broth. Combine with remaining ingredients except paprika in greased large casserole; mix well. Sprinkle with paprika. Bake at 350 degrees for 30 minutes. Yield: 10 servings.

Virginia Hutto
Jonesboro, Texas

Poultry

EASY DILLED CHICKEN-RICE CASSEROLE

    2   10-oz. packages frozen broccoli
          spears, thawed, drained
    1/2 lb. fresh mushrooms, sliced
    3/4 c. chopped onion
    1 med. clove of garlic, crushed
    1/3 c. butter
    2   10 1/2-oz. cans chicken gravy
    3 c. cooked rice
    2 c. chopped cooked chicken
    2 c. sliced celery
    2 tbsp. dry Sherry
    3/4 tsp. dillweed, crushed
    1/4 tsp. salt
    1/4 tsp. white pepper

Trim broccoli flowerets; reserve for garnish. Coarsely chop stalks; set aside. Saute mushrooms, onion and garlic in butter in saucepan over medium heat for 5 minutes, stirring occasionally. Stir in chicken gravy, rice, chicken, celery, chopped broccoli stalks, Sherry, dillweed, salt and white pepper. Cook, covered, over low heat for 5 minutes, stirring constantly. Pour chicken mixture into 3-quart casserole. Bake, covered, at 400 degrees for 30 minutes. Arrange flowerets over casserole. Bake, uncovered, for 10 minutes or until center is bubbly.

Photograph for this recipe on this page.

CREAMED CHICKEN WITH BAKED RICE SQUARES

    1 c. chopped green pepper
    1/4 c. chopped onion
    1/2 c. butter
    1/3 c. flour
    2 tsp. salt
    1/4 tsp. pepper
    3 c. chicken stock
    3 c. milk
    6 to 8 c. chopped cooked chicken
    1/2 c. chopped pimento
    Baked Rice Squares

Saute green pepper and onion in butter in saucepan until tender; remove from heat. Add flour, 2 teaspoons salt and 1/4 teaspoon pepper; mix well. Stir in chicken stock and milk gradually. Cook over medium heat until thickened, stirring constantly. Cook for 2 minutes longer. Stir in chicken and pimento. Heat to serving temperature, stirring occasionally. Spoon over Baked Rice Squares.
Yield: 20 servings.

BAKED RICE SQUARES

    5 eggs, slightly beaten
    4 c. milk
    2 c. shredded Cheddar cheese
    1/2 c. chopped onion
    2 tsp. salt
    1/4 tsp. pepper
    3 c. rice, cooked

Combine first 6 ingredients in bowl; mix well. Add rice; mix well. Pour into greased 11 x 14-inch baking pan. Bake at 325 degrees for 1 1/4 hours or until set. Cut into squares.

Jean Roche
Carson City, Nevada

WILD RICE-CHICKEN CASSEROLE

    1/2 c. chopped onion
    1/2 c. chopped celery
    2 tbsp. butter
    1 can cream of mushroom soup
    1/2 c. sour cream
    1/3 c. dry white wine
    1/2 tsp. curry powder
    2 c. chopped cooked chicken
    1   6-oz. package long grain and wild
          rice mix, cooked

Saute onion and celery in butter in skillet until tender. Add soup, sour cream, wine and curry powder; mix well. Stir in chicken and rice. Spoon into greased 7 x 12-inch baking dish. Bake at 350 degrees for 35 to 40 minutes or until bubbly. Stir before serving.
Yield: 4 servings.

Yolanda Martinez
Tornillo, Texas

Poultry

BROWN RICE-CHICKEN CASSEROLE

1 can cream of chicken soup
1/2 c. mayonnaise
1 tbsp. lemon juice
1/4 c. milk
1/4 tsp. salt
3 hard-boiled eggs, chopped
1 c. cooked brown rice
1 8-oz. can sliced water chestnuts (opt.)
1 2-oz. jar chopped pimentos (opt.)
1/2 c. chopped celery
2 c. chopped cooked chicken
1 tbsp. finely chopped onion
1/4 c. crushed cornflakes
1/4 c. slivered almonds
1 tbsp. butter, melted

Combine first 11 ingredients in bowl; mix well. Spoon into lightly greased 8 x 12-inch casserole. Combine onion, cornflakes, almonds and butter in bowl; mix well. Sprinkle over casserole. Bake at 375 degrees for 20 minutes or until bubbly. Yield: 8 servings.

Fran Gillespie
Seattle, Washington

CHICKEN-ALMOND OVERNIGHT CASSEROLE

1 can cream of chicken soup
1/2 c. mayonnaise
1 1/2 c. chopped cooked chicken
1 c. chopped celery
1 tbsp. chopped onion
1/2 c. slivered almonds
1 1/2 c. cooked rice
1 tsp. each salt and pepper
3 hard-boiled eggs, chopped
1 can French-fried onion rings

Combine soup, mayonnaise and 1/2 cup water in bowl; mix well. Add remaining ingredients except onion rings; mix well. Spoon into greased 9 x 13-inch casserole. Chill overnight. Arrange onion rings over top. Bake at 350 degrees for 20 minutes or until heated through. Yield: 6 servings.

Willie Ruth Hobbs
Belhaven, North Carolina

FAMILY FAVORITE CHICKEN-BROCCOLI CASSEROLE

1 onion, chopped
1/2 c. chopped celery
1/4 c. butter
1 pkg. frozen chopped broccoli, thawed, drained

1 can cream of mushroom soup
1/4 c. chicken broth
1 can sliced water chestnuts, drained
1 8-oz. jar jalapeno Cheez Whiz
2 c. cooked rice
3 to 4 c. chopped cooked chicken
1 8-oz. can sliced mushrooms

Saute onion and celery in butter in large skillet. Add broccoli, soup and broth. Simmer for several minutes, stirring constantly. Add remaining ingredients; mix well. Place in greased casserole. Bake at 325 degrees for 30 minutes. Yield: 8 servings.

Jill Weinheimer
San Antonio, Texas

QUICK AND EASY CHICKEN CASSEROLE

1 pkg. wild rice, cooked
3 c. chopped cooked chicken
1 can French-style green beans, drained
1 c. mayonnaise
1 med. jar pimento, drained
1 onion, chopped
1 can cream of celery soup

Combine all ingredients in greased casserole; mix well. Bake at 350 degrees for 30 to 45 minutes or until bubbly. Yield: 10-12 servings.

Lucy Van Pelt
Atmore, Alabama

CHICKEN WITH EGGPLANT CASSEROLE

1 eggplant, peeled, cubed
1 med. green pepper, chopped
1 sm. onion, chopped
3 tbsp. oil
2 to 3 c. chopped cooked chicken
1 1/2 c. cooked rice
1 16-oz. can tomatoes, chopped
1 c. shredded Cheddar cheese
1 clove of garlic, crushed
1 tsp. salt
1/4 tsp. lemon-pepper seasoning

Saute eggplant, green pepper and onion in oil in skillet until tender. Combine with remaining ingredients in bowl; mix well. Pour into greased 2-quart baking dish. Bake at 350 degrees for 30 minutes. Yield: 6 servings.

Clarissa Mayfield
Houston, Texas

Poultry

CHEESY MEXICAN CHICKEN CASSEROLE

2 cans cream of chicken soup
1 can cream of mushroom soup
1 10-oz. can Ro-Tel
1 lg. package taco-flavored corn chips
3 to 4 c. chopped cooked chicken
1 med. onion, chopped
1 clove of garlic, chopped
1 1/2 c. grated Cheddar cheese

Combine first 3 ingredients in saucepan. Heat until well blended, stirring frequently. Alternate layers of corn chips, chicken, onion, garlic, cheese and soup mixture in casserole until all ingredients are used, ending with soup mixture. Bake at 350 degrees until bubbly.

Jean Ellington
Arvada, Oklahoma

LAYERED CHICKEN ENCHILADA CASSEROLE

1 15-oz. can tomato sauce
1 6-oz. can tomato paste
4 c. chopped tomatoes
1 4-oz. can chopped green chilies
1 4-oz. can sliced olives
1 pkg. taco seasoning mix
1 onion, chopped
1/2 tsp. each salt and pepper
1 tsp. garlic powder
3 to 4 c. chopped cooked chicken
1 pkg. corn tortillas, cut into wedges
1 lb. Cheddar cheese, grated

Combine first 10 ingredients in saucepan. Simmer for 15 minutes, stirring frequently. Add chicken. Alternate layers of tortillas, sauce and cheese in greased 9 x 13-inch baking dish until all ingredients are used, ending with cheese. Bake, covered, at 350 degrees for 30 minutes. Yield: 8 servings.

Shannon Kibby
Glenn, California

CHICKEN MONTEREY

1 c. chopped onion
2 tbsp. butter
3 8-oz. cans tomato sauce
1 4-oz. can chopped green chilies, drained
1 tsp. hot chili powder
1 tsp. dried parsley
1 tsp. salt
1 8-oz. package taco-flavored tortilla chips, broken
1 1/2 c. shredded Monterey Jack cheese
2 c. chopped cooked chicken
1 c. sour cream
1/2 c. shredded Cheddar cheese

Saute onion in butter in skillet until lightly browned. Add tomato sauce, chilies, chili powder, parsley and salt. Simmer for 5 minutes. Alternate layers of tortilla chips, Monterey Jack cheese, chicken and sauce in buttered 1 1/2-quart casserole ending with sauce. Bake at 350 degrees for 25 minutes. Spread sour cream over top; sprinkle with Cheddar cheese. Bake for 5 minutes longer or until cheese is melted. Yield: 6 servings.

Photograph for this recipe below

TACO CHICKEN

1/4 c chopped onion
1 stick butter
1 can cream of mushroom soup
1 can cream of chicken soup
1 can Ro-Tel
4 chicken breasts, cooked, sliced
1 c. chicken broth
1 16-oz. package taco-flavored corn chips, crushed
1 1/2 c. grated cheese

Saute onion in butter in skillet. Add soups, Ro-Tel, chicken and broth; mix well. Bring to a boil. Layer corn chips and chicken mixture in greased 9 x 13-inch baking dish. Top with cheese. Bake at 350 degrees for 15 minutes or until cheese is melted. Yield: 12 servings.

Gracie Duran
Buda, Texas

44

Poultry

CHICKEN DINNER PIE

2 c. flour
1 tsp. salt
2/3 c. shortening
2 tbsp. melted margarine
2 tbsp. flour
1 c. chicken broth
1/2 c. cream
1 can peas, drained
1 c. chopped cooked carrots
2 c. chopped cooked chicken
Salt and pepper to taste

Combine 2 cups flour and 1 teaspoon salt in bowl. Cut in shortening until crumbly. Add 6 tablespoons cold water; mix well. Roll into two 10-inch circles on floured surface. Fit 1 circle into 9-inch pie plate. Blend margarine with 2 tablespoons flour in saucepan. Stir in broth and cream. Cook over medium heat until thickened, stirring constantly. Add vegetables, chicken and salt and pepper to taste. Pour into prepared pie plate. Top with remaining pastry, sealing edges and cutting vents. Bake at 350 degrees for 45 to 50 minutes or until browned.
Yield: 6-8 servings.

Debra Bowen
Pilot Mountain, North Carolina

CHICKEN PIE WITH VEGETABLES

1 can refrigerator biscuits
1 can cream of mushroom soup
2 c. chopped chicken
1 c. carrots, cooked
1 can sweet peas
1/2 c. chopped celery

Roll biscuits thinly on lightly floured surface. Line 2-quart casserole; reserve several biscuits for top crust. Combine remaining ingredients in bowl; mix well. Spoon into prepared casserole. Top with reserved biscuits. Bake at 350 degrees until golden brown. Yield: 4 servings.

Karen Conder
Monroe, North Carolina

FAVORITE HOT CHICKEN SALAD

4 c. chopped cooked chicken
2 tbsp. lemon juice
2 c. chopped celery
1 tsp. minced onion
4 hard-boiled eggs, sliced
3/4 c. cream of chicken soup
2 pimentos, finely chopped

3/4 c. mayonnaise
1 tsp. salt
1 c. grated cheese
1 1/2 c. crushed potato chips
2/3 c. chopped almonds

Combine first 9 ingredients in bowl; mix well. Spoon into 9 x 13-inch baking dish. Top with cheese, chips and almonds. Chill overnight in refrigerator. Bake at 400 degrees for 20 minutes or until heated through. Yield: 8 servings.

Barbara Johnson
Youngstown, Ohio

CHICKEN SALAD WITH WALNUTS

5 c. chopped cooked chicken
2 cans cream of chicken soup
2 c. celery
1 c. chopped walnuts
1 tsp. salt
1/2 tsp. pepper
2 tsp. lemon juice
1 1/2 c. mayonnaise
3 or 4 hard-boiled eggs, finely chopped
4 tsp. grated onion
2 c. crushed potato chips

Combine all ingredients except chips in bowl; mix well. Spoon into greased 9 x 13-inch casserole. Top with potato chips. Bake at 350 degrees for 45 minutes to 1 hour.
Yield: 10 servings.

Wilma Yancy
Bartlesville, Oklahoma

CRUNCHY HOT CHICKEN SALAD

2 c. chopped cooked chicken
2 c. chopped celery
1/2 tsp. salt
1 c. mayonnaise
2 tbsp. lemon juice
1/2 c. sliced almonds
2 tsp. grated onion
1 c. sliced water chestnuts
1 c. crushed potato chips
1/2 c. grated Cheddar cheese

Combine chicken, celery, salt, mayonnaise, lemon juice, almonds, onion and water chestnuts in bowl; mix well. Spoon into buttered baking dish. Top with potato chips and cheese. Bake at 350 degrees until bubbly.
Yield: 6 servings.

Rosa Black
Sacramento, California

Poultry

CREAMY CHICKEN TETRAZZINI

1/2 c. sliced mushrooms
1/2 c. thinly sliced onion
1/2 c. butter
1/2 c. flour
2 c. chicken broth
1 c. light cream
1 tsp. salt
1/4 tsp. pepper
1/2 tsp. poultry seasoning
8-oz. spaghetti, cooked
3 c. chopped cooked chicken
1/2 c. shredded Cheddar cheese

Saute mushrooms and onion in butter in skillet. Stir in flour. Cook until bubbly. Stir in broth and cream. Add salt, pepper and poultry seasoning. Bring to a boil, stirring frequently. Alternate layers of spaghetti, chicken and sauce in greased 2-quart casserole, ending with spaghetti. Sprinkle cheese over top. Bake at 400 degrees for 20 minutes. Yield: 8 servings.

Clara Josten
Hobbs, New Mexico

ALMOND-CHICKEN TETRAZZINI

2 tbsp. flour
3 tbsp. melted butter
2 c. chicken broth
1 c. milk
1 1/2 c. shredded Cheddar cheese
1/4 c. chopped pimento
3 c. chopped cooked chicken
1/2 c. sliced almonds
1 8-oz. package spaghetti, cooked
1 c. buttered bread crumbs

Blend flour and butter in saucepan. Cook until bubbly. Stir in broth gradually. Cook until thickened, stirring constantly. Add milk and cheese. Cook until cheese is melted, stirring constantly. Combine with remaining ingredients except bread crumbs. Spoon into greased 2-quart casserole; mix well. Sprinkle with bread crumbs. Bake at 350 degrees for 45 minutes. Yield: 6 servings.

Pat Linz
Sheridan, Wyoming

CHICKEN AND WALNUT CHILI

3 c. coarsely chopped Spanish onion
3 cloves of garlic, finely chopped
3 c. English walnuts, finely chopped
1/2 c. corn oil

2 30-oz. cans pinto beans
1 15-oz. can garbanzo beans
1 c. tomato sauce
2 3-oz. cans chopped green chilies
2 tbsp. cumin
2 tbsp. oregano
2 tbsp. Masa Harina
1 c. vinegar
Salt and pepper to taste
3 to 4 c. chopped cooked chicken
2 c. black coffee
Tabasco sauce to taste

Saute onion, garlic and walnuts in corn oil in skillet until walnuts are golden. Add pinto beans, garbanzo beans, tomato sauce, chopped green chilies, cumin, oregano, Masa Harina, vinegar, salt and pepper. Simmer for 1 to 2 hours. Add chicken, coffee and Tabasco sauce. Heat to serving temperature.

Carol Johnson
Leadville, Colorado

CHINGALINGAS

1 sm. onion, chopped
1 green pepper, chopped
1 clove of garlic, minced
1 tbsp. shortening
1 can Ro-Tel, drained, mashed
1 tsp. chicken bouillon
1 tsp. each cumin, chili powder
3 to 4 c. shredded cooked chicken
24 flour tortillas
Oil for deep frying

Saute onion, green pepper and garlic in shortening in skillet until tender. Add Ro-Tel, bouillon, cumin and chili powder. Simmer for 15 to 20 minutes or until nearly dry. Stir in chicken. Steam tortillas until softened. Spoon 2 tablespoons chicken mixture onto each tortilla. Roll to enclose filling; tuck in ends and secure with toothpicks. Deep-fry in 375-degree oil for 3 to 4 minutes or until browned, turning once. Drain on paper towels; remove toothpicks. Serve with sour cream and guacamole. Yield: 24 servings.

Joyce Bark
San Angelo, Texas

CHICKEN CREPES

1 1/4 c. flour
3 eggs, beaten
1 1/2 c. milk
2 tbsp. melted butter
Salt to taste

1 can cream of mushroom soup
2 c. chopped cooked chicken
1 4-oz. can sliced mushrooms
1 8-oz. can sliced water chestnuts
1/4 c. finely chopped celery
1 tbsp. finely chopped pimento
1/4 c. white wine
Dash each of white pepper, paprika

Combine flour, eggs, milk, butter and salt in blender container. Process until smooth. Let stand for 1 hour. Pour a small amount of batter at a time into crepe pan, tilting to coat bottom. Cook until brown on both sides. Mix remaining ingredients and pinch of salt in saucepan. Cook until heated through. Do not boil. Spoon onto crepes; roll to enclose filling. Place in buttered 9 x 13-inch baking dish. Bake at 350 degrees for 10 to 15 minutes or until heated through.

Susan J. Kerr
New Stanton, Pennsylvania

CHICKEN CROQUETTES

3 tbsp. butter, melted
1/4 c. flour
1/4 c. milk
1/2 c. chicken broth
1 tbsp. minced parsley
1 tsp. lemon juice
1 tsp. grated onion
1/4 tsp. salt
Dash each of paprika, nutmeg and pepper
1 1/2 c. finely chopped cooked chicken
3/4 c. (or more) fine dry bread crumbs
1 egg, beaten
Oil for deep frying

Blend butter and flour in saucepan. Add milk and chicken broth. Cook until thickened, stirring constantly. Cook for 1 minute longer. Add parsley, lemon juice, onion and seasonings; cool. Add chicken; mix well. Chill thoroughly. Shape by 1/4 cupfuls into balls with wet hands. Roll in crumbs; shape into cones. Dip into mixture of egg and 2 tablespoons water; roll in remaining crumbs. Fry in 365-degree deep fat for 2 1/2 to 3 minutes. Drain on paper towels.

May Hyden
Ashland, Kentucky

GRANDMOTHER'S CHICKEN AND DRESSING WITH GIBLET GRAVY

10 c. corn bread crumbs
10 c. bread crumbs
5 c. hot chicken broth
1/4 c. sage
1 bunch green onions, chopped
1/2 bunch celery, chopped
Salt and pepper to taste
4 eggs, beaten
1/2 c. melted margarine
10 c. chopped cooked chicken
3 to 5 hard-boiled eggs, chopped
1 to 2 c. milk
Giblets of 3 chickens, cooked chopped
1/4 c. margarine

Combine bread crumbs and broth in large bowl; mash with potato masher until well mixed. Add sage; mix well. Simmer green onions and celery in a small amount of water in saucepan until tender. Add to crumb mixture; mix well. Stir in seasonings, eggs and 1/2 cup margarine. Reserve 1 cup mixture. Spread remaining mixture in greased baking pan. Arrange chicken over dressing. Bake at 350 degrees for 1 1/2 hours. Combine hard-boiled eggs, milk, giblets, reserved dressing, 1/4 cup margarine and 1/2 cup water in saucepan. Simmer until thickened, stirring frequently. Yield: 15-20 servings.

Alicia Hampton
Omaha, Texas

ENCHILADAS VERDE

6 green peppers, peeled, chopped
1 10-oz. can tomatillos
1 tbsp. parsley
1 c. whipping cream
1 egg, beaten
1/8 tsp. salt
Pepper to taste
1 pkg. corn tortillas
1/4 c. oil
6 chicken breasts, cooked, shredded
4 oz. cream cheese, softened
1 onion, finely chopped
1/8 tsp. cumin (opt.)

Simmer green peppers in salted water in saucepan for 5 minutes; drain. Combine with tomatillos, parsley and a small amount of tomatillo liquid in blender container. Process until pureed. Add cream, egg, salt and pepper. Pour into saucepan. Heat to serving temperature, stirring constantly. Soften tortillas in hot oil in skillet. Dip tortillas in sauce. Mix chicken, cream cheese, onion and cumin in bowl. Spoon mixture onto tortillas. Roll to enclose filling. Serve with sauce. Garnish with sliced radishes and sour cream. Yield: 10 servings.

Jane Olson
Shasta, California

Poultry

JAPANESE STACK-UP DINNER

4 c. chicken broth
4 tsp. cornstarch
1 can cream of chicken soup
3 to 4 c. cooked rice
1 lg. can chow mein noodles
4 to 5 c. chopped cooked chicken
1 1/2 c. chopped celery
1 20-oz. can crushed pineapple, heated
3/4 c. chopped green onions
1 pkg. flaked coconut
1 c. sliced almonds
1 1/2 lb. Cheddar cheese, finely grated

Blend broth with cornstarch in saucepan. Cook until thickened, stirring constantly. Stir in soup. Place remaining ingredients in individual bowls for buffet serving. Layer rice and remaining ingredients in order given for each serving. Top with hot gravy. Yield: 10 servings.

R. Jeanette Elmore
Olathe, Kansas

CHICKEN WIGGLY

1 c. chopped celery
1 c. chopped green pepper
1 c. chopped onion
1 jar chopped pimento
4 c. (or more) chicken stock
1 lg. can English peas, drained
2 cans cream of mushroom soup
1 12-oz. package noodles
3 to 4 c. chopped cooked chicken

Combine celery, green pepper, onion, pimento and chicken stock in saucepan. Cook until tender. Add peas, soup, noodles and chicken. Cook for 20 minutes or until noodles are tender. Yield: 10-12 servings.

Linda Guip
Hartwell, Georgia

Turkey

TURKEY CACCIATORE

1 1/2 lb. boneless turkey breast, sliced
1/2 tsp. Italian seasoning
1 tsp. salt
1/4 tsp. pepper
1 med. onion, chopped
1 1/2 tsp. minced garlic
1 c. tomato juice
2 c. sliced mushrooms
1 lg. green pepper, coarsely chopped
1/4 tsp. basil

Sprinkle turkey with Italian seasoning, salt and pepper. Saute onion and garlic in a small amount of oil in skillet until tender. Add turkey. Brown on both sides. Stir in remaining ingredients. Simmer, covered, for 15 minutes or until turkey is tender. Yield: 4 servings.

Wendy Galvan
Stoneville, North Carolina

TURKEY PICCATA

4 slices fresh turkey breast
2 tbsp. flour
1 clove of garlic, crushed
1/4 c. corn oil margarine
1/4 c. dry vermouth
1 tbsp. lemon juice

Pound turkey with wooden mallet until very thin. Coat with flour; shake off excess. Brown garlic in 3 tablespoons margarine in skillet; discard garlic. Brown turkey in garlic oil for 1 to 2 minutes on each side. Arrange on serving plate. Add remaining 1 tablespoon margarine, vermouth and lemon juice to skillet. Simmer for 3 minutes, scraping skillet. Spoon sauce over turkey. Garnish with lemon slices.
Yield: 4 servings.

Cindy Bell
Hampton, Virginia

TURKEY CURRY

2 turkey wings and legs with thighs
1 tsp. salt
2 med. onions, chopped
2 apples, minced
1/2 c. butter
1/4 c. curry powder
1/4 tsp. pepper
6 stalks celery, minced
1/2 tsp. Tabasco sauce
1/2 tsp. ginger
1 tbsp. Worcestershire sauce
1/4 c. flour
1 c. coconut milk
2 c. heavy cream
3 egg yolks, well beaten

Cook turkey pieces with salt in 1 1/2 quarts boiling water until tender. Drain. Reserve 4 cups stock; bone turkey. Saute onions and apples in butter in skillet; add curry powder. Cook for 5 minutes. Stir in pepper, celery, Tabasco sauce, ginger, Worcestershire sauce and reserved stock. Simmer for 20 minutes. Mix flour, 1/2 cup water and coconut milk in small bowl; stir into stock with turkey. Cook for 4 minutes or until thickened, stirring constantly. Remove from heat; let stand for 3 hours. Add cream and egg yolks; mix well. Heat to serving temperature, stirring constantly. Serve with rice.

Judith Evans
Wamsutter, Wyoming

PLANTATION TURKEY

1 pkg. corn bread mix
1/4 c. flour
1/4 c. melted butter
2 c. hot milk
1 tsp. salt
2 c. grated Swiss cheese
1/4 lb. country ham, sliced
1 1/2 lb. sliced cooked turkey breast
1 4-oz. can mushrooms, drained
1/2 c. grated Swiss cheese

Prepare and bake corn bread according to package directions, using deep 9-inch baking dish. Blend flour with butter in saucepan. Stir in milk and salt gradually. Cool until thickened, stirring constantly. Add 2 cups cheese. Cook until melted, stirring constantly. Layer 2/3 cup sauce, ham, 2/3 cup sauce, turkey, mushrooms and remaining sauce over baked corn bread layer. Sprinkle 1/2 cup cheese over top. Bake at 375 degrees until brown and bubbly.

Lula B. Fitzgerald
Smithfield, North Carolina

GOBBLE-IT-UP CASSEROLE

2 10-oz. packages frozen
   broccoli, thawed
8 to 10 slices cooked turkey
2 cans cream of chicken soup
3/4 c. mayonnaise
1 tbsp. lemon juice
1 c. grated Cheddar cheese
1/2 c. buttered croutons

Layer broccoli and turkey in greased 8 x 10-inch baking pan. Blend soup, mayonnaise and lemon juice in bowl. Pour over layers. Top with cheese and croutons. Bake at 350 degrees for 40 minutes. Yield: 4 servings.

Marianne Griffith
Alameda, California

TURKEY CUTLET PACIFICA

6 thick slices cooked turkey
1/4 c. flour
1 egg, beaten
1/2 c. milk
1/2 c. dry bread crumbs
1/4 c. butter
Salt and pepper to taste
1 1-lb. can puree-pack chopped tomatoes
1/2 tsp. oregano
1/2 tsp. sugar
6 slices Swiss cheese
2 California avocados, sliced

Coat turkey slices with flour; dip in mixture of egg and milk. Roll in bread crumbs to coat. Brown on both sides in butter in large heavy skillet. Sprinkle with salt and pepper. Place in greased shallow baking dish. Mix tomatoes with oregano and sugar. Spoon over cutlets. Top with cheese. Broil for several minutes or until cheese is bubbly. Arrange avocado slices on top. Yield: 6 servings.

Photograph for this recipe below.

Poultry

HARVEST TURKEY DINNER

1 10-lb. turkey
Salt and pepper
2 tbsp. butter
6 to 8 med. Louisiana yams
1 16-oz. jar spiced crab apples
2 tbsp. melted butter
2 tbsp. cornstarch
1/2 c. Rhine wine
1 6-oz. can unsweetened pineapple juice
1/2 c. dark corn syrup
1 1/2 tsp. lemon juice

Sprinkle turkey cavity with salt and pepper. Place on rack in shallow roasting pan. Brush with 2 tablespoons melted butter. Roast at 325 degrees for 2 hours. Drain. Cook yams in boiling salted water until almost tender. Drain, peel and cut into halves. Arrange around turkey. Drain crab apples, reserving syrup. Combine reserved syrup, 2 tablespoons butter, 1/4 teaspoon salt, cornstarch and next 4 ingredients in saucepan; mix well. Cook until thickened, stirring constantly. Brush turkey and yams with sauce. Roast for 30 minutes longer or to 185 degrees on meat thermometer, basting once with sauce. Heat crab apples in remaining sauce. Serve with turkey and yams.
Yield: 6-8 servings.

Photograph for this recipe above.

SMOKED TURKEY WITH
APRICOT GLAZE

1 14-lb. turkey
1/4 c. salt
1 c. apricot nectar
1 c. honey

Rub turkey inside and out with salt. Place in roasting pan. Bake at 350 degrees for 2 hours. Drain, reserving 1 cup drippings. Place on barbecue grill over low coals and hickory chips. Combine reserved drippings with apricot nectar and honey; blend well. Smoke turkey, covered, for 10 to 12 hours or until tender, basting with honey mixture at 1-hour intervals.
Yield: 25 servings.

Catherine Ward
Forest Park, Georgia

ROAST TURKEY
WITH GIBLET GRAVY

1 12-lb. turkey
1 c. chopped celery with leaves
1/2 c. chopped onion
1/2 c. butter
1/4 c. chopped parsley
1/4 tsp. each basil, rosemary and thyme
2 8-oz. packages stuffing mix
Turkey giblets
1 slice onion
1 stalk celery
1/4 tsp. each salt and pepper
Chicken broth
6 tbsp. flour

Wash turkey in cold running water; pat inside dry with paper towels. Leave outside of turkey moist. Saute chopped celery and onion in butter in skillet until tender. Add parsley, basil, rosemary, thyme, stuffing mix and water according to package directions; mix well. Stuff and truss turkey. Place in roaster; tent with foil. Bake at 325 degrees for 3 1/2 hours. Remove foil. Bake for 1 hour longer or to 190 degrees on meat thermometer. Simmer giblets with onion slice, celery stalk, salt, pepper and water to cover in saucepan for 2 hours or until tender. Drain and chop giblets. Combine pan drippings with enough broth to measure 3 cups in saucepan. Add flour mixed with a small amount of cold water. Cook until thickened, stirring constantly. Add giblets. Heat to serving temperature. Serve with turkey.

Willa Dailey
Gibbon, Nebraska

ROTISSERIE-BARBECUED TURKEY

1/2 c. oil
2 tbsp. chopped onion
2 cloves of garlic, crushed
2 tsp. sugar
1 tsp. salt

1 tsp. chili powder
1 tsp. paprika
1/4 tsp. pepper
Dash of cayenne pepper
1/2 tsp. dry mustard
2 tbsp. vinegar
2 tsp. Worcestershire sauce
1 tsp. hot sauce
1 8 to 10-lb. turkey
Melted shortening

Combine oil, onion, seasonings and 1 1/4 cups water in saucepan. Simmer for 30 minutes. Brush sauce over turkey cavity. Tie wings and legs securely. Do not stuff turkey. Place on rotisserie spit using manufacturer's directions. Cook over hot coals for 3 1/2 to 4 hours or to 180 degrees on meat thermometer, basting occasionally with melted shortening. Baste generously with sauce during last 30 to 45 minutes cooking time.

Winona Walker
Baker, Florida

TURKEY-CHEESE CASSEROLE

1/2 c. chopped onion
1/4 c. butter
1/4 c. flour
1 tbsp. instant chicken bouillon
2 1/2 c. milk
1/2 lb. American cheese, chopped
3 c. chopped cooked turkey
2 c. cooked elbow macaroni
2 tbsp. chopped pimento
1 c. soft buttered bread crumbs
1/4 lb. American cheese, shredded

Saute onion in butter in medium saucepan until tender. Stir in flour and bouillon. Add milk and 1/2 pound cheese; mix well. Cook until cheese is melted and sauce is thickened, stirring constantly; remove from heat. Combine turkey, macaroni, pimento and cheese sauce in lightly greased 2-quart baking dish. Sprinkle bread crumbs over top. Bake at 350 degrees for 25 minutes or until bubbly. Sprinkle shredded cheese over top. Bake for 5 minutes longer or until cheese melts. Yield: 8 servings.

Melba Smith
Grandview, Texas

TURKEY AND SPINACH LASAGNA
WITH WHITE SAUCE

3 tbsp. butter, melted
3 tbsp. flour

2 1/2 c. milk
Salt and pepper to taste
Pinch of nutmeg
2 10-oz. packages frozen chopped
   spinach, cooked, well drained
8 lasagna noodles, cooked
1 7 1/2-oz. carton ricotta cheese
1 1/2 c. chopped cooked turkey
1/2 c. grated Parmesan cheese
1/4 c. Italian-seasoned bread crumbs

Blend butter and flour in saucepan. Add milk gradually. Cook over low heat until thickened, stirring constantly. Season with salt, pepper and nutmeg. Mix half the sauce with spinach; set aside. Pour a small amount of remaining white sauce into greased shallow baking dish. Alternate layers of noodles, spinach mixture, ricotta, turkey and sauce until all ingredients are used, ending with sauce. Sprinkle with Parmesan cheese and bread crumbs. Bake at 375 degrees for 30 minutes or until lightly browned and bubbly. Yield: 4-6 servings.

Flora Fry
Coleman, Texas

TURKEY RATATOUILLE

1 lg. onion, coarsely chopped
1 clove of garlic, minced
2 tbsp. oil
1 sm. eggplant, peeled, cubed
1 green pepper, chopped
1 c. thinly sliced zucchini
2 tomatoes, seeded, chopped
1 c. sliced fresh mushrooms
3 c. chopped cooked turkey
1 tsp. Italian seasoning
2 1/2 c. herb-seasoned croutons, crushed
2 c. shredded Swiss cheese

Saute onion and garlic in oil in skillet until tender. Add eggplant, green pepper and zucchini. Cook for 5 minutes, stirring constantly. Add tomatoes and mushrooms. Stir in turkey and Italian seasoning. Cook for 1 minute. Spread croutons and 1/2 cup cheese in greased 7 x 12-inch baking dish. Layer half the turkey mixture, 1 cup cheese and remaining turkey mixture over croutons. Bake, covered, at 350 degrees for 30 minutes. Top with remaining 1/2 cup cheese. Bake for 10 minutes longer. Let stand for 5 minutes before serving. Yield: 10 servings.

Carie Hayhurst
Strawn, Texas

Game Birds

Handsome, stout-bodied game birds and sleek waterfowl have been a favorite on American tables for generations. These include grouse, quail, squab or pigeon, plus larger pheasant, wild ducks or geese, and the native wild turkey. In addition to the succulent meat and rich, wild flavor of game birds, there is something very satisfying about preparing and enjoying the prized catch of the hunter in the family.

At a glance, these are the characteristics of a few favorites: Quail, or partridge, is a delectable migratory bird that weighs less than ½ pound. Grouse is prized for its clean eating habits and resulting mild yet wild flavor. Dove, squab and pigeon are all dark meat delicacies.

Pheasant, introduced to this part of the world by Ben Franklin's son-in-law, is the aristocrat of wild fowl. Served on the best of fine occasions, it is a white meat bird with very mild flavor. The pheasant hen is the most succulent. The wild turkey is a truly American game bird, prized by hunters both because it is fast and wary and because its flavor is wild, yet delectable. The flavor takes on a whole new personality when a wild turkey is smoked rather than roasted.

Cornish game hens are a popular delicacy, elegant and somewhat expensive, but truly delectable. Greatly favored by gourmets for their fine flavor and delicate texture, domestic duck and goose are rich and succulent and an excellent choice for very special dinner occasions.

Wild fowl contribute value, variety and taste appeal to any cook's choice of foods to serve family and friends, and are an excellent choice for special occasion meals. And, because they reflect nature's bounty so well, they should be served whenever possible!

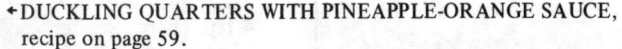
◄DUCKLING QUARTERS WITH PINEAPPLE-ORANGE SAUCE,
recipe on page 59.

Game Birds

SMOTHERED DOVE BREASTS

12 to 18 dove breasts
1 med. onion, chopped
2 tbsp. butter
1 can cream of mushroom soup
1/4 to 1/2 c. chicken broth
Pinch each of oregano, rosemary
Salt and pepper to taste
1 c. sour cream

Place dove breasts meaty side down in greased baking dish. Do not crowd. Saute onion in butter in skillet. Add remaining ingredients except sour cream. Pour over dove breasts. Bake, covered, at 325 degrees for 1 hour, turning occasionally. Stir sour cream into sauce. Bake for 20 minutes longer. Yield: 6 servings.

Cresta Witt
Yakima, Washington

BRAISED DOVE BREASTS

1 onion, chopped
1/4 c. butter, softened
16 dove breasts
1 tsp. each salt and pepper
2 tsp. Worcestershire sauce
1/4 tsp. thyme
1/2 c. red wine
1 c. beef bouillon
2 tbsp. flour
2 tbsp. butter, softened

Saute onion in 1/4 cup butter in skillet until tender; add dove breasts. Brown on both sides. Add seasonings; reduce heat. Arrange breasts meaty side up. Add wine. Cook until sauce is reduced by half. Add bouillon. Cook, covered, for 45 minutes or until tender. Remove dove from skillet; place on heated platter. Mix flour and 2 tablespoons butter in small bowl. Add to sauce in skillet. Cook until thickened, stirring constantly. Serve with dove.

Susie Lund
Huntsville, Alabama

DOVE AND WILD RICE DRESSING

12 to 16 dove breasts
2 c. flour
Salt, pepper and paprika to taste
1/2 c. wild rice
1/4 lb. sausage
1 onion, chopped
1/2 tsp. sage
1/2 c. wine

Coat dove with flour seasoned with salt, pepper and paprika. Brown in shortening in skillet. Arrange in circle in casserole. Cook wild rice in 2 cups boiling salted water in saucepan until tender. Brown sausage with onion and sage in skillet; drain. Add to rice; mix well. Spoon into center of casserole. Pour mixture of wine and 3/4 cup water over all. Bake, covered, at 350 degrees for 1 hour or until dove breasts are tender. Yield: 4-6 servings.

Camille Pilcher
Charlotte, North Carolina

BAKED CORNISH GAME HENS

6 Cornish game hens
Salt, pepper, red pepper and garlic
    powder to taste
1 stick butter, sliced
1/2 green pepper, chopped
2 stalks celery, chopped
1 clove of garlic, chopped
1 onion, chopped
3 slices bacon
1 c. chicken broth
1/2 c. chopped green onion tops
1/2 c. chopped parsley
1   8-oz. can sliced mushrooms
1 tbsp. flour
1 tbsp. Worcestershire sauce
2 tbsp. currant jelly

Wash game hens; pat dry inside and out. Sprinkle with seasonings inside and out. Stuff with butter, green pepper, celery, garlic and onion. Place breast side up in baking dish. Arrange bacon slices over game hens. Add broth. Bake, covered with foil, at 325 degrees for 30 minutes or until tender. Pour pan juices into skillet. Bake hens, uncovered, at 500 degrees until browned. Saute onion tops and parsley in pan juices. Drain mushrooms, reserving liquid. Blend flour with reserved liquid and Worcestershire sauce. Add with mushrooms and jelly to skillet. Cook until thickened, stirring constantly. Pour over game hens. Yield: 6 servings.

Alice Waters
Galveston, Texas

GLAZED CORNISH GAME HENS

2/3 c. light corn syrup
1/2 c. prepared mustard
4 tsp. curry powder
2 cloves of garlic, minced
4 Cornish game hens

Combine first 4 ingredients in bowl; mix well. Wash game hens; pat dry inside and out. Place on rack in baking pan; brush with syrup mixture. Bake at 350 degrees for 1 1/2 hours or until tender, basting occasionally.
Yield: 4 servings.

Senemia Braswell
Marion, Ohio

CORNISH GAME HENS WITH HERBED RICE

    2 tbsp. honey
    2 tbsp. unsalted margarine, melted
    2 tbsp. orange juice
    4 Cornish game hens
    1/4 c. chopped celery
    1/4 c. chopped onion
    2 tbsp. chopped parsley
    1 tsp. grated orange rind
    1/8 tsp. each rosemary, thyme
    1 c. dry-roasted unsalted peanuts
    1 c. rice
    1/2 c. orange juice

Combine honey, margarine and 2 tablespoons orange juice in small bowl. Wash game hens; pat dry inside and out. Place on rack in baking pan. Bake at 375 degrees for 1 hour or until tender, basting frequently with honey mixture. Saute celery and onion in saucepan until tender. Add remaining ingredients and 1 1/2 cups water; mix well. Simmer, covered, until rice is tender. Place game hens on serving platter. Spoon rice around game hens. Yield: 4 servings.

Felamia Johnson
Wheeling, Ohio

CORNISH GAME HENS WITH HONEYED RICE STUFFING

    1/2 c. chopped onion
    1/2 c. chopped celery
    1 tbsp. butter, melted
    1 c. cooked rice
    1/4 c. raisins
    1/4 c. walnuts
    2 tbsp. honey
    1 tbsp. lemon juice
    Salt, pepper and cinnamon to taste
    2 Rock Cornish game hens
    1 tbsp. melted butter
    1/2 tsp. paprika

Combine onion, celery and 1 tablespoon butter in glass bowl. Microwave on High for 1 to 2 minutes or until tender. Add next 5 ingredients

and seasonings. Spoon into game hen cavities; truss. Place breast side up on rack in glass baking dish. Brush with mixture of 1 tablespoon butter and paprika. Microwave on High for 18 minutes or until tender, turning dish and basting hens every 6 minutes. Cover tightly with foil. Let stand for 10 minutes.

Photograph for this recipe below.

ROAST CORNISH GAME HENS WITH ORANGE STUFFING

    2 20 to 24-oz. Cornish game hens
    1/2 tsp. each salt, ginger
    1/4 tsp. pepper
    1/4 c. dry Sherry
    1/3 c. orange juice
    1/2 tsp. Worcestershire sauce
    1 tsp. soy sauce
    2 1/4 c. cubed sourdough bread
    1 tsp. grated orange rind
    1 egg yolk
    2 tbsp. melted butter
    2 tbsp. finely chopped parsley
    1/4 c. orange juice

Wash game hens; pat dry inside and out. Cut in half. Season with salt, ginger and pepper. Place skin side down in broiler pan. Roast at 375 degrees for 30 minutes. Combine next 4 ingredients in bowl; mix well. Brush over game hens. Turn hens; brush with Sherry mixture. Combine bread and remaining ingredients in bowl; mix lightly. Spoon into baking pan. Roast hens and stuffing for 30 minutes or until game hens are tender, basting several times. Spoon stuffing onto serving plate. Arrange game hens around stuffing. Garnish with orange slices.
Yield: 4 servings.

Nina Washburn
Ely, Nevada

Game Birds

MANDARIN CORNISH GAME HENS

4 Cornish game hens
Salt to taste
2 sm. cans mandarin oranges, drained
2 c. croutons
1/2 c. butter
1/2 c. white wine
1 tsp. garlic salt
1 tsp. onion salt

Wash game hens; pat dry inside and out. Sprinkle cavities with salt. Stuff with mixture of oranges and croutons. Place on large piece of foil in baking pan. Combine remaining ingredients in saucepan. Bring to a boil. Pour over hens. Seal foil. Bake at 350 degrees for 45 minutes. Open foil. Bake for 15 minutes longer or until game hens are brown and tender.

Barbara Pentz
Goldendale, Ohio

CORNISH GAME HENS WITH SESAME RICE

1/2 c. brown rice
1 sm. onion, minced
3 tbsp. butter
1 c. chicken broth
1 tbsp. sesame seed
2 Cornish game hens
Salt and pepper to taste
1/4 c. melted butter

Saute rice and onion in 3 tablespoons butter in saucepan until onion is tender and rice is golden. Add chicken broth. Cook, covered, over low heat for 15 minutes or until rice is tender. Add sesame seed; mix well. Wash game hens; pat dry inside and out. Sprinkle with salt and pepper. Stuff with rice mixture; truss. Place in baking pan. Brush with 1/4 cup butter. Roast at 350 degrees for 1 hour or until very tender. Yield: 2-4 servings.

Jimmie Lee Cupton
Danville, Virginia

SPANISH-ROASTED GAME HENS

4 Cornish game hens
Salt and pepper to taste
1 lb. small fresh mushrooms
2/3 c. chopped pimento-stuffed olives
2 slices bacon
1/2 tsp. paprika
1/3 c. chopped filberts
4 tbsp. melted butter
1/3 c. finely chopped onion
1 c. rice

2 c. chicken broth
1/2 c. grated Swiss cheese
1/3 c. chopped pimento-stuffed olives

Wash game hens; pat dry inside and out. Sprinkle cavities with salt and pepper. Stuff with mixture of mushrooms and 2/3 cup olives. Secure with pins; truss. Place in roasting pan; place 1/2 slice bacon on each. Roast at 450 degrees for 20 minutes. Reduce temperature to 350 degrees. Remove bacon. Stir paprika into pan drippings. Brush over Cornish hens. Roast until browned and tender. Saute filberts in 2 tablespoons butter in skillet; remove filberts. Add remaining 2 tablespoons butter, onion and rice. Saute until rice is very lightly browned, stirring occasionally. Add broth. Simmer, covered, for 15 minutes or until rice is tender. Stir in cheese, 1/3 cup olives and sauteed filberts. Spoon onto serving platter. Arrange game hens on top. Garnish with whole stuffed olives. Serve with pan juices.

Christine Cross
Blackwell, Oklahoma

CORNISH GAME HENS WITH BLUEBERRIES

8 Cornish game hens
Salt and pepper to taste
1/4 c. oil
1/4 c. lemon juice
4 c. fresh blueberries, rinsed, drained
4 tsp. sugar
1/2 c. butter, softened
8 bay leaves

Wash game hens; pat dry inside and out. Sprinkle inside and out with salt and pepper. Mix oil and lemon juice in bowl. Brush inside and outside of game hens. Fill each with 1/2 cup blueberries and 1/2 teaspoon sugar. Skewer opening; place in shallow baking pan. Spread with butter; place 1 bay leaf on each breast. Roast at 350 degrees for 1 hour or until tender. Remove bay leaves. Garnish with additional blueberries. Yield: 8 servings.

Freda Johnson
Salem, Oregon

CORNISH GAME HENS A LA BOURBON

8 Cornish game hens
3/4 c. chopped onion
1/4 c. melted butter
4 1/2 c. cooked wild rice
2/3 c. chopped toasted almonds

1/2 tsp. thyme
Salt to taste
1/2 c. melted butter
1/4 tsp. pepper
1/2 c. Bourbon
1 c. butter
1/2 c. bouillon (opt.)
1/2 c. currant jelly, melted

Wash game hens; pat dry inside and out. Saute onion in 1/4 cup butter in skillet. Add wild rice, almonds, thyme and salt; mix well. Stuff game hens with wild rice mixture. Place breast side up in greased shallow baking dish. Mix 1/2 cup butter, salt and pepper; pour over game hens. Roast at 425 degrees for 20 minutes, basting with mixture of Bourbon and 1 cup butter every 5 minutes. Reduce temperature to 350 degrees. Roast for 30 minutes, basting twice. Turn game hens breast side down. Roast for 15 minutes, basting several times; add bouillon if necessary. Turn game hens; pour melted jelly over breasts. Roast for 30 minutes longer.

Matilda Cunningham
Crossville, Tennessee

CANARD CONCORDE

1   4 to 5-lb. duckling with giblets
1/2 lemon
Salt and pepper
1 stalk celery
1 carrot
1 sm. onion
1/2 c. apricot Brandy
1/2 c. Concord grape preserves
1/2 tsp. finely chopped candied ginger
2 tbsp. cornstarch

Rub duckling with lemon half. Season cavity with salt and pepper. Place on rack in roasting pan. Roast at 350 degrees for 15 minutes per pound. Do not baste. Season with salt and pepper; prick skin with fork to drain fat. Roast for 20 to 25 minutes longer or to desired degree of doneness. Combine giblets, celery, carrot, onion, 3 cups water, salt and pepper in saucepan. Bring to a boil; reduce heat. Simmer for 30 minutes. Strain, reserving 2 cups broth. Remove duck to heated serving platter. Drain roasting pan, reserving 2 tablespoons drippings. Deglaze roasting pan with Brandy. Add reserved broth, preserves and ginger. Cook for several minutes, stirring occasionally. Blend 1/4 cup water and cornstarch until smooth. Stir into sauce. Cook until thickened and smooth, stirring constantly. Serve with duck. Garnish with apricots.
Yield: 4 servings.

Photograph for this recipe on page 3.

DUCKLING WITH OLD-FASHIONED APRICOT SAUCE

8 oz. dried apricots
1/4 tsp. ground cloves
2 c. packed brown sugar
2 tsp. salt
1 duckling, quartered
Salt and pepper to taste
Soy sauce

Soak apricots in 5 cups water in saucepan overnight. Simmer until soft. Pour into blender container. Puree until smooth. Pour into saucepan. Add cloves, brown sugar and salt. Simmer for 5 minutes. Place duckling quarters, skin side down, on baking sheet. Season with salt and pepper; turn. Brush skin with soy sauce. Roast at 350 degrees for 1 hour and 45 minutes or until tender. Serve sauce over duckling.

Cheryl Forbes
Grand Junction, New Mexico

DUCK WITH BRANDIED PEACHES

1   4 to 5-lb. duck
1/2 tsp. each salt, pepper, rosemary
   and basil
1 stalk celery, chopped
1 carrot, chopped
1 onion, chopped
1 c. beef broth
4 peach halves
1/4 c. Brandy
3 tbsp. sugar
1 tbsp. butter
1/3 c. vinegar
1 c. peach juice
1/2 tsp. cornstarch

Wash duck; pat dry inside and out. Rub duck with seasonings; prick skin in several places. Place on rack in roasting pan. Roast at 450 degrees for 1 1/2 hours. Drain drippings, reserving 2 tablespoons; split duck in half. Saute vegetables in reserved drippings in saucepan for 10 minutes. Add broth. Cook for 5 minutes; strain. Marinate peaches in Brandy in bowl. Cook sugar and butter in saucepan until brown; add vinegar. Cook until reduced by half. Add strained sauce, peach juice and cornstarch dissolved in 1 tablespoon water. Simmer for 10 minutes. Add peaches and Brandy. Simmer for 5 minutes longer. Place duck on serving platter. Arrange peach halves around duck; top with sauce.

June Hamilton
Macon, Georgia

Game Birds

DUCK WITH AVOCADO-ORANGE SAUCE

1 c. melted butter
1/4 tsp. ginger
1/2 tsp. salt
Dash of pepper
1 duck, cut up
1 tbsp. cornstarch
1   6-oz. can frozen orange juice
   concentrate, thawed
1 tsp. soy sauce
1/4 tsp. ginger
1 avocado, sliced

Blend butter, 1/4 teaspoon ginger, salt and pepper in bowl. Wash duck; pat dry. Brush duck with seasoned butter. Arrange in greased baking pan. Bake at 375 degrees for 1 hour, turning occasionally. Remove duck to warm platter. Stir cornstarch into pan drippings; add orange juice concentrate, soy sauce and 1/4 teaspoon ginger. Cook until thickened, stirring constantly. Mix avocado slices into orange sauce quickly; pour sauce over duck. Serve with hot buttered rice. Yield: 4 servings.

Allison Davis
Bakersfield, California

CAJUN DUCK

4 to 6 mallard ducks
2 tsp. red pepper
1/4 c. salt
2 bunches celery, coarsely chopped
6 onions, coarsely chopped
2 green peppers, coarsely chopped
2 lb. lean mild pork sausage
2 1/2 c. wild rice, cooked

Wash ducks; pat dry inside and out. Sprinkle with mixture of red pepper and salt. Let stand for 20 minutes. Place in saucepan. Add celery, onions, green peppers and 1/2 to 1 cup water. Simmer until ducks and vegetables are tender. Brown sausage in skillet, stirring frequently; drain. Place ducks on serving platter. Add sausage and wild rice to vegetables. Heat to serving temperature, stirring frequently. Serve with ducks. Yield: 6 servings.

Cappy Smithson
Pendleton, Oregon

CHARCOAL-BROILED DUCK BREASTS

4 duck breast filets
4 slices bacon
Salt and pepper to taste
2 beef bouillon cubes
1 tbsp. red currant jelly
1/2 tsp. dry mustard
1 tbsp. Sherry
1 tbsp. Brandy
Pinch of marjoram (opt.)
Pinch of oregano (opt.)
Grated rind of 1 orange

Wrap each duck breast filet with bacon as for filet mignon. Season with salt and pepper. Broil over hot coals for exactly 2 minutes per side. Dissolve bouillon cubes in 1 cup water in chafing dish or electric skillet. Blend in next 6 ingredients. Simmer until slightly thickened; stir in orange rind. Place charcoal-broiled filets in chafing dish. Cook for 5 minutes or until medium-rare, basting constantly.

Johnnie Witson
Decatur, Alabama

FRUIT-STUFFED DUCKLING WITH LEMON GLAZE

1 duckling
1/2 tsp. salt
1 1/2 c. sliced celery
3 tbsp. butter
4 c. bread cubes
1 tsp. grated lemon rind
1 tsp. grated orange rind
1/3 c. light raisins

1/3 c. chopped pecans
2/3 c. drained chopped orange sections
1 tsp. grated lemon rind
1/4 c. lemon juice
1/4 c. honey

Wash duckling; pat dry. Sprinkle with 1/2 teaspoon salt inside and out. Saute celery in butter in skillet until tender. Add bread, 1 teaspoon lemon rind and next 4 ingredients; mix well. Spoon into neck and body cavities; truss. Place breast side up on rack in roasting pan. Bake at 350 degrees for 45 minutes per pound. Blend 1 teaspoon lemon rind, lemon juice and honey in saucepan. Simmer for 5 minutes. Baste duckling with glaze several times during final 30 minutes of baking. Yield: 4 servings.

Photograph for this recipe on opposite page.

PLUM GOOD DUCK

1 onion, minced
2 tbsp. butter
1   17-oz. can purple plums, pureed
1   6-oz. can frozen lemonade, thawed
1/3 c. chili sauce
1/4 c. soy sauce
1 tsp. Worcestershire sauce
1 tsp. ginger
2 tsp. mustard
Onion salt and garlic salt to taste
Tabasco sauce to taste
4 ducks
4 oranges, sliced

Saute onion in butter in saucepan until tender. Add next 4 ingredients and seasonings. Simmer for 15 minutes, stirring frequently. Wash ducks; pat dry inside and out. Place on rack in baking pan; cover with orange slices. Bake, covered, at 350 degrees for 1 1/2 hours. Spoon half the sauce over ducks. Bake for 1 1/2 hours longer or until tender. Serve with remaining sauce.

Billie Bryson
Los Angeles, California

ROAST DUCK
WITH CITRUS GARNISH

1   4 to 5-lb. duck
1 tsp. salt
1/2 tsp. pepper
2 oranges, cut into halves
2 sprigs of parsley
2 celery tops
4 tsp. chicken broth

4 tsp. each soy sauce, honey and vinegar
1 tsp. grated orange rind
1 tsp. each sugar, cinnamon
1 tsp. salt
1/2 tsp. aniseed, crushed
1 1/4 c. orange juice
1/3 c. chicken broth
2 tsp. cornstarch
2 oranges
2 grapefruit, sliced

Wash duck; pat dry inside and out. Sprinkle inside with 1 teaspoon salt and pepper. Stuff with orange halves, parsley and celery. Place duck in roasting pan. Combine 4 teaspoons chicken broth with soy sauce, honey, vinegar, orange rind, sugar, cinnamon, 1 teaspoon salt and aniseed in bowl; mix well. Brush marinade over duck. Let stand for 1 hour. Add 1 cup water. Bake at 350 degrees for 2 hours, brushing frequently with marinade and turning duck occasionally. Place on serving platter. Drain drippings into saucepan. Combine drippings with orange juice and 1/3 cup chicken broth in saucepan. Mix cornstarch with 2 teaspoons cold water. Blend into orange mixture. Simmer for 5 minutes. Slice remaining oranges. Place with grapefruit on baking sheet. Brush with remaining marinade. Bake at 350 degrees for 5 minutes. Arrange around duck. Serve with sauce. Yield: 4 servings.

Noel Page
Keene, New Hampshire

DUCKLING QUARTERS WITH
PINEAPPLE-ORANGE SAUCE

1   5-lb. duckling, quartered
1/2 tsp. salt
1   6-oz. can frozen pineapple-orange
     juice concentrate, thawed
1/4 c. light corn syrup
2 tbsp. cornstarch
1 tbsp. lemon juice
2 tsp. soy sauce
1/2 tsp. ginger

Wash duckling; pat dry. Sprinkle with salt. Place skin side up on rack in shallow roasting pan. Bake at 350 degrees for 2 hours, turning several times. Combine remaining ingredients with 3/4 cup water in saucepan; blend well. Cook until thickened, stirring constantly. Baste duckling with sauce. Bake for 30 minutes longer, basting several times with sauce. Serve duckling over hot cooked rice with remaining sauce. Yield: 4 servings.

Photograph for this recipe on page 52.

Game Birds

SHERRIED SPICED DUCKLING

    1   4 to 5-lb. duckling
    Salt to taste
    2 leeks, sliced
    1 c. dry Sherry
    1/4 c. dark soy sauce
    1 whole star anise
    1 lg. piece of dried tangerine rind
    1 tbsp. corn syrup
    1 tbsp. cornstarch

Wash duckling; pat dry inside and out. Sprinkle with salt. Place on rack in roasting pan. Roast at 350 degrees over pan of water until tender. Prick with fork. Place layer of leeks in saucepan. Stuff remaining leeks into duck cavity. Place duck breast side up over leeks. Add Sherry, soy sauce and 2 1/2 cups hot water. Simmer for 1 hour, basting frequently. Add anise, tangerine rind and corn syrup. Simmer for 1 hour longer. Remove duckling to platter. Skim sauce; strain into saucepan. Add cornstarch blended with 1 tablespoon cold water. Cook until thickened, stirring constantly. Pour over duckling.

Cora Wheeler
Meridian, Mississippi

WINE-SPICED WILD DUCK

    1 c. white wine
    1 clove of garlic
    1 c. oil
    1 tsp. each thyme, oregano, seasoned
        salt and pepper
    4 duck breast filets
    4 slices bacon

Combine wine, garlic, oil and seasonings in bowl; mix well. Add duck breasts. Marinate in refrigerator for several days. Place duck with marinade in saucepan. Simmer, covered, for 2 hours or until tender, adding water if necessary. Place duck on rack in broiler pan. Top with bacon. Broil for 3 to 5 minutes or until bacon is crisp.

Erica Taylor
Minot, North Dakota

WILD DUCK WITH WINE SAUCE

    2 wild ducks, cut into halves
    2 tbsp. butter
    2 tbsp. Sherry
    2 tbsp. tomato paste
    2 tbsp. flour
    1 1/2 c. bouillon
    1/2 c. dry red wine
    1 tsp. salt
    1/4 tsp. pepper
    1/2 lb. mushrooms, sliced
    1 bay leaf
    2 c. cooked wild rice

Wash ducks; pat dry. Brown ducks in butter in large skillet. Pour Sherry over ducks; remove ducks. Blend tomato paste and flour with pan juices. Stir in bouillon and wine gradually. Bring to a boil, stirring constantly. Add ducks, salt, pepper, mushrooms and bay leaf. Cook, covered, over low heat for 2 hours or until tender. Place ducks on warm serving platter. Pack hot wild rice into 4 molds; unmold. Alternate rice molds and duck halves on platter. Skim and strain pan juices. Serve with ducks.

Fern Falwell
Seaton Hall, Kentucky

HONEY-BAKED DUCK
WITH MUSHROOM RICE

    4 wild ducks, cut in half
    1/2 c. butter, softened
    Salt and pepper to taste
    3 tbsp. honey
    2 tsp. soy sauce
    1 c. rice
    2 c. boiling chicken broth
    1 c. sliced fresh mushrooms
    1/2 c. chopped onion
    2 tbsp. butter

Wash ducks; pat dry inside and out. Coat with 1/2 cup butter. Sprinkle with salt and pepper. Place skin side up on rack in roasting pan. Roast at 350 degrees for 1 to 1 1/2 hours or until tender. Brush with mixture of honey and soy sauce. Roast for 15 minutes longer. Brush with remaining honey mixture. Combine rice and broth in buttered 2-quart casserole; mix well. Bake, covered, at 350 degrees for 30 minutes or until rice is tender. Saute mushrooms and onion in 2 tablespoons butter in skillet for 5 minutes or until onion is tender. Stir into rice. Season with salt and pepper. Spoon onto serving platter. Arrange ducks over top.

Cassie Stonewell
Montpelier, New Hampshire

WILD DUCK STROGANOFF

    1/4 c. flour
    Salt and pepper
    4 duck breast filets, slivered
    2 tbsp. butter

1 c. consomme
1 c. sliced mushrooms
Dash of nutmeg
1 c. sour cream

Combine flour with a generous amount of salt
and pepper. Coat duck with seasoned flour.
Brown in butter in skillet. Stir in consomme,
mushrooms and nutmeg. Simmer, covered, for
1 hour or until duck is tender, adding a small
amount of water if necessary. Blend in sour
cream. Cook until heated through. Do not boil.
Serve over wild rice or noodles.

Stephanie Sunderman
Eagle Lake, Wisconsin

WILD DUCK WITH ORANGE STUFFING

1   5-lb. duck
2 to 3 c. bread cubes, toasted
2/3 c. orange pulp
2 c. chopped celery
1/4 c. melted butter
1 egg, beaten
1/2 tsp. salt
Dash of pepper
1/4 tsp. poultry seasoning
2 tsp. grated orange rind
1/2 c. oil (opt.)

Wash duck; pat dry inside and out. Mix bread
with 1/2 cup hot water in bowl. Let stand for
15 minutes. Add remaining ingredients except
oil; mix lightly. Stuff duck with bread mixture.
Place in roasting pan. Roast at 325 degrees for
2 to 3 hours or until tender, basting occasionally with mixture of oil and 1 cup hot water.

Wilona Fireling Luper
Greensboro, North Carolina

BAKED WILD DUCKS IN SWEET AND SOUR SAUCE

2 wild ducks
Orange, apple slices
2 tbsp. oil
2 tbsp. brown sugar
1/4 c. Worcestershire sauce
3/4 c. catsup
2 tbsp. lemon juice
1/2 c. grated onion
1/2 tsp. paprika
1/4 c. white vinegar
Salt and pepper to taste

Wash ducks; pat dry inside and out. Stuff duck
cavities with fruit slices. Rub ducks with oil.

Place in baking dish. Combine remaining ingredients in bowl; mix well. Spoon sauce over
ducks. Cover tightly with foil. Bake at 325 degrees for 2 hours. Uncover. Bake until tender.

Mrs. Marion T. Mills
Morehead City, North Carolina

BAKED GOOSE

1 goose
Salt
1 apple, quartered
1 tbsp. butter
1/4 c. honey
1/4 c. orange juice
1 tsp. grated orange rind
1/4 tsp. ginger

Wash goose; pat dry inside and out. Sprinkle
with salt inside and out. Stuff with apple. Place
on large sheet of foil in baking pan. Heat remaining ingredients in saucepan. Pour half the
honey mixture into cavity and remainder over
goose; seal foil. Bake at 350 degrees for 2 1/2
hours. Bake, uncovered, until browned.

Pam Battey
Muscatine, Iowa

STILLWATER GOOSE BREAST

1 goose breast, boned, skinned
1 c. flour
Salt and pepper to taste
3 tbsp. olive oil
1 clove of garlic, crushed
1/4 lb. mushrooms, sliced
1 med. onion, chopped
1/2 c. dry white wine
1 tbsp. tomato paste
1 tsp. thyme
1 c. chicken stock
2 tbsp. butter

Slice goose breast into eight 1/4-inch thick filets. Pound with meat mallet to 1/8-inch thickness. Coat with mixture of flour, salt and pepper. Brown in olive oil in skillet for 3 minutes
on each side. Remove filets to oven to keep
warm. Saute garlic, mushrooms and onion in
pan drippings and a small amount of additional
olive oil if necessary. Add wine; deglaze skillet.
Stir in remaining ingredients. Cook until reduced by half. Place filets in sauce. Simmer,
covered, for 20 to 30 minutes adding a small
amount of additional stock if necessary. Adjust
seasonings. Serve over noodles or wild rice.

Daniela Barrett
Ft. Wayne, Indiana

Game Birds

GOOSE CACCIATORE

2 goose breast filets
3 tbsp. flour
1 clove of garlic, minced
1/4 c. olive oil
1/4 c. Italian tomato sauce
1/2 c. dry white wine
1 tsp. salt
1/4 tsp. white pepper
3/4 c. chicken broth
1 bay leaf
1/8 tsp. each thyme, marjoram
1/2 tsp. basil
1/4 c. chopped scallions
1 c. sliced mushrooms
1/4 c. Brandy

Slice goose filets 1/2 inch thick as for London broil. Coat with flour. Saute with garlic in olive oil in skillet for 5 minutes on each side. Combine remaining ingredients in bowl; mix well. Pour into skillet. Simmer, covered, for 1 hour or until tender. Yield: 4 servings.

George E. Meagher, III
Ambler, Pennsylvania

CHRISTMAS GOOSE

1   5-lb. goose
1 1/2 tsp. salt
3/4 lb. sausage
1 tbsp. butter
1 1/2 c. finely chopped onions
1/4 tsp. pepper
1 tsp. sage
2 tbsp. chopped parsley
1 tsp. Beau Monde seasoning
4 c. toasted bread cubes
1/2 c. milk
1 egg, slightly beaten
1/2 c. chopped carrot
1/2 c. chopped celery
1 c. chicken stock
1 1/2 c. currant jelly
1 tsp. onion powder
1/2 tsp. salt
1/4 tsp. pepper
2 tbsp. arrowroot

Wash goose well; pat dry inside and out. Sprinkle 1 teaspoon salt inside cavity and 1/2 teaspoon salt over outer skin. Saute sausage in butter in skillet until well browned. Add onions. Saute until tender. Add 1/4 teaspoon pepper and next 6 ingredients; mix well. Spoon into goose cavity. Place goose in Dutch oven. Add carrot, celery and chicken stock. Bake, covered, at 425 degrees for 1 1/2 hours or until tender.

Remove goose to heated serving platter. Skim excess fat. Add jelly, onion powder, 1/2 teaspoon salt, 1/4 teaspoon pepper and 2 cups water to pan juices. Cook until well blended, stirring constantly. Combine arrowroot with 1 cup water. Stir into jelly mixture. Cook until thickened, stirring constantly. Serve over goose and stuffing.

Phoebe S. deReynier
Katonah, New York

GOLDEN STUFFED GOOSE

1   10 to 12-lb. goose
1 1/2 c. maple syrup
2 tbsp. lemon juice
1/2 c. chopped celery
1/2 c. chopped onion
1/4 c. melted butter
3 c. bread cubes
1 c. chopped apples
1/4 c. chopped parsley
1/2 tsp. salt
1/2 tsp. savory
Dash of pepper
16 sm. onions
8 potatoes, peeled, quartered

Soak goose in salted water to cover for 2 hours. Wash goose; pat dry inside and out. Combine maple syrup and lemon juice in small bowl. Brush cavity with 1/2 cup syrup mixture. Saute celery and onion in butter in skillet until tender. Add bread cubes, apples, parsley, salt, savory and pepper; mix well. Fill cavity loosely with stuffing; truss. Place breast side up on rack in roasting pan. Bake at 325 degrees for 1 1/2 hours. Pour off drippings. Place goose on bottom of pan. Arrange onions and potatoes around goose. Bake for 1 1/2 hours or until goose and vegetables are tender, basting frequently with remaining syrup mixture. Yield: 8-10 servings.

Marka Flood
Tupelo, Mississippi

ROASTED GROUSE
WITH WINE SAUCE

1 grouse, dressed
1 onion, quartered
1 apple, quartered
1 stalk celery, chopped
1/4 c. oil
Salt pork, thinly sliced
1/4 c. melted butter

62

Game Birds

Flour
1 tbsp. instant chicken bouillon
1/2 c. Marsala
Salt and pepper to taste
1/2 lb. mushrooms, thinly sliced
4 shallots, minced
1/2 c. chopped parsley
1/4 c. melted butter

Wash grouse; pat dry inside and out. Stuff grouse with onion, apple and celery. Place on rack in shallow roasting pan. Brush with oil; cover with salt pork. Bake at 300 degrees for 45 minutes. Remove salt pork; brush with butter. Coat lightly with flour. Bake at 500 degrees for 5 to 10 minutes or until brown. Remove to warm serving platter. Skim fat from pan juices. Add bouillon, Marsala, salt, pepper and 1 1/2 cups water. Cook over high heat for 5 minutes or until liquid is reduced by one-third, stirring occasionally. Saute mushrooms, shallots and parsley in 1/4 cup butter in skillet. Add to pan juices; mix well. Serve over grouse.

Bonnie Alderson
Hartford, Connecticut

HUNTSMAN-STYLE PARTRIDGE

3 young partridge, cut up
Seasoned flour
7 oz. Brandy
1 onion, chopped
2 carrots, sliced
1 can mushrooms
1 tsp. mixed dry seasoning
1 c. canned consomme

Wash partridge; pat dry. Coat with seasoned flour. Brown in oil in skillet. Add Brandy. Ignite. Add vegetables and seasoning; mix gently. Add consomme. Simmer, covered, for 45 minutes or until partridge is tender. Yield: 4-6 servings.

Anne Wilson
Kingston, West Virginia

PARTRIDGE WITH ARTICHOKE HEARTS

4 partridge
Salt and pepper to taste
6 tbsp. butter
6 tbsp. oil
6 tomatoes, peeled
2 onions, sliced
2 cloves of garlic, chopped
2 pkg. frozen artichoke hearts, thawed

2 bay leaves
3 c. beef broth

Wash partridge; pat dry inside and out. Sprinkle inside and out with salt and pepper. Brown in mixture of 4 tablespoons butter and 4 tablespoons oil in skillet. Place partridge in greased casserole. Add remaining butter and oil to pan drippings. Saute tomatoes, onions and garlic until onions are golden. Spoon sauteed vegetables over partridge. Add artichoke hearts, bay leaves and broth. Bake, covered, at 400 degrees for 1 hour. Discard bay leaves. Split partridge lengthwise. Serve with vegetables and pan juices.

Mary Kay Blanchard
Chippewa Falls, Wisconsin

BAKED PHEASANT WITH OYSTER DRESSING

1 pheasant
1/2 c. chopped celery
1/2 c. chopped onion
1/4 c. margarine
3 c. chopped oysters
6 c. dry bread crumbs
2 eggs, beaten
Salt and pepper to taste

Cook pheasant in water in saucepan for 45 minutes or until tender. Drain, reserving 1 3/4 cups broth. Saute celery and onion in margarine in skillet. Add oysters, bread crumbs, eggs, seasonings and reserved broth; mix well. Stuff pheasant with bread crumb mixture. Place in roasting pan. Spoon any remaining dressing around pheasant. Bake at 350 degrees for 45 minutes. Yield: 4-6 servings.

Elva Kaenig
Waterloo, Iowa

PHEASANT SUPREME

2 pheasant, cut into quarters
Salt and pepper to taste
8 thin slices Canadian bacon
1 can cream of mushroom soup
1 can sliced mushrooms

Wash pheasant; pat dry. Place skin side up in greased 9 x 12-inch baking dish. Sprinkle with salt and pepper. Place 1 piece of Canadian bacon on each quarter. Spread soup over pheasant. Top with mushrooms. Bake at 300 degrees for 2 hours or until tender. Yield: 6-8 servings.

Jessica Winkler
Applegate, Michigan

63

Game Birds

SPIT-ROASTED PHEASANT

1 c. coarsely chopped cashews
1 c. chicken broth
4 slices crisp-fried bacon, crumbled
Salt and pepper
1/4 tsp. each sage, poultry seasoning
1 tsp. butter
2 pheasant
8 slices bacon

Simmer cashews in chicken broth in saucepan until cashews are tender and liquid is absorbed. Add crumbled bacon, 1/4 teaspoon salt, dash of pepper, sage, poultry seasoning and butter. Rinse pheasant; pat dry inside and out. Sprinkle cavities with salt and pepper; stuff with cashew stuffing. Truss as for chicken. Wrap bacon slices over wings, legs, thighs and breasts of pheasant, tying in place with cord. Thread pheasant onto spit; place on rotisserie. Grill over medium coals for 1 1/4 hours or until brown and tender.

Photograph for this recipe above.

PHEASANT-BARLEY CASSEROLE

1 c. barley
1 can mushroom soup
1 c. chopped celery
1 c. chopped onion
Salt and pepper to taste
1 pheasant, cut up
1 can mushroom soup

Brown barley in a small amount of oil in Dutch oven. Add 1 can soup and 1/2 soup can water; mix well. Add celery, onion and seasonings; mix well. Brown pheasant in skillet. Place in Dutch oven. Spoon 1 can soup over pheasant. Bake, covered, at 325 degrees for 30 minutes. Bake, uncovered, for 30 minutes longer or until pheasant is tender.
Note: May substitute wild rice for barley.

Fran Lefke
Stockton, California

PHEASANT WITH NUTTED RICE

3 1 1/2-lb. pheasant
1/2 lemon
Salt and pepper to taste
1/3 c. butter, softened
Juice of 3 oranges
1 c. white raisins
1 tsp. grated lemon rind
1 c. chicken broth
1/3 c. Muscatel
1 c. rice
2 c. chicken broth
2 tbsp. butter
2/3 c. chopped nuts
2 tbsp. minced parsley

Rinse pheasant inside and out with warm water; drain well. Rub pheasant cavities with lemon. Season with salt and pepper. Place breast side up in baking dish. Spread with 1/3 cup butter. Add orange juice, raisins, lemon rind, 1 cup chicken broth and Muscatel. Bake at 350 degrees for 45 minutes, basting every 10 minutes. Combine rice and 2 cups chicken broth in saucepan. Bring to a boil. Cook, covered, over low heat for 15 minutes or until rice is tender and liquid is absorbed. Remove from heat. Stir in 2 tablespoons butter, nuts and parsley. Season to taste. Serve with pheasant.

Rebecca Brown
Troy, Texas

PHEASANT IN WINE AND CREAM

Thighs and boned breasts of 3 pheasant
1/2 c. half and half
Flour
Garlic salt, pepper and paprika to taste
3 tbsp. butter
1 1/2 c. half and half
1 1/2 c. Sauterne
1 4-oz. jar button mushrooms

Dip pheasant pieces into half and half. Coat with flour seasoned with garlic salt, pepper and paprika. Repeat process a second time. Brown in butter in skillet. Place in greased 3-quart casserole. Combine 1 1/2 cups half and half, Sauterne and mushrooms in bowl; mix well. Pour over pheasant. Bake, covered, at 250 degrees for 3 hours or until tender.

Candace Longworth
Costa Mesa, California

ROAST PHEASANT WITH WILD RICE

1 pheasant
Salt and pepper to taste

Game Birds

1 c. wild rice
1 c. apricot juice

Wash pheasant; pat dry inside and out. Rub cavity with salt and pepper. Place in baking pan lined with large piece of foil. Sprinkle wild rice over pheasant. Pour apricot juice over all. Seal foil. Bake at 325 degrees for 1 hour or until pheasant and rice are tender. Yield: 4 servings.

Velma Wood
Ardmore, Oklahoma

WILD PHEASANT AND VEGETABLES

1 pheasant, cut up
1 pkg. Uncle Ben's wild rice mix
4 med. carrots, sliced
1 med. onion, chopped
6 stalks celery, diced
1 sm. jar chopped pimento
1 sm. can corn (opt.)

Wash pheasant; pat dry. Combine rice mix with water using package directions in large baking dish. Add remaining ingredients; mix well. Arrange pheasant over top. Bake, covered, at 350 degrees for 30 to 45 minutes or until pheasant is tender. Yield: 6 servings.

Mildred Genelle Cady
Houston, Texas

QUAIL BAKED IN MUSHROOM SAUCE

8 quail, cut into halves
Salt and pepper to taste
Flour
6 tbsp. oil
1 6-oz. can sliced mushrooms, drained
2 cans cream of mushroom soup
1 soup can white wine
2 c. sour cream

Wash quail; pat dry. Season quail with salt and pepper; coat with flour. Brown on both sides in oil in skillet. Arrange in greased shallow baking dish. Combine remaining ingredients in bowl; blend well. Pour over quail. Bake at 350 degrees for 1 hour. Yield: 4 servings.

Ann Senfert
College Grove, North Carolina

SHERRIED QUAIL

6 quail
Salt to taste
Flour
3/4 c. Sherry

3 tbsp. Worcestershire sauce
1/3 c. lemon juice

Wash quail; pat dry inside and out. Sprinkle with salt. Coat with flour. Brown in oil in skillet. Place in casserole. Combine remaining ingredients in bowl; mix well. Pour over quail. Bake, covered, at 350 degrees for 1 hour. Yield: 6 servings.

Linda S. Barnes
Anderson, Indiana

SOUR CREAM QUAIL

6 to 8 quail, cut up
1 c. flour
Salt and pepper to taste
2 lg. cartons sour cream
1 can mushroom soup
1 or 2 med. green peppers, coarsely chopped
Mozzarella cheese, sliced
2 bay leaves

Wash quail; pat dry. Coat with flour. Arrange in greased 8 x 10-inch baking pan. Sprinkle with salt and pepper. Bake at 350 degrees for 40 minutes or until lightly browned. Combine sour cream, soup and green peppers in blender container. Process until smooth. Pour over quail. Top with cheese. Add bay leaves. Bake, covered, until cheese melts. Bake, uncovered, until cheese is lightly browned. Remove bay leaves. Yield: 4-6 servings.

Marie Johnson
Pontiac, Michigan

ROAST SQUAB WITH WILD RICE

4 shallots, chopped
16 mushrooms, chopped
1/4 c. melted butter
2 c. cooked wild rice
4 slices crisp-fried bacon, crumbled
4 tsp. minced parsley
4 jumbo squab
1 c. melted butter
1 c. white wine

Saute shallots and mushrooms in 1/4 cup butter in skillet. Stir in wild rice, bacon and parsley. Wash squab; pat dry inside and out. Stuff with wild rice mixture; truss. Place in roasting pan. Brush with butter. Bake at 350 degrees for 45 minutes or until tender. Add wine to remaining melted butter. Baste squab every 10 minutes. Yield: 4 servings.

Fleda Lambert
Duncanville, Texas

65

Seafood

Fantastic flavor variety and unbeatable nutrition — that's what fish have to offer the homemaker planning today's meals. There are so many choices and they're all easy to prepare in a host of different ways. Fish can be baked whole, or cut into fillets or steaks and fried, broiled, grilled or put into casseroles, so they can be prepared to suit most any taste or any occasion. Altogether, it sounds like fish are a cook's dream food!

Depending on where you live, inland or on the coast, near a river or on a lake, there are delicious fresh fish available that are particular to your area. And, whether you have a fisherman in the family or a good fish market in the neighborhood, the supply of local fish should be abundant and economical. Family fisherman, fish market or not, you can shop your local supermarket for both fresh and frozen varieties of fish from all parts of the world. And, don't overlook the canned or dried fish available in most any grocery store.

Many people consider shellfish to be the seafood with the most personality and flavor. And, it's often true that in both popular and elegant restaurants, it's the shrimp, crab, lobster, scallops, oyster and other shellfish recipes that comprise many of the finer dishes.

It's not that shellfish is particularly rare, because our coastlines and bays have always provided an abundance. Shellfish is often expensive because it must be shipped live from the Atlantic, Pacific or Gulf coasts to be at its tastiest. More than anything else, it's the uniquely delicate and intriguing flavors of shellfish that are truly prized. And, the fine dishes they produce are within the reach of virtually any cook.

Today's emphasis on creative cookery makes cooks more enthusiastic than ever before to include seafood in their menu plans as often as possible. Plus, it is low in calories and combines well with other "lean" foods to create everything from hors d'oeuvres, salads and sandwiches to casseroles, grilled entrees, gumbo and more.

◄SPANISH FILLET OF SOLE, recipe on page 87.

Seafood

CREAMY CLAM CHOWDER

3 med. onions, chopped
3 tbsp. bacon drippings
1/2 lb. sliced bacon, crisp-fried, crumbled
3 lg. potatoes, cut into 1/2-in. cubes
Salt and pepper to taste
1 tsp. each basil, thyme
2 tbsp. melted butter
1/4 c. flour
4 7-oz. cans minced clams, drained
2 c. heavy cream
2 c. milk

Saute onions in bacon drippings in skillet until tender. Combine with bacon, potatoes, seasonings and 1 cup water in saucepan. Simmer until potatoes are tender. Stir in mixture of butter and flour. Cook until thickened, stirring constantly. Add clams, cream and milk. Heat to serving temperature. Yield: 4 servings.

Louise Raymond
Phoenix, Arizona

CROCK•POT CLAM CHOWDER

4 cans cream of potato soup
2 cans evaporated milk
2 cans chopped clams
3/4 c. chopped carrots
1 c. finely chopped onion
1/4 lb. bacon, chopped

Combine all ingredients in Crock-Pot. Cook on High for 8 hours. Yield: 6-8 servings.

Beverly Kagele
Yakima, Washington

NEW ENGLAND CLAM CHOWDER

3 oz. diced salt pork
2 med. potatoes, peeled, chopped
2 med. onions, chopped
1/2 c. finely chopped leek
2 doz. cherrystone clams
1/2 to 1 c. milk
Salt and pepper to taste
1 tbsp. butter
1 tbsp. chopped parsley
1/2 tsp. paprika

Place salt pork in heavy saucepan with water to cover. Cook until water evaporates and pork is golden. Drain pork on paper towels; reserve drippings. Saute potatoes, onions and leek in reserved drippings until tender-crisp. Do not brown. Shuck and chop clams, reserving liquor. Add clam liquor to sauteed vegetables. Add

enough water to cover. Simmer, covered, for 25 minutes or until potatoes are tender. Mash potatoes lightly. Stir in clams. Cook for several minutes or until clams are just firm. Add enough milk to make of desired consistency. Heat to serving temperature. Add remaining ingredients. Spoon into serving bowl. Top with reserved pork. Yield: 4 servings.

Nancy Raynor
Raleigh, North Carolina

MANHATTAN CLAM CHOWDER

1/4 c. finely chopped onion
1/4 c. butter
2 8-oz. cans minced clams
2 c. finely chopped potatoes
1/3 c. chopped celery
1 16-oz. can whole tomatoes
2 tsp. minced parsley
1 tsp. salt
1/4 tsp. thyme
1/8 tsp. pepper

Saute onion in butter in large saucepan. Drain clams, reserving liquid. Add clam liquid, potatoes, 1 cup water and celery to sauteed onion. Cook for 10 minutes or until potatoes are tender. Add clams, tomatoes with liquid and remaining ingredients. Bring to a boil, stirring occasionally. Yield: 4-6 servings.

Billie Gay
Moultrie, Georgia

DOWN-HOME FISH STEW

1 c. chopped onion
2 cloves of garlic, chopped
2 tbsp. oil
1 16-oz. can tomatoes, drained
3 tbsp. chopped canned green chilies
1/2 c. Florida grapefruit juice
1 vegetable bouillon cube
3/4 tsp. thyme
1/2 tsp. salt
1 10-oz. package frozen lima
    beans, thawed
1 1-lb. package frozen cod fillets,
    partially thawed, cut into chunks
2 med. Florida grapefruit, sectioned

Saute onion and garlic in oil in saucepan until tender. Stir in tomatoes, chilies, grapefruit juice, bouillon cube, thyme and salt. Simmer for 20 minutes. Add lima beans and cod. Cook for 5 to 10 minutes or until fish flakes easily. Add grapefruit sections; mix gently.

Photograph for this recipe on Cover.

EASY FISH CHOWDER

1 1/2 lb. haddock fillets
1 lg. onion, sliced
1/4 c. butter
3 cans cream of potato soup
Salt to taste
3 qt. milk
8 lg. saltine crackers

Cook haddock in a small amount of salted water in saucepan until haddock flakes easily. Saute onion in butter in skillet. Add to haddock with soup, salt and enough milk to make of desired consistency. Simmer until heated through. Place 1 warm cracker in each chowder bowl. Pour chowder over cracker. Garnish with paprika. Yield: 8 servings.

Sally Riley
Wheaton, Illinois

NEW ENGLAND FISH AND VEGETABLE CHOWDER

1/4 lb. bacon, chopped
2 med. onions, sliced
1 leek, sliced
1/4 c. chopped green pepper
1 stalk celery, chopped
1 clove of garlic, crushed
2 lb. haddock, cut into chunks
2 med. potatoes, peeled, chopped
2 tbsp. chopped parsley
1/2 tsp. thyme
1/4 tsp. each basil, salt and pepper
3 c. milk
Dash of hot sauce (opt.)

Saute bacon in saucepan until crisp; remove bacon. Add onions, leek, green pepper, celery and garlic. Saute until tender. Add haddock, potatoes, parsley, seasonings and 4 cups water. Simmer for 15 minutes or until potatoes are tender. Add milk, bacon and hot sauce. Heat to serving temperature.

Emma Craig
Rawlesburg, West Virginia

PUGET SOUND SALMON CHOWDER

1/2 c. chopped celery
1/2 c. chopped onion
1/2 c. chopped green pepper
1 clove of garlic, minced
3 tbsp. margarine
1 c. chopped potatoes
1 c. shredded carrots
2 c. chicken broth
1 1/2 tsp. salt
1/2 tsp. each pepper, dillweed
1 c. flaked cooked salmon
1 17-oz. can cream-style corn
1 lg. can evaporated milk

Saute celery, onion, green pepper and garlic in margarine in saucepan. Add potatoes, carrots, broth and seasonings. Simmer for 20 minutes. Stir in salmon, corn and evaporated milk. Simmer for 10 minutes or until heated through.

Sara J. Paeth
St. Helens, Oregon

SHRIMP CREOLE LOUISIANNE

1 sm. green pepper, chopped
2 stalks celery, chopped
1/2 clove of garlic, minced
1 med. onion, chopped
1 1/2 tbsp. oil
2 16-oz. cans tomatoes, mashed
1 tsp. parsley flakes
1/8 tsp. red pepper
Dash of allspice
3 whole cloves
2 bay leaves
1 lb. shrimp, peeled

Saute green pepper, celery, garlic and onion in oil in skillet. Add tomatoes and 2 cups water. Stir in seasonings. Simmer for 1 to 1 1/2 hours. Add shrimp. Simmer for 10 minutes. Remove bay leaves and cloves. Serve over hot cooked rice.

Rhoda G. Warren
Pensacola, Florida

EASY MICROWAVE SHRIMP CREOLE

1 16-oz. can tomatoes, chopped
1 green pepper, chopped
1/2 tsp. chili powder
1 med. onion, chopped
1 bay leaf
1/2 tsp. salt (opt.)
1/2 tsp. pepper
1 lb. shrimp, peeled

Combine all ingredients except shrimp in 1 1/2-quart glass casserole. Microwave, covered, on High for 8 to 12 minutes or until green pepper is tender, stirring once. Stir in shrimp. Microwave, covered, on High for 3 to 5 minutes or just until shrimp are pink. Do not overcook. Let stand for 3 to 5 minutes; remove bay leaf. Serve over hot cooked rice. Yield: 4 servings.

Peggy Moore
Flagstaff, Arizona

Seafood

EASY SEAFOOD GUMBO

1 clove of garlic, finely chopped
2 c. chopped onions
1 c. chopped green pepper
3 tbsp. oil
2 16-oz. cans whole peeled tomatoes
2 tsp. salt
1/4 tsp. pepper
2 drops of Tabasco sauce
1 bay leaf
1 10-oz. package frozen whole baby okra,
    partially thawed, cut into 1-in. pieces
1/4 c. rice
1 1-lb. package frozen shrimp
1 7-oz. package frozen cooked crab
    meat, thawed
1 7-oz. can frozen oysters, thawed
3 tbsp. chopped parsley
1 tsp. file (opt.)
Hot cooked rice

Saute garlic, onions and green pepper in oil in saucepan until tender. Add tomatoes, 3 cups water, salt, pepper, Tabasco sauce, bay leaf, okra and uncooked rice. Bring to a boil. Simmer, covered, for 10 minutes. Add shrimp. Simmer, covered, for 5 minutes. Add crab meat, oysters and parsley. Simmer for 3 minutes. Remove bay leaf. Place about 1/8 teaspoon file in each soup bowl. Add 1 scoop hot cooked rice. Ladle gumbo into each bowl; stir gently. Sprinkle with additional parsley.
Yield: 8-10 servings.

Rowena Ballew
Ft. Worth, Texas

SHRIMP GUMBO

1 1/2 c. chopped onions
3 tbsp. oil
1/4 c. flour
1 16-oz. can tomatoes, chopped
1 10-oz. package frozen sliced okra
2 tsp. salt
1/4 tsp. each red pepper, black pepper
Pinch each of marjoram, savory, basil,
    thyme, sage, rosemary and oregano
1 lb. shrimp, cleaned
1 3/4-oz. package dried shrimp
1 tbsp. file

Saute onions in oil in saucepan. Blend in flour. Cook until browned, stirring constantly. Add 4 cups water, tomatoes, okra, seasonings and mixture of spices tied in cheesecloth; mix well. Cook, covered, for 30 minutes. Stir in shrimp. Cook for 10 minutes longer or until shrimp are

pink. Remove seasoning bag. Stir in file just before serving. Serve with rice. Yield: 8 servings.

Gloria Cooper
Houston, Texas

CALIFORNIA PAELLA

1 3-lb. chicken, cut up
1/4 c. oil
1 c. long grain rice
1 onion, chopped
1 stalk celery, chopped
2 cloves of garlic, minced
1 chicken bouillon cube
1/2 c. white wine
2 tsp. salt
1/8 tsp. white pepper
1 tbsp. chopped parsley
1 bay leaf
1/8 tsp. saffron (opt.)
1 c. pitted ripe olives
1 10-oz. can whole clams
1 4 1/2-oz. can shrimp
1 c. frozen peas

Brown chicken in oil in skillet; remove chicken. Brown rice in pan drippings, stirring constantly. Add onion, celery and garlic. Saute for several minutes. Add 1 1/4 cups hot water, bouillon cube, wine and seasonings. Bring to a boil. Add olives, clams and shrimp. Pour into greased 2 1/2-quart baking dish. Arrange chicken over top. Bake, covered, at 350 degrees for 35 minutes. Stir in peas. Bake, covered, for 5 minutes longer. Yield: 6 servings.

Photograph for this recipe below.

COMPANY JAMBALAYA

1 1/2 c. chopped pork
1 c. chopped green onions
1 c. chopped onion
1 c. chopped celery
1 c. chopped green pepper
3 tbsp. butter
9 lg. tomatoes, chopped
2 6-oz. cans tomato paste
2 cloves of garlic, minced
1/2 tsp. thyme
Tabasco sauce to taste
3 bay leaves
1/4 tsp. red pepper
1 tsp. salt
Pepper to taste
2 c. chicken broth
1 1/2 lb. shrimp, chopped
1/2 c. chopped green pepper
1/2 c. chopped celery

Saute first 5 ingredients in butter in skillet. Add tomatoes, tomato paste, garlic, seasonings and broth; mix well. Simmer for 30 minutes. Add shrimp, 1/2 cup green pepper and 1/2 cup celery. Simmer for 30 minutes longer, adding a small amount of water, if necessary. Serve over hot cooked rice. Yield: 10-12 servings.

Marjane Telck
Rock Springs, Wyoming

MICROWAVE SHRIMP JAMBALAYA

3 tbsp. oil
3 tbsp. flour
2 c. finely chopped onion
1/2 c. finely chopped green pepper
4 cloves of garlic, finely chopped
1 10-oz. can chopped tomatoes
2 c. shrimp, peeled
2 c. diced ham
3 c. cooked rice
1 tbsp. chopped parsley
1 tbsp. chopped green onion tops

Mix oil and flour in 3-quart glass casserole. Microwave on High for 5 to 6 minutes or until lightly browned. Add onion, green pepper and garlic; mix well. Microwave on High for 3 minutes. Add tomatoes, shrimp and 1 1/2 cups hot water; mix well. Microwave on High for 7 minutes or until shrimp are pink. Stir in ham and rice. Microwave, covered, on High for 3 minutes. Sprinkle parsley and onion tops over top. Yield: 6 servings.

Kitty Cardwell
St. Louis, Missouri

CREOLE JAMBALAYA

1 lb. link sausage, chopped
1 tbsp. shortening
1/2 med. onion, chopped
1/2 med. green pepper, chopped
1 6-oz. can tomato paste
1 8-oz. can tomato sauce
1 3/4-oz. package dried shrimp
1 tsp. salt
1/2 tsp. each black pepper, red pepper
3 c. cooked rice

Brown sausage in skillet. Add shortening, onion and green pepper. Saute until tender. Stir in tomato paste, tomato sauce, shrimp and 2 cups water. Simmer, covered, for 20 minutes, stirring occasionally. Add remaining ingredients; mix well. Simmer until heated through. Garnish with parsley. Yield: 6 servings.

Felicia Thibodeaux
Houston Texas

CIOPPINO

1/2 c. chopped green pepper
1/2 c. chopped celery
2 cloves of garlic, finely chopped
1/4 c. oil
1 tsp. each oregano, marjoram
1/2 tsp. basil
2 tsp. parsley
1/2 tsp. paprika
1/8 tsp. pepper
1 16-oz. can stewed tomatoes
1 c. tomato sauce
3 oz. tomato paste
3 chicken bouillon cubes
1/2 c. Sherry
1 crab, cleaned, cracked
1 lb. clams
1 lb. prawns
1 lb. white fish

Combine green pepper, celery, garlic and oil in 6-quart stock pot. Add oregano, marjoram, basil and parsley. Saute for 10 minutes, stirring occasionally. Add paprika, pepper, 2 cups water and next 5 ingredients. Simmer for 40 minutes. Add crab, clams and prawns. Simmer for 15 minutes. Add fish. Simmer for 15 minutes longer. Serve with sourdough bread and salad. Yield: 4 servings.

Mary L. Gomez
San Joaquin, California

Seafood

EASY OYSTER STEW

1 pt. oysters
1/2 c. melted butter
3 c. milk, scalded
1 c. light cream, heated
1/2 tsp. each salt, paprika
Pepper to taste

Combine oysters, oyster liquid and butter in saucepan. Cook until edges curl. Add milk and cream. Cook over low heat until heated through. Do not boil. Stir in salt, paprika and pepper. Yield: 4 servings.
Note: May thicken by stirring 1 or 2 tablespoons flour into oysters and butter before adding milk.

Nola McCombs
Watertown, New York

HOLIDAY OYSTER STEW

1/3 c. chopped onion
2 tbsp. bacon drippings
2   12-oz. cans oysters
Light cream
1 can frozen cream of potato soup
1 1/4 tsp. salt
Dash of white pepper
2 slices crisp-fried bacon, crumbled
2 tbsp. chopped parsley

Saute onion in bacon dripping in large saucepan. Drain oysters, reserving liquid. Add enough cream to reserved liquid to measure 4 cups. Add cream mixture, soup and seasonings to onion. Heat to near boiling point. Do not boil. Add bacon and oysters. Heat for 3 minutes or until oysters begin to curl. Sprinkle with parsley. Yield: 6 servings.

Photograph for this recipe below.

CRAWFISH ETOUFFEE

1 lb. crawfish tails, shelled
1 tsp. salt
1/2 c. melted butter
1 tbsp. paprika
1 onion, chopped
1/2 green pepper, chopped
2 cloves of garlic, chopped
1 tbsp. Worcestershire sauce
Pinch of red pepper
1/2 tsp. chili powder
1 tsp. each thyme, basil
1 bay leaf, crushed
1 tbsp. chopped green onion tops
1 tbsp. parsley
2 tbsp. cornstarch
2 c. long grain rice, cooked

Season crawfish with salt. Saute in butter and paprika for 5 minutes; remove crawfish. Add next 3 ingredients; saute for 10 minutes. Add crawfish, 2 cups water and next 6 ingredients. Simmer for 40 minutes, stirring occasionally. Add onion tops and parsley. Stir in cornstarch blended with a small amount of water. Cook until slightly thickened, stirring constantly. Serve over rice.

Monica Osberg
Butte, California

SHRIMP ETOUFFEE

1 onion, finely chopped
2 green onions, finely chopped
1/4 c. finely chopped celery
3 or 4 cloves of garlic, minced
1/2 c. butter
2 tbsp. flour
1   10-oz. can tomato puree
1 tbsp. Worcestershire sauce
1 tsp. salt
1/2 tsp. thyme
2 bay leaves
4 drops of Tabasco sauce
1/2 tsp. sugar
1/4 tsp. pepper
1 lb. fresh shrimp, cooked
2 hard-boiled eggs, quartered

Saute first 4 ingredients in butter in skillet until tender. Stir in flour. Cook until lightly browned. Add next 8 ingredients with 2 1/2 cups water. Simmer for 35 minutes or until thickened, stirring occasionally. Add shrimp. Heat to serving temperature. Garnish with eggs. Serve over rice.

Nan Murphy
Lafayette, Alabama

LOBSTER SOUP

2 8-oz. frozen lobster tails,
  partially thawed
1/3 c. chopped onion
1/3 c. chopped green pepper
1/3 c. chopped celery
1 tbsp. butter
6 c. chicken broth
1 7-oz. can tomatoes, chopped
1 tbsp. minced parsley
1/4 tsp. salt
Dash of pepper
1/3 c. small pasta shells
4 c. torn fresh spinach leaves

Split lobster tails in half lengthwise. Cut in half crosswise to make 8 portions. Saute onion, green pepper and celery in butter in saucepan until tender. Do not brown. Add chicken broth, undrained tomatoes, parsley, salt and pepper. Bring to a boil. Add pasta. Cook until pasta is tender. Reduce heat. Add lobster and spinach. Cook for 5 minutes longer or until lobster is tender. Yield: 4 servings.

Luella Clark
Solway, New York

RUSSIAN SOLIANKA

1 onion, sliced
1 cucumber, peeled, chopped
2 tomatoes, chopped
1/4 c. butter, melted
8 c. chicken broth
2 6-oz. rock lobster tails
1 8-oz. can minced clams
2 gherkins, thinly sliced
12 pitted ripe olives, sliced
1 tbsp. capers
1 tbsp. chopped fresh dill
Salt and pepper to taste

Saute onion, cucumber and tomatoes in butter in large saucepan for 5 minutes. Stir in chicken broth. Cut away underside membrane of rock lobster tails with scissors. Remove lobster meat in 1 piece; slice crosswise 1 inch thick. Add lobster, clams, gherkins, olives, capers and dill to soup mixture. Bring to a boil. Season with salt and pepper. Garnish with sour cream and sprigs of fresh dill. Yield: 6 servings.

Alena Logan
Biloxi, Mississippi

TASTY TUNA SALAD

1 7-oz. can water-pack tuna
1 c. French-style green beans

2 stalks celery, chopped
1 sm. onion, chopped
1 or 2 unpeeled apples, chopped
3 ripe olives, minced
5 tbsp. salad dressing

Combine all ingredients in bowl; mix well. Serve on lettuce-lined plates. Yield: 4 servings.

Amanda Laramee
West Burke, Vermont

CORONADO TUNA SALAD

2 7-oz. cans tuna, drained, flaked
2 carrots, peeled, grated
2/3 c. mayonnaise
1 tsp. curry powder

Combine tuna, carrots, mayonnaise and curry powder in bowl; mix well. Chill until serving time. Spoon into shallow dish. Garnish with parsley.

Clara Null
Calchester, Illinois

TUNA-MACARONI SALAD

2 c. elbow macaroni, cooked
1 c. chopped celery
1/2 c. chopped onion
1 13-oz. can tuna
1 tbsp. lemon juice
1/2 c. (about) mayonnaise
Pepper to taste

Combine all ingredients in bowl; mix well. Chill until serving time. Yield: 10-12 servings.

Ernestine Nold
Savannah, Missouri

TUNA-GREEN PEA SALAD

1 can green peas, drained
1 lg. can tuna, drained
1 sm. sweet onion, chopped
2 hard-boiled eggs, chopped
1 tbsp. wine vinegar
2 tbsp. sugar
1/2 to 3/4 c. mayonnaise

Combine all ingredients in bowl; mix well. Chill in refrigerator. Yield: 6 servings.

Roma Perrine
Fayette, North Carolina

Seafood

SEAFOOD SALAD SUPREME

1 1-lb. box macaroni, cooked
2 lb. jumbo shrimp, cooked
1 c. chopped celery
1 green pepper, chopped
1 can tuna
1 1-lb. can crab meat
Old Bay Seafood seasoning to taste
2 hard-boiled eggs, chopped

Combine all ingredients in bowl; toss to mix. Pack into ring mold. Chill until firm. Unmold onto serving plate. Garnish with green and black olives and radish roses.
Note: Use toothpicks to secure garnishes.

Duetta Edwards
Salem, Missouri

CRAB MEAT-MACARONI SALAD

1/4 c. sugar
3 c. macaroni, cooked, cooled
1 can crab meat, flaked
3 onions, chopped
3 green peppers, chopped
2 sm. red peppers, chopped
2 tbsp. celery seed
1/2 c. chopped sweet pickles
Salad dressing

Sprinkle sugar over macaroni in bowl. Add next 6 ingredients with enough salad dressing to moisten; mix well. Garnish with parsley and pimento.

Gwendolyn V. Deville
Prince George, Maryland

NORTHWEST CRAB SALAD BOWL

1/2 c. mashed avocado
1/3 c. sour cream
2 tbsp. lemon juice
1/2 tsp. sugar
1/4 tsp. chili powder
1/4 tsp. salt
1/4 tsp. hot pepper sauce
1 clove of garlic, crushed
1 lb. king crab meat, broken into
    bite-sized pieces
4 c. mixed salad greens
2 tomatoes, cut into wedges
1 c. corn chips
1/2 c. sliced ripe olives
1/4 c. chopped green onion
1/2 c. shredded Cheddar cheese

Combine first 8 ingredients in bowl; mix well. Chill until serving time. Combine crab meat, greens, tomatoes, corn chips, olives and onion in large bowl. Add dressing; mix well. Sprinkle with cheese. Garnish with whole pitted ripe olives. Yield: 6 servings.

Mary Wodrich
Rapelye, Montana

SALAD OF THE STATES

1 c. chopped lettuce
1 c. chopped romaine
1/2 c. chopped watercress
1 1/2 c. chopped lobster
1/2 c. chopped green onions
4 lg. pimento-stuffed olives, sliced
1 grapefruit, peeled, sectioned
1 med. avocado, cubed
1/4 to 1/3 c. mayonnaise
Salt to taste
4 lg. tomatoes, thinly sliced

Combine lettuce, romaine, watercress, lobster, green onions, olives and grapefruit in large bowl; toss to mix. Chill in refrigerator. Add avocado, mayonnaise and salt; toss to mix. Place tomato slices on lettuce-lined plates. Spoon lobster mixture over tomatoes.
Yield: 4-6 servings.

Augusta Kueber
Mt. Vernon, Indiana

NEW ORLEANS SHRIMP SALAD

1 c. cold cooked rice
1 c. chopped cooked shrimp
3/4 tsp. salt
1 tbsp. lemon juice
1/4 c. slivered green pepper
1 tbsp. minced onion
1 tbsp. chopped olives
3/4 c. chopped fresh cauliflower
2 tbsp. French dressing
Dash of pepper
1/3 c. mayonnaise

Combine rice, shrimp, salt, lemon juice, green pepper, onion, olives and cauliflower in salad bowl; toss to mix. Blend French dressing, pepper and mayonnaise in bowl. Spoon over shrimp mixture; toss lightly. Chill in refrigerator. Serve on lettuce-lined plates.
Yield: 4 servings.

Wilma Rehwinkle
Oshkosh, Wisconsin

TOASTED CLAM ROLLS

3 6 1/2-oz. cans minced clams, drained
1/3 c. thinly sliced green onions
1/2 c. mayonnaise
6 tbsp. Parmesan cheese
1 tsp. Worcestershire sauce
3/4 tsp. garlic powder
1/2 to 3/4 tsp. hot pepper sauce
1 lg. loaf thinly sliced sandwich
    bread, crusts trimmed
6 tbsp. melted butter

Mix clams, green onions, mayonnaise, Parmesan cheese, Worcestershire sauce, garlic powder and hot pepper sauce in bowl. Roll bread slices until very thin. Spread 1 tablespoon mixture over each. Roll as for jelly roll. Brush with butter. Place seam-side down on greased baking sheet. Bake at 425 degrees for 12 minutes or until lightly browned. Yield: 6 servings.

Jeri Laveder
Napa, California

BAKED CRAB SANDWICHES

2 cans crab meat
2 tbsp. Worcestershire sauce
1/2 c. chopped red onion
2 tbsp. lemon juice
4 eggs, beaten
2 c. milk
1/2 c. chopped celery
1/2 c. chopped green pepper
12 slices bread, crusts trimmed, buttered
6 slices Monterey Jack cheese

Combine crab meat, Worcestershire sauce, onion and lemon juice in bowl; mix well. Blend eggs and milk in bowl. Stir in celery and green pepper. Layer half the bread, crab mixture and cheese slices in greased 9 x 13-inch baking pan. Top with remaining bread slices. Pour egg mixture over top. Bake at 350 degrees for 45 minutes. Yield: 6 servings.

Carol Litfin
Stanislaus, California

CHEESY CRAB BUNS

2 c. shredded cheese
1/3 c. margarine
1 7-oz. can crab meat, drained
6 hamburger buns, split

Heat cheese and margarine in saucepan over low heat until melted; remove from heat. Stir in crab meat. Spread crab meat mixture on buns; place on rack in broiler pan. Broil 4 to 5 inches from heat source for 2 minutes or until browned and bubbly. Yield: 6 servings.

Clara Burns
South Bend, Indiana

CRAB MUFFINS

1 jar Old English cheese spread, softened
1/2 c. mayonnaise
1 stick margarine, softened
1/2 tsp. garlic salt
1/2 lb. fresh crab meat, flaked
12 English muffins, split

Combine cheese spread, mayonnaise, margarine and garlic salt in bowl; mix well. Stir in crab meat. Spread over muffin halves. Place on baking sheet. Freeze until firm. Bake at 350 degrees for 10 minutes to thaw. Broil until brown. Yield: 6 servings.

Betty Lee Pratt
Ames, Iowa

TUNA BUNWICHES

2 tbsp. minced onion
1/2 c. chopped celery
2 tbsp. butter
2 tbsp. flour
1/4 tsp. salt
3/4 c. evaporated milk
1 tbsp. lemon juice
1 7-oz. can tuna, drained, flaked
1 hard-boiled egg, chopped
1 tbsp. chopped parsley
1 10-count can refrigerator biscuits
2 oz. cheese, cut into 20 strips

Saute onion and celery in butter in saucepan until tender. Blend in flour and salt. Stir in evaporated milk gradually. Cook until thickened, stirring constantly. Stir in lemon juice, tuna, egg and parsley. Roll each biscuit into 4-inch circle on lightly floured surface. Place 1 heaping tablespoonful tuna mixture on each biscuit. Pull edges to center to enclose filling; seal. Place on baking sheet. Bake at 375 degrees for 12 to 15 minutes or until lightly browned. Place 2 strips cheese in crisscross pattern on each roll. Bake for 2 minutes longer or until cheese melts. Serve in basket with pickle and carrot sticks. Yield: 5 servings.

Helen Jackson
Williamsburg, Virginia

Seafood

SHRIMP SANDWICHES

1 c. chopped cooked shrimp
1/4 c. mayonnaise
1/4 c. crushed pineapple
2 tsp. chives
1 tsp. lemon juice
1/8 tsp. hot pepper sauce
1/8 tsp. salt
2 tbsp. chopped walnuts
4 croissants, split

Combine first 8 ingredients in bowl; mix well.
Spoon onto croissants. Top with lettuce leaves.

Nelda Miles
Minden, Louisiana

TUNA CHEESIES

1   6-oz. can tuna, drained
1 c. chopped celery
1/2 c. diced Velveeta cheese
1 tbsp. instant minced onion
1/4 tsp. salt
1/8 tsp. pepper
1/4 c. mayonnaise
6 hamburger buns, split, buttered

Combine tuna, celery, cheese, onion, salt, pepper and mayonnaise in bowl; mix well. Spoon
onto buns. Wrap individually in foil; seal. Place
on baking sheet. Bake at 350 degrees for 20
minutes. Yield: 6 sandwiches.

Georgia McLellan
Westboro, Massachusetts

Fish

ALBACORE WITH TOMATO SAUCE

2 lb. 1 1/2-inch albacore steaks
Salt and pepper
1 onion, sliced
1 clove of garlic
1 tbsp. chopped parsley
1/4 c. olive oil
1/2 c. tomato paste

Season albacore with salt and pepper. Saute
onion, garlic and parsley in olive oil in skillet
until tender. Add tomato paste and 2 cups hot
water. Simmer, covered, for 20 minutes. Add
albacore. Cook, covered, for 15 minutes or
until tender. Yield: 4 servings.

Wilma Mitchell
Smithville, Ohio

BROILED ALBACORE

6   8-oz. albacore steaks
1/2 c. olive oil
1/2 c. salad oil
Juice of 2 lemons
1 tsp. rosemary
Dash each of salt, pepper and garlic powder
Lemon butter
Watercress

Remove skin and any dark fish near bone of
albacore. Combine olive oil, salad oil, lemon
juice, rosemary, salt, pepper and garlic powder
in shallow dish. Arrange albacore in marinade.
Marinate for 2 hours, turning once. Drain. Grill
albacore over medium coals for 4 to 5 minutes
on each side. Serve with lemon butter and garnish with watercress. Yield: 6 servings.

Rachel C. Falk
Wilmington, North Carolina

EASY BAKE STRIPED BASS

1   2 to 3-lb. striped bass, boned
1 clove of garlic, minced
1 tsp. marjoram
1/2 tsp. salt
Dash of pepper
2 tbsp. oil
2 tsp. lemon juice

Place fish on greased heavy foil. Combine garlic,
marjoram, 1/2 teaspoon salt and pepper. Sprinkle cavity of fish with garlic mixture. Brush
mixture of oil and lemon juice over fish. Seal
foil. Place in shallow baking pan. Bake at 350
degrees for 45 minutes. Open foil. Bake for 10
minutes longer or until fish flakes easily.
Yield: 4-6 servings.

Missy Cardwell
Medicine Lake, Montana

SPICED SEA BASS

2 lb. bass fillets
1/4 tsp. salt
1/8 tsp. pepper
1 clove of garlic, minced
1/4 c. melted margarine
3 tbsp. soy sauce
3 tbsp. lime juice
1/4 tsp. red pepper
1 lemon, sliced

Rub fish with salt, pepper and garlic. Place in
greased 9 x 13-inch baking dish. Combine next

4 ingredients in bowl; mix well. Pour over fish. Top with lemon slices. Bake at 400 degrees for 30 to 45 minutes or until fish flakes easily. Yield: 6 servings.

Katie Ramfield
Scottsdale, Arizona

BARBECUED CATFISH

6 med. catfish
1 tsp. Worcestershire sauce
1/8 tsp. paprika
1/2 c. oil
1/4 c. white vinegar
1/4 c. catsup
2 tbsp. sugar
1/4 tsp. each salt, pepper

Fillet and skin catfish; place in shallow dish. Combine remaining ingredients in bowl; mix well. Pour over catfish. Marinate for 20 minutes. Drain, reserving marinade. Place catfish 4 inches above hot coals on greased grill. Cook for 5 minutes on each side or until fish flakes easily, basting frequently with the reserved marinade.

Cynthia Evers
Paducah, Kentucky

CATFISH IN BEER BATTER

1 lb. catfish fillets
1/4 c. biscuit mix
1/2 tsp. salt
1 egg, beaten
1/2 c. beer
1 c. biscuit mix
Oil for deep frying

Coat fish lightly with 1/4 cup biscuit mix. Combine salt, egg, beer and 1 cup biscuit mix in bowl; mix well. Dip fish into batter; drain off excess batter. Fry in 1 1/2-inch 350-degree oil for 2 minutes on each side or until golden brown. Drain on paper towels. Yield: 4 servings.

Sherri Wilson
Stephens, Oklahoma

FRIED CATFISH

6 catfish
Salt and pepper to taste
2 c. bread crumbs
1 egg, beaten
Oil for deep frying

1 1/2 tbsp. shortening, melted
1 tbsp. flour
1 c. milk
2 green peppers, chopped
6 dill pickles, chopped

Cut catfish into small serving pieces. Season with salt and pepper. Coat with crumbs. Dip in egg; coat with remaining crumbs. Deep-fry until browned. Drain on paper towels. Blend shortening and flour in saucepan. Add milk gradually. Cook until thickened, stirring constantly. Stir in green peppers and pickles. Serve with catfish.

Victoria Poole
Savannah, Georgia

COD CUTLETS KIEV

1/4 c. butter, softened
1/4 c. finely chopped green onions
1/4 c. minced parsley
3 tsp. dillweed
1/2 tsp. salt
2 lb. thick cod fillets with pockets
1/4 c. cornstarch
2 eggs, beaten
1/2 to 2/3 c. sesame seed
2 to 4 tbsp. butter
2 to 3 tbsp. oil

Cream first 5 ingredients in bowl; spread about 2 teaspoonfuls in each fish pocket. Coat fish with cornstarch; dip in beaten eggs. Sprinkle about 1 tablespoon sesame seed over each. Set aside to dry. Fry in mixture of 2 tablespoons butter and 2 tablespoons oil in heavy skillet for 3 to 5 minutes on each side or until fish flakes easily. Yield: 6-8 servings.

Photograph for this recipe below.

Seafood

BAKED COD WITH VEGETABLE SAUCE

4 cod fillets
Salt, pepper and garlic powder to taste
1 c. chopped onion
1 c. chopped green pepper
1 can stewed tomatoes
Oregano to taste

Place fish in baking dish. Layer remaining ingredients in order given over fish. Bake at 350 degrees for 30 minutes or until fish tests done. Yield: 4 servings.

Marilou Lindall
Blair, Nebraska

CREOLE FLOUNDER

1 lb. flounder fillets
1 med. tomato, chopped
1/2 sm. green pepper, chopped
3 tbsp. lemon juice
1 1/2 tsp. oil
1 tsp. salt
1 tsp. finely chopped onion
1/2 tsp. basil
1/8 tsp. coarsely ground pepper
2 drops of red pepper sauce

Arrange fillets in greased 9 x 13-inch baking dish. Combine remaining ingredients in bowl; mix well. Spoon over fillets. Bake at 400 degrees for 10 minutes or until fish flakes easily. Garnish with green pepper rings and tomato wedges. Yield: 5-6 servings.

Joan Boutwell
Thomasville, Georgia

EASY MICROWAVE FLOUNDER ROSEMARY

1 sm. onion, thinly sliced
1 tbsp. butter
1 clove of garlic, minced
1/4 tsp. rosemary
1/8 tsp. pepper
1 can Cheddar cheese soup
1/2 c. drained chopped canned tomatoes
1 lb. flounder fillets

Combine first 5 ingredients in glass casserole; mix well. Microwave on High for 3 minutes or until onion is tender. Add soup and tomatoes; mix well. Arrange fillets in single layer in shallow glass baking dish. Pour sauce over top. Microwave on High for 15 minutes or until fish flakes easily. Yield: 4 servings.

Kathy Bell
Bray, Connecticut

FLOUNDER AND ASPARAGUS ROLLS

4 flounder fillets
2 tbsp. butter
1 8-oz. package frozen asparagus spears, cooked
1 c. chopped peeled tomatoes
1/2 c. sliced mushrooms
1/4 c. thinly sliced celery
1/4 c. chopped onion
1/4 c. dry white wine
1 clove of garlic, minced
2 tsp. minced fresh mint
1/2 tsp. basil
1/4 tsp. salt

Dot fillets with butter. Arrange asparagus spears across fillets; roll to enclose spears and secure with toothpicks. Place seam side down in large skillet. Add remaining ingredients. Simmer, tightly covered, for 6 minutes or until fish flakes easily. Remove to serving platter. Cook sauce, uncovered, until reduced to desired consistency. Spoon over fillets.

Rosemarie Barns
Saugerties, New York

SAUCY FLOUNDER

1 pkg. frozen flounder fillets, thawed
1 lg. can artichoke hearts, drained
1 can mushroom soup
1 c. heavy cream
Sherry to taste
4 c. shredded Cheddar cheese
1 8-oz. package herb-seasoned stuffing mix

Roll up each piece of flounder; place in greased casserole. Arrange artichoke hearts around flounder. Blend soup, cream and Sherry in bowl. Cover flounder completely with soup mixture. Sprinkle with cheese. Top with stuffing mix. Bake, covered, at 350 degrees for 30 minutes. Bake, uncovered, for 30 minutes longer. Yield: 4 servings.

Mary Jackson
Bad Axe, Michigan

BAKED FLOUNDER IN WINE SAUCE

3 c. thinly sliced cooked potatoes
1 4-oz. can sliced mushrooms, drained
1 tsp. paprika

1/2 tsp. salt
1/4 tsp. pepper
1 c. sour cream
1/2 c. dry white wine
2 tbsp. flour
1 tbsp. grated onion
2 lb. flounder fillets

Layer potatoes and mushrooms in greased casserole. Sprinkle half the combined seasonings over vegetables. Mix sour cream, wine, flour and onion in bowl. Spread half the mixture over mushrooms. Arrange flounder over top. Sprinkle with remaining seasonings. Spread remaining sour cream mixture over flounder. Bake at 350 degrees for 35 minutes or until flounder flakes easily. Let stand for 10 minutes before serving. Yield: 6 servings.

Adrian Alexander
Knoxville, Kentucky

STEAMED FLOUNDER

2 tbsp. soy sauce
2 tbsp. Sherry
1 tbsp. oil
1 tsp. minced fresh gingerroot
1 lb. frozen flounder fillets, thawed
3 lemon slices

Combine first 4 ingredients with 2 tablespoons water in wok. Bring to a boil. Arrange flounder in wok. Top with lemon slices. Simmer, covered, for 10 minutes. Arrange on serving plate; spoon pan juices over fillets. Garnish with cucumber slices and chopped green onions.

Kay Banks
Crab Orchard, Tennessee

FLOUNDER WITH SPINACH-RICOTTA FILLING

2 lb. flounder fillets
2 10-oz. packages frozen chopped
   spinach, cooked
1 c. ricotta cheese
1/2 tsp. basil
2 tbsp. butter, melted
2 tbsp. flour
1/4 tsp. salt
Dash of pepper
1 c. milk
1/4 c. Parmesan cheese
1/2 c. dry white wine
1 tsp. lemon juice
1/4 c. Parmesan cheese

Arrange half the fillets in greased 9 x 13-inch baking dish. Mix drained spinach, ricotta cheese and basil in bowl. Spoon over fillets. Top with remaining fillets. Blend butter, flour, salt and pepper in saucepan. Add milk gradually. Cook until thickened, stirring constantly. Add 1/4 cup cheese, wine and lemon juice. Spoon over top. Bake at 350 degrees for 20 minutes or until fish flakes easily. Sprinkle with 1/4 cup cheese. Broil until lightly browned.
Yield: 6 servings.

Audrey Young
East Troy, Wisconsin

FLOUNDER AND VEGETABLE CASSEROLE

1 c. finely chopped celery
1/2 c. finely chopped onion
1 tbsp. butter
5 c. coarsely chopped fresh spinach
1/4 tsp. dillweed
Dash of pepper
8 oz. medium egg noodles, cooked
4 fresh flounder fillets

Saute celery and onion in butter in skillet for 5 minutes. Place spinach in even layer over onion mixture; sprinkle with dillweed and pepper. Cook, covered, for 3 minutes or until spinach just begins to wilt. Reserve 1 cup mixture. Combine remaining spinach mixture with noodles in greased casserole. Top with flounder fillets. Sprinkle with reserved spinach mixture. Bake, covered, at 375 degrees for 25 minutes or until fish flakes easily. Yield: 4 servings.

Photograph for this recipe below.

Seafood

BAKED GROUPER FILLETS

1 lemon, sliced
1 onion, sliced
Salt and pepper to taste
2 lb. fresh grouper fillets
1 c. sour cream
1 tsp. prepared mustard
1/4 tsp. paprika

Arrange lemon and onion slices in greased baking pan. Sprinkle with salt and pepper. Top with grouper fillets. Bake, covered, at 400 degrees for 20 minutes. Combine sour cream, mustard, paprika and salt to taste in bowl; mix well. Spread over fillets. Broil 3 inches from heat source until brown. Yield: 4 servings.

Angela Antonuccia
Somerville, Massachusetts

BAKED HADDOCK WITH LEMON-MUSHROOM SAUCE

2 pkg. frozen haddock fillets
1 can cream of mushroom soup
1/2 c. milk
1 can sliced mushrooms
1 lg. onion, chopped
2 tbsp. lemon juice
1 tsp. paprika
1/2 tsp. salt
1/4 tsp. oregano
1/4 tsp. pepper
1 bay leaf, crushed
1 c. buttered crumbs
Poultry seasoning to taste
2 tbsp. butter

Place frozen fillets in greased shallow baking dish. Combine soup, milk, mushrooms, onion, lemon juice and seasonings in saucepan; mix well. Simmer for 10 minutes. Pour over fillets. Top with crumbs seasoned with poultry seasoning; dot with butter. Bake at 375 degrees for 45 minutes. Yield: 6 servings.

Barbara Peugh
Knoxville, Tennessee

CREAMY BAKED HADDOCK

1 1/2 lb. haddock fillets
3/4 c. heavy cream
1/4 c. chopped green onion
1/4 c. minced parsley
1 clove of garlic, minced
2 tbsp. Parmesan cheese
3 tbsp. dry white wine
1/2 tsp. salt

Dash of pepper
1/4 c. Parmesan cheese

Arrange fillets in greased 7 x 12-inch baking dish. Combine heavy cream with next 7 ingredients in bowl; mix well. Spoon over fillets. Bake at 350 degrees for 20 minutes or until fish flakes easily. Sprinkle with Parmesan cheese. Broil until lightly browned. Yield: 4 portions.

Charline Jones
Hammond, Louisiana

SAUCY BAKED FILLETS

1 1/2 lb. haddock fillets
Salt, pepper and paprika to taste
1 chicken bouillon cube
3 tbsp. flour
1 1/2 c. milk
1 tsp. Worcestershire sauce
1 1/2 tbsp. Sherry
1/2 tsp. rosemary
1/2 c. chopped mushrooms

Place fillets in greased shallow casserole. Sprinkle with salt, pepper and paprika. Dissolve bouillon cube in 1/4 cup hot water in saucepan. Blend in flour. Add milk; blend well. Simmer until thickened, stirring constantly. Stir in remaining ingredients. Cook until heated through. Pour over fillets. Bake at 350 degrees for 25 minutes or until fish flakes easily.
Yield: 6 servings.

Pearl V. Reed
Dallas, Texas

SEAFOOD TERIYAKI

1 egg, beaten
1 tsp. salt
2 lb. haddock fillets, cut into 1-in. cubes
2 c. cornflake crumbs
1 c. oil
2 green peppers, cut into 1 1/2-in. squares
6 pineapple slices, cut into quarters
1 c. mashed Ocean Spray jellied
    cranberry sauce
1/2 c. Japanese soy sauce
1/3 c. cider vinegar
1/3 c. dry Sherry
2 cloves of garlic, crushed
1 tbsp. grated fresh gingerroot

Beat egg with salt in bowl. Dip haddock cubes in egg; coat with crumbs. Brown on all sides in hot oil in skillet; drain on paper towels. Pour off oil, reserving 2 tablespoons. Saute green peppers in reserved oil. Add pineapple and remaining ingredients. Simmer for 5 minutes. Combine sauce and haddock in chafing dish to keep warm. Serve over wild rice. Yield: 6 servings.

Photograph for this recipe on this page.

FOIL-BAKED HALIBUT

    1 16-oz. package frozen halibut
        fillets, thawed
    Salt and pepper to taste
    Paprika
    4 tsp. lemon juice
    2 carrots, cut into julienne strips
    1 sm. green pepper, cut into rings
    1 med. onion, sliced

Cut fish into 4 portions. Place in centers of 4 pieces foil. Sprinkle with salt, pepper, paprika and lemon juice. Top with vegetables. Fold foil; seal edges. Bake at 450 degrees for 25 minutes or until fish flakes easily. Yield: 4 servings.

Anne Miller
Morganton, North Carolina

HALIBUT WITH WINE-MUSHROOM SAUCE

    1 med. carrot, chopped
    1 stalk celery, coarsely chopped
    1 sm. onion, coarsely chopped
    2 tbsp. butter
    6 halibut steaks
    3/4 c. chicken broth
    1/2 c. dry white wine
    1/2 tsp. thyme
    4 egg yolks, slightly beaten
    1/2 c. heavy cream
    1 4-oz. can sliced mushrooms, drained

Saute carrot, celery and onion in butter in skillet until tender-crisp. Arrange halibut steaks over vegetables. Add broth, wine and thyme. Simmer, covered, for 5 minutes or until fish flakes easily. Remove to warm platter. Strain pan juices. Cook pan juices until reduced to 1 cup. Stir half the hot mixture into mixture of egg yolks and cream; stir egg yolks into hot mixture. Add mushrooms. Simmer for 2 minutes. Spoon over fish. Yield: 6 servings.

Marilyn Clarkson
Grand Coteau, Louisiana

SMOKED HERRING

    4 smoked herring
    2 tbsp. lemon juice

    1/8 tsp. sugar
    1/8 tsp. salt
    Dash of pepper

Remove and discard heads from herring. Place herring in skillet. Add 1/2 cup water, lemon juice, sugar, salt and pepper. Cook, covered, over medium heat for 10 minutes or until herring are heated through and liquid has evaporated. Garnish with parsley. Yield: 4 servings.

Ruth Romesberg
Rockwood, Pennsylvania

BROILED SPANISH MACKEREL FILLETS

    6 Spanish mackerel fillets
    Salt and pepper to taste
    3 tbsp. lemon juice
    Mayonnaise to taste

Place fillets on foil on broiler rack. Shape foil to form edge. Sprinkle fillets with salt, pepper and lemon juice. Spread with mayonnaise. Broil 6 inches from heat source for 10 minutes or until fish flakes easily.

Jean Heil
Moulton, Texas

GRILLED POMPANO

    6 8-oz. pompano fillets
    Oil
    Salt to taste

Brush fillets with oil; season with salt. Place on grill over hot coals. Cook for 3 minutes on each side or until fish tests done. Serve with lemon wedges and a generous amount of melted butter.

Hyacinth Horsch
Norfolk, Nebraska

Seafood

BAKED SALMON WITH SOUR CREAM

1 4 to 5-lb. salmon
Salt and pepper to taste
Sour cream

Rub salmon inside and out with salt and pepper. Spread sour cream in cavity and over both sides of salmon, coating completely. Wrap in foil; place on baking sheet. Bake at 375 degrees for 1 1/2 hours.

Jessie Russell
Houston, Texas

LEMONY BAKED SALMON

1 8 to 10-lb. salmon
Lemon-pepper seasoning
2 lemons, sliced
1 onion, sliced
1/4 c. melted butter

Wash salmon; pat dry inside and out. Rub cavity with lemon-pepper. Place lemon and onion slices in cavity; drizzle with butter. Wrap in foil. Bake at 350 degrees for 1 1/2 hours or until fish flakes easily. Yield: 10-12 servings.

Barbara Stalick
Corvallis, Oregon

SALMON-MACARONI CASSEROLE

1 c. elbow macaroni
1 tsp. salt
1/4 c. chopped onion
2 tbsp. margarine
1/2 c. milk
1 can cream of mushroom soup
3/4 c. grated Cheddar cheese
1 8-oz. can salmon, drained, flaked
1/4 c. bread crumbs
1 tbsp. melted margarine
1/4 c. grated Cheddar cheese

Cook macaroni in 2 quarts salted water in saucepan for 10 to 12 minutes or until tender; drain. Saute onion in 2 tablespoons margarine in skillet. Stir in milk, soup, 3/4 cup cheese, macaroni and salmon; mix well. Pour into greased 1 1/2-quart casserole. Mix crumbs with melted margarine. Sprinkle crumbs and 1/4 cup cheese over casserole. Bake at 350 degrees for 30 minutes.

Maschil Offenberger
Lowell, Ohio

PARTY SALMON CREPES

1 1/4 c. milk
1 tbsp. butter, melted
1 egg, slightly beaten
1 c. pancake mix
1/4 c. minced onion
1/2 c. chopped celery
1/4 c. butter
1/4 c. flour
1/2 tsp. salt
2 1/4 c. milk
2/3 c. Parmesan cheese
2 7 1/2-oz. cans flaked salmon
1 c. canned peas with liquid

Combine 1 1/4 cups milk, 1 tablespoon butter and egg in bowl; mix well. Stir into pancake mix in bowl. Do not overmix. Pour 1/3 cup batter at a time onto hot lightly buttered griddle. Bake until set. Turn. Bake until lightly browned. Saute onion and celery in 1/4 cup butter in skillet until tender. Remove from heat; blend in flour and salt. Stir in 2 1/4 cups milk gradually. Cook until thickened, stirring constantly. Remove from heat; add cheese. Stir until cheese is melted. Reserve 1 1/3 cups sauce. Add salmon and peas to remaining sauce. Cook until heated through, stirring constantly. Spread each pancake with salmon mixture; roll to enclose filling. Place seam side down in greased shallow 9 x 11-inch baking dish. Bake at 350 degrees for 15 to 20 minutes. Heat reserved sauce to serving temperature. Pour over crepes. Yield: 4 servings.

Photograph for this recipe above.

SALMON CROQUETTES

1 can pink salmon, drained, flaked
2 eggs, slightly beaten
2 tbsp. flour
1/2 c. bread crumbs

3 tbsp. sweet pickle juice
3 tbsp. chopped onion
1/3 c. cornmeal
1/3 c. flour
Oil fof frying

Combine salmon, eggs, 2 tablespoons flour, crumbs, pickle juice and onion in bowl; mix well. Shape into patties. Coat with mixture of cornmeal and 1/3 cup flour. Chill on waxed paper for 2 hours or longer. Fry in oil in skillet until brown on both sides. Yield: 4 servings.

Sue Young
Lake Placid, New York

SALMON FLORENTINE

1 med. onion, chopped
2 tbsp. butter
Salt and pepper to taste
1 tsp. sugar
2 tbsp. flour
1 c. milk
2 pkg. frozen chopped spinach, cooked,
   well drained
1 can salmon, drained
2 tbsp. flour
2 tbsp. melted butter
1 c. milk
1/2 c. grated cheese

Saute onion in 2 tablespoons butter in skillet. Stir in salt, pepper, sugar and 2 tablespoons flour. Add 1 cup milk gradually. Cook until thickened, stirring constantly. Add spinach; mix well. Spread in greased pie plate. Arrange salmon over spinach mixture. Blend 2 tablespoons flour and 2 tablespoons melted butter in saucepan. Add 1 cup milk gradually. Cook until thickened, stirring constantly. Add cheese. Cook until cheese is melted, stirring constantly. Pour over salmon. Bake at 350 degrees for 15 minutes or until bubbly.

Carole Greer
Fredericksburg, Virginia

SALMON SALAD LOAF

1 15-oz. can salmon
2 eggs, beaten
1 c. fine bread crumbs
1/2 c. milk
1 tbsp. minced onion
1/4 c. chopped pimento-stuffed olives
1/2 tsp. dry mustard
1 tsp. lemon juice

Drain and flake salmon, reserving liquid. Combine salmon, eggs, crumbs, milk, onion, olives, mustard, lemon juice and salmon liquid in bowl; mix well. Spoon into buttered loaf pan. Bake at 350 degrees for 40 minutes.
Yield: 6 servings.

Sarah Cook
Payne, Oklahoma

SALMON PUFF

2 tbsp. margarine, melted
1/2 c. milk
4 slices bread, torn
1 15-oz. can salmon, drained, flaked
2 eggs, separated
3 tbsp. lemon juice
2 tsp. finely chopped onion
1 tsp. salt
1/2 tsp. pepper
Paprika

Combine first 3 ingredients in bowl; mix well. Add salmon, egg yolks, lemon juice, onion, salt and pepper; mix well. Fold stiffly beaten egg whites gently into salmon mixture. Spoon into greased 1 1/2-quart round glass casserole. Sprinkle with paprika. Microwave on High for 5 minutes or until top is dry and set.

Lurlene Byars
Manitowoc, Wisconsin

SALMON QUICHE

1 15-oz. can red salmon
1 unbaked 9-in. pie shell
3 eggs, beaten
1 c. cottage cheese
2 tsp. Dijon mustard
3/4 tsp. salt
1/2 c. half and half
1 4-oz. can sliced mushrooms, drained
1/2 c. shredded carrots
1/4 c. sliced green onions

Drain and flake salmon reserving 2 tablespoons liquid. Prick bottom and side of pie shell. Bake at 375 degrees for 15 minutes. Combine eggs with cottage cheese, mustard and salt in large bowl; beat well. Add half and half, salmon liquid and mushrooms; mix well. Stir in carrots, onions and salmon. Spoon mixture into partially baked pie shell. Bake for 45 minutes or until knife inserted in center comes out clean. Let stand for 10 minutes. Cut into wedges; serve warm. Yield: 6 servings.

Elizabeth Richmond
Sheffield, Alabama

Seafood

SALMON ROMANOFF

1/2 c. chopped green onions
1 clove of garlic, crushed
2 tbsp. butter
1 c. cottage cheese
2 c. sour cream
5 dashes of Tabasco sauce
1/2 tsp. salt
1 lb. cooked fresh salmon
1 6-oz. package noodles, cooked
1 c. shredded cheese

Saute green onions and garlic in butter in skillet until tender. Remove from heat. Add cottage cheese, sour cream, Tabasco sauce and salt. Add salmon; mix lightly. Stir in noodles. Place in buttered casserole. Bake at 350 degrees for 15 minutes. Top with cheese. Bake for 15 to 20 minutes longer.

Jackie Rawlings
St. Paul, Nebraska

BAKED STUFFED SALMON

1 5 to 6-lb. salmon, backbone removed
1 tbsp. oil
1 tbsp. lemon juice
1 med. onion, chopped
2 tbsp. butter
2 c. croutons
1 c. shredded sharp cheese
1 c. chopped fresh parsley
1 sprig of dill
1/8 tsp. dry mustard
Salt and pepper to taste

Brush salmon inside and out with oil and lemon juice. Saute onion in butter in skillet until tender. Stir in remaining ingredients; mix well. Stuff into salmon cavity; secure with string. Wrap in heavy foil. Place in baking pan. Bake at 375 degrees for 1 hour or until fish flakes easily.

Pattie Jacks
Oakland, Washington

SEAFOOD-STUFFED SALMON

1/2 lb. crab meat, flaked
1/2 lb. cooked shrimp, chopped
2 tbsp. parsley flakes
1/2 c. chopped celery
1/4 c. chopped onion
4 c. bread crumbs
1/2 c. melted butter
1/2 c. (or more) chicken bouillon
1 4 to 6-lb. salmon

1/4 c. fresh lemon juice
1/4 c. melted butter

Combine first 7 ingredients with enough bouillon to moisten in bowl; mix well. Fill salmon cavity; fasten with skewers. Place in baking pan. Bake at 300 degrees for 2 hours, basting several times with mixture of lemon juice and 1/4 cup butter. Yield: 8-10 servings.

Carolyn Barranco
Birmingham, Alabama

POACHED SALMON STEAKS

1 c. chopped celery
1 carrot, cut into 1-in. pieces
1 med. onion, quartered
3 tbsp. butter
1 bay leaf
4 whole black peppercorns
3 whole cloves
4 sprigs of parsley
1/2 tsp. rosemary
4 tsp. salt
1/2 lemon, sliced
8 6-oz. salmon steaks

Saute celery, carrot and onion in butter in saucepan for 5 minutes. Add next 6 seasonings, lemon and 1 1/2 quarts cold water. Simmer for 30 minutes. Strain. Place salmon in saucepan; cover with strained hot liquid. Simmer over low heat for 7 minutes or until fish flakes easily. Remove skin. Serve hot or cold with mayonnaise or sour cream. Garnish with lemon wedges and watercress. Yield: 8 servings.

Elinor Siecke
Littleton, Colorado

SPANISH SARDINE OMELETS

    1 lg. sweet green pepper, coarsely chopped
    1 lg. sweet red pepper, coarsely chopped
    1/4 c. olive oil
    3 lg. cloves of garlic, minced
    5 tbsp. dry white wine
    1/2 tsp. salt
    1/4 tsp. red pepper
    4 tsp. butter
    8 eggs, beaten
    2   3 3/4-oz. cans Norway
        sardines, drained
    2 sm. tomatoes, cut into wedges

Saute peppers in olive oil in large skillet over medium-high heat for 5 minutes. Add garlic. Cook for 1 minute. Stir in wine, salt and red pepper. Cook for 3 minutes or until reduced slightly. Melt 1 teaspoon butter in 6-inch omelet pan. Add 2 beaten eggs; stir lightly. Cook over medium-low heat until almost set, lifting edges gently. Slide open-faced onto heated serving plate; keep warm. Repeat with remaining eggs and butter. Spoon hot pepper mixture over omelets. Arrange sardines and tomato wedges on each. Serve immediately. Yield: 4 servings.

Photograph for this recipe on opposite page.

BARBECUED TROUT

    2 c. soft bread crumbs
    2 c. chopped cucumbers, drained
    2 eggs, beaten
    1/2 c. chopped onion
    1/4 c. melted margarine
    Seasonings to taste
    1   4 to 6-lb. trout, boned
    Barbecue sauce

Combine bread crumbs, cucumbers, eggs, onion, margarine and seasonings in bowl; mix well. Spoon into trout cavity; secure with skewers. Place stuffed trout on foil. Brush generously with barbecue sauce; seal foil. Grill over hot coals for 1 hour or until fish flakes easily. Garnish with pineapple slices. Yield: 8-10 servings.

Arlene Maisel
Highland Park, New Jersey

BAKED TROUT

    1/4 lb. mushrooms, sliced
    2 tbsp. sliced green onion
    2 tbsp. minced parsley

    Salt and pepper to taste
    4 freshwater trout
    1/4 c. melted butter
    1/4 c. fine dry bread crumbs

Layer mushrooms, green onion and parsley in greased baking dish. Season with salt and pepper. Brush trout with butter. Season with salt and pepper. Coat with crumbs. Place in baking dish. Drizzle with remaining butter. Bake at 375 degrees for 20 to 25 minutes or until fish flakes easily.

Barbara Nezer
Woburn, Massachusetts

CRISPY FRIED RAINBOW TROUT

    5 rainbow trout
    1/4 c. evaporated milk
    1 1/2 tsp. salt
    Dash of pepper
    1/2 c. flour
    1/4 c. yellow cornmeal
    1 tsp. paprika
    Oil for frying

Wash trout; pat dry. Blend evaporated milk, salt and pepper in bowl. Combine flour, cornmeal and paprika. Dip trout into milk mixture; roll in flour mixture to coat. Fry in hot oil in skillet over medium heat for 4 to 5 minutes or until brown. Turn carefully. Fry for 4 to 5 minutes longer or until fish flakes easily. Drain on paper towel. Arrange trout on heated serving platter; garnish with parsley, lemon slices and pimento. Yield: 5 servings.

Madeline Godlin
Highgate Center, Vermont

SOUTHERN-GRILLED TROUT

    4 lg. speckled trout
    Salt and pepper to taste
    1/2 c. melted butter
    1/3 c. lemon juice
    5 tbsp. chopped parsley
    1/2 c. grated onion
    1/2 tsp. paprika
    5 tbsp. Worcestershire sauce
    1/8 tsp. cayenne pepper

Season trout with salt and pepper. Place each trout on piece of foil. Drizzle mixture of remaining ingredients over trout; seal foil. Grill over hot coals for 30 minutes or until fish flakes easily, turning occasionally.

Mamie Payne
DeSoto, Kansas

Seafood

CRISP TROUT FILLETS

Pancake mix
Lemon-lime carbonated beverage
8 trout fillets
Oil for deep frying

Combine enough pancake mix and carbonated beverage to make thick batter. Coat fillets with batter. Deep-fry at 350 degrees for 10 minutes or until golden brown.

Nancy Laine
Suffolk, Virginia

TROUT MEUNIERE

4 brook trout
3/4 c. flour
Salt to taste
Freshly ground pepper to taste
1/8 tsp. thyme
1/2 stick margarine
1/2 stick butter
1/2 c. chopped mushrooms
1 tbsp. lemon juice
1/4 c. chopped parsley
1 tbsp. chopped chives

Coat trout with flour seasoned with salt, pepper and thyme. Brown in margarine in skillet. Place on heated serving plate. Cook butter in saucepan until browned. Add mushrooms. Saute for 5 minutes. Add lemon juice, parsley and chives. Simmer for several minutes. Serve over trout.

Helen Reed
San Antonio, Texas

GRILLED RED SNAPPER

1/2 c. butter, melted
1/4 c. lemon juice
3/4 tsp. Worcestershire sauce
1/4 tsp. onion salt
2 lb. red snapper

Combine first 4 ingredients in small bowl; mix well. Grill snapper over hot coals for 5 to 8 minutes on each side or until fish flakes easily, basting frequently with butter mixture. Serve with remaining mixture. Yield: 6-8 servings.

Earlene Jefferson
Mt. Ada, Florida

KEY LIME RED SNAPPER

4 med. red snapper fillets
1 c. Key lime juice
1 1/2 c. Italian bread crumbs

Dash of salt
Dash of lemon-pepper seasoning
1 egg, slightly beaten
4 cloves of garlic, crushed
1/2 lb. butter, melted

Marinate fillets in lime juice in covered glass bowl in refrigerator for 1 hour. Mix bread crumbs, salt and lemon-pepper. Dip fillets in beaten egg; coat with bread crumb mixture. Saute garlic in butter in skillet until browned; remove garlic. Cook fillets in garlic butter until browned and easily flaked. Yield: 4 servings.

Annie Clark
Westminster, Maryland

STUFFED RED SNAPPER

2 med. onions, chopped
1/4 c. margarine
2 c. dry bread cubes
1 c. coarsely shredded carrot
3 oz. mushrooms, chopped
1/2 c. minced parsley
4 tsp. lemon juice
1 egg
1 clove of garlic, finely chopped
2 tsp. salt
1/4 tsp. dried marjoram leaves
1/4 tsp. pepper
1   8 to 10-lb. red snapper
Salt and pepper to taste
1/2 c. melted margarine
1/4 c. lemon juice

Saute onions in 1/4 cup margarine in skillet until tender. Combine with next 10 ingredients in bowl; mix well. Sprinkle red snapper cavity with salt and pepper. Spoon stuffing into cavity; secure with skewers. Brush with mixture of 1/2 cup margarine and lemon juice. Place in shallow roasting pan. Bake at 350 degrees for 1 1/2 hours or until fish flakes easily, basting occasionally.

Margaret Coopy
Champlain, New York

SAN FRANCISCO SOLE

2 lb. sole fillets
Salt to taste
Dash of white pepper
1/2 c. chopped onion
2 tbsp. butter
1/4 c. dry white wine
1/4 c. grape liquid
3/4 c. half and half
1 egg yolk, beaten

1 tbsp. flour
Dash of nutmeg
1 8 3/4-oz. can seedless green
   grapes, drained

Sprinkle fillets with salt and white pepper. Roll fillets; secure with toothpicks. Saute onion in butter in skillet until tender. Add fillets, wine and grape liquid. Simmer, covered, for 8 to 10 minutes or until fish flakes easily. Place fillets on warm platter. Remove picks; reserve liquid. Combine half and half, egg yolk, flour and nutmeg in bowl; mix well. Add to hot liquid gradually. Cook until thickened, stirring constantly. Add grapes. Pour over fillets. Garnish with paprika. Broil 5 inches from heat source for 5 minutes or until browned. Yield: 6 servings.

Dot Patrick
Zion, Illinois

FILLET OF SOLE
WITH DILL SAUCE

   1 lb. fillet of sole
   1 carrot, cut into julienne strips
   1 sm. zucchini, cut into julienne strips
   2 green onions, cut into julienne strips
   1/2 tsp. salt
   2 tsp. cornstarch
   1/4 c. sour cream
   1/4 tsp. dillweed

Cut fillets into serving-sized pieces. Arrange in shallow greased baking dish. Bake at 400 degrees for 10 minutes or until fish flakes easily. Stir-fry vegetables with salt in large saucepan for 2 minutes. Add 1 cup water. Simmer, covered, for 5 minutes. Remove vegetables to bowl with slotted spoon. Blend cornstarch with 1 tablespoon water; stir into vegetable pan juices. Cook until thick, stirring constantly; remove from heat. Stir in sour cream and dillweed. Spoon half the dill sauce into serving plate; arrange fish over sauce. Top with vegetables. Stir fish pan juices into remaining dill sauce. Spoon over vegetables. Yield: 4 servings.

Carolyn Rose
Amherst, Ohio

SPANISH FILLET OF SOLE

   1/3 c. chopped onion
   1/2 c. chopped celery
   2 tbsp. butter
   1/3 c. chopped toasted almonds (opt.)
   2 tbsp. chopped parsley

1/2 c. chopped pimento-stuffed olives
6 med. fillets of sole
1/2 tsp. salt
Dash of pepper
1/3 c. melted butter
2 tbsp. lemon juice
1/3 c. sliced pimento-stuffed olives

Saute onion and celery in 2 tablespoons butter in small skillet over low heat until golden. Stir in almonds, parsley and chopped olives. Place stuffing mixture at end of each fillet; roll as for jelly roll. Sprinkle lightly with salt and pepper. Place seam side down in greased shallow baking pan. Combine 1/3 cup melted butter with lemon juice. Pour over fillets. Bake at 350 degrees for 15 minutes. Add sliced olives. Bake for 10 minutes longer or until fish flakes easily. Yield: 6 servings.

Photograph for this recipe on page 66.

FILLET OF SOLE FLORENTINE

   2 10-oz. packages frozen chopped
      spinach, thawed, drained
   6 tbsp. butter
   1 lb. mushrooms, chopped
   3 green onions, finely chopped
   1/2 tsp. salt
   1/4 tsp. white pepper
   1/4 c. dry white wine
   1/2 c. bread crumbs
   2 tbsp. chopped parsley
   1/4 c. melted butter
   5 to 8 lg. fillets of sole
   1/2 c. flour
   1/2 c. bread crumbs
   1 c. medium white sauce
   1/2 c. ricotta cheese
   1/4 c. grated Cheddar cheese

Press excess moisture from spinach. Combine 6 tablespoons butter, spinach, mushrooms, green onions, salt, pepper and wine in skillet; mix well. Cook for several minutes, stirring frequently. Spoon into buttered 9 x 13-inch baking dish. Sprinkle with mixture of 1/2 cup bread crumbs and parsley. Drizzle with 1/4 cup butter. Coat fillets with mixture of flour and 1/2 cup bread crumbs. Arrange in prepared dish. Combine white sauce and cheeses in saucepan. Heat until cheese melts, stirring constantly. Pour over fillets. Bake at 375 degrees for 30 minutes or until fish flakes easily. Yield: 5 servings.

Elaine Carrington
Placer, California

87

Seafood

PARSLEY-BUTTERED TORSK

1/3 c. sugar
1 tsp. salt
1 lb. torsk fillets
1/4 c. butter
1 tbsp. lemon juice
1 tbsp. minced parsley
1/4 tsp. salt
1/8 tsp. red pepper sauce

Combine sugar and salt with 1 1/2 inches water in 10-inch skillet. Bring to a boil. Arrange fish in single layer in skillet. Simmer for 4 minutes or until fish flakes easily. Combine remaining ingredients in saucepan. Cook over low heat until butter is melted; mix well. Serve with fish.

Louise Massey
Camden, Arkansas

SPICY BROILED TURBOT

4 5-oz. turbot fillets
1 tbsp. lemon juice
1 pkg. Hidden Valley Ranch salad
   dressing mix

Place fillets on rack in broiler pan. Sprinkle with lemon juice and salad dressing mix. Broil for 6 minutes on each side or until fish flakes easily. Yield: 4 servings.

Roberta Andrews
Cumberland, Tennessee

AEGEAN TUNA CASSEROLE

2 7-oz. cans oil-pack tuna
1 c. chopped onion
1 clove of garlic, minced
2 1/2 c. chopped peeled seeded tomatoes
2 10-oz. packages frozen chopped
   spinach, thawed
2 tbsp. chopped parsley
1/2 tsp. salt
1/4 tsp. dried dillweed
1/8 tsp. pepper
1 1/2 tbsp. lemon juice
1 c. yogurt
4 c. hot cooked rice
2 tbsp. butter, melted
1 tbsp. lemon juice
1/4 c. chopped parsley

Drain tuna, reserving 2 tablespoons oil. Saute onion and garlic in reserved oil in skillet until tender. Add tomatoes, spinach, parsley, salt, dillweed, pepper, lemon juice and tuna. Cook for 10 minutes. Stir in yogurt. Mix rice with remaining ingredients. Serve tuna mixture over rice. Yield: 6 servings.

Photograph for this recipe on opposite page.

CHEESY TUNA AND RICE MUFFINETTES

2 c. cooked rice
1 c. shredded Cheddar cheese
1 6-oz. can tuna, drained, flaked
1 4-oz. can chopped mushrooms
1 tbsp. chopped onion
2 eggs, beaten
2 tbsp. milk
1/4 c. melted butter
1 tbsp. lemon juice
1/2 tsp. parsley flakes
Salt and pepper to taste

Combine first 7 ingredients in bowl; mix well. Spoon into greased muffin cups. Bake at 375 degrees for 15 minutes or until lightly browned. Remove from pan. Arrange on serving plate. Blend remaining ingredients in small bowl. Spoon over muffinettes. Yield: 6 servings.

Barbara Schnelle
Mt. Blanchard, Ohio

CREAMY TUNA CASSEROLE

1 8-oz. package cream cheese, softened
1/2 c. sour cream
1/2 c. cottage cheese
1/4 c. sliced green onions
1/4 tsp. garlic salt
1 8-oz. package macaroni shells,
   cooked, drained
1 7-oz. can tuna, drained, flaked
2 tomatoes, peeled, sliced
1/4 tsp. salt
1 c. grated Cheddar cheese

Combine cream cheese, sour cream, cottage cheese, green onions and garlic salt in bowl; mix well. Spread half the hot macaroni in greased 2-quart casserole. Add layers of half the cream cheese mixture, all the tuna, remaining macaroni and remaining cream cheese mixture. Arrange sliced tomatoes over top. Sprinkle with salt. Bake at 350 degrees for 30 minutes. Sprinkle cheese over tomatoes. Bake for 3 to 5 minutes longer or until cheese is melted.
Yield: 6 servings.

Jeanette Hulsey
Monticello, Arkansas

TUNA CREPES

1 6-oz. can tuna, drained
1 15-oz. can tomato sauce
1/2 c. chopped celery
1 egg
1 c. cottage cheese
1/2 tsp. garlic salt
1/8 tsp. pepper
Crepes
1 c. shredded mozzarella cheese

Combine first 3 ingredients in saucepan. Cook until heated through. Pour 1/3 of the tuna mixture into ungreased 9 x 13-inch baking dish. Combine egg, cottage cheese and seasonings in bowl; mix well. Spoon onto Crepes. Sprinkle with half the cheese. Roll up to enclose filling. Place seam side down in prepared dish. Pour remaining tuna mixture over top. Sprinkle with remaining cheese. Bake at 350 degrees for 30 minutes. Yield: 6 servings.

CREPES

1/2 c. flour
1/2 tsp. salt
2 eggs
2 tsp. oil

Combine all ingredients and 1/2 cup water in bowl. Pour 2 tablespoons at a time into buttered 7-inch skillet. Rotate skillet until batter covers bottom. Cook for 30 seconds. Stack between layers of waxed paper.

June Fletcher
Litchfield, Illinois

TUNA DIVAN

1 10-oz. package frozen broccoli
1 9-oz. can tuna
1/4 c. flour
1 tsp. salt

2 c. milk
1/3 c. Parmesan cheese
1 tbsp. lemon juice

Cook broccoli using package directions until tender-crisp; drain. Drain oil from tuna into saucepan. Add flour and salt; stir until smooth. Stir in milk. Cook until thickened, stirring constantly. Add cheese and lemon juice. Stir until cheese is melted. Layer broccoli, tuna and cheese sauce in greased casserole. Bake at 375 degrees for 20 minutes or until bubbly. Yield: 6 servings.

Jessie Fayette
Fales, New Hampshire

GOURMET TUNA CASSEROLE

1 16-oz. carton ricotta cheese
2 6-oz. cans tuna, drained
1 8-oz. carton sour cream
2 cans cream of mushroom soup
1 onion, chopped
1 c. chopped celery
2 cloves of garlic, minced
1 tsp. salt
1/4 tsp. pepper
1 tbsp. Worcestershire sauce
1 12-oz. package large shell macaroni, cooked
1/4 c. Parmesan cheese

Combine first 10 ingredients in large bowl; mix well. Stir in macaroni. Spoon into greased shallow 2 1/2-quart baking dish. Sprinkle with Parmesan cheese. Bake at 350 degrees for 1 1/4 hours. Yield: 8 servings.

James Saco
San Joaquin, California

QUICK TUNA CASSEROLE

1 1/2 c. broken egg noodles, cooked, drained
1 can cream of chicken soup
1/2 c. milk
1 7-oz. can tuna, drained
1 c. grated Cheddar cheese
1/3 c. chopped onion
1/2 c. crushed potato chips
1/2 c. grated Cheddar cheese

Combine noodles, soup, milk, tuna, 1 cup cheese and onion in bowl; mix well. Pour into greased 1 1/2-quart baking dish. Top with chips and 1/2 cup cheese. Bake at 425 degrees for 15 minutes or until bubbly. Yield: 4 servings.

Dana Arthaud
Cimarron, Oklahoma

Seafood

TUNA LOAF

1 lg. can evaporated milk
1/2 tsp. salt
1 tsp. dry mustard
1 tbsp. horseradish
8 oz. cheese, grated
4 eggs, slightly beaten
1/2 c. sliced stuffed olives
2 tbsp. grated onion
2 6-oz. cans tuna, drained, flaked
1/4 c. melted butter
1 c. soft bread crumbs
1 8-oz. package macaroni, cooked

Combine first 4 ingredients in saucepan. Cook over low heat for 2 minutes. Add cheese. Cook until cheese is melted, stirring constantly. Combine eggs and remaining ingredients in bowl; mix well. Stir in cheese sauce. Spoon into loaf pan lined with buttered foil. Bake at 350 degrees for 50 to 60 minutes or until set.

Erleen Johnson
Oregonia, Ohio

TUNA-NOODLE CRISPY

8 oz. cheese, cubed
1 can cream of mushroom soup
1/2 c. milk
2 c. noodles, cooked, drained
1 6-oz. can tuna, drained
Dash of pepper
1/2 c. coarse cracker crumbs
2 tbsp. melted margarine

Combine cheese, soup and milk in saucepan. Cook over low heat until cheese melts, stirring constantly. Add noodles, tuna and pepper; mix well. Spoon into greased 2-quart casserole. Toss cracker crumbs with margarine. Sprinkle over casserole. Bake at 325 degrees for 20 minutes. Yield: 4 servings.

Jeannie Walrath
Gainesville, Missouri

TUNA-MACARONI CASSEROLE

2 1/2 c. cooked macaroni, drained
1/3 c. chopped onion
1 7-oz. can tuna, drained
3 tbsp. chopped pimento
3/4 tsp. salt
1 1/2 c. grated Cheddar cheese
1/2 tsp. chili powder
1 tbsp. chopped green chilies
2 eggs, well beaten
1 1/2 c. milk

3/4 c. sour cream
2 tbsp. melted butter
1 c. soft bread crumbs
1/2 c. grated Cheddar cheese
3/4 tsp. paprika

Combine first 5 ingredients with 1 1/2 cups cheese in bowl. Add chili powder, chilies, eggs and milk; mix well. Spoon into 2-quart casserole. Bake at 350 degrees for 45 minutes or until bubbly. Spread sour cream over top. Mix butter and bread crumbs in small bowl. Sprinkle bread crumbs and 1/2 cup cheese over sour cream. Sprinkle with paprika. Broil for 1 to 2 minutes or until cheese is melted.
Yield: 4 servings.

Lana Giehl
Groveport, Ohio

TUNA-NOODLE NEWBURG

1 can cream of celery soup
2/3 c. evaporated milk
1/2 c. shredded cheese
1/3 c. mayonnaise
1/4 c. dry Sherry
2 7-oz. cans tuna, drained
4 oz. medium noodles, cooked
1 c. thinly sliced celery
1/4 c. chopped pimento

Combine soup and evaporated milk in saucepan. Bring to a boil, stirring frequently. Add cheese. Stir until cheese is melted. Add remaining ingredients; mix well. Spoon into greased 1 1/2-quart casserole. Bake, covered, at 350 degrees for 30 minutes. Yield: 4 servings.

Elva Ring
Buckholts, Texas

TUNA QUICHE

1 c. whole wheat flour
2/3 c. shredded sharp Cheddar cheese
1/4 c. chopped almonds
1/2 tsp. salt
1/4 tsp. paprika
6 tbsp. oil
2 cans water-pack tuna
3 eggs, beaten
1 c. sour cream
1/4 c. mayonnaise
1/2 c. shredded sharp Cheddar cheese
1 tbsp. grated onion
1/4 tsp. dillweed
3 drops of hot pepper sauce

Combine flour, 2/3 cup cheese, almonds, salt and paprika in bowl; mix well. Stir in oil; blend well. Reserve 1/2 cup crust mixture. Press remaining crust mixture over bottom and side of 9-inch pie plate. Bake at 400 degrees for 10 minutes. Drain tuna, reserving liquid. Add enough water to liquid to measure 1/2 cup. Combine liquid with eggs, sour cream and mayonnaise in bowl; mix well. Add 1/2 cup cheese, tuna and remaining ingredients; mix well. Spoon into prepared crust. Sprinkle with reserved crust mixture. Bake at 325 degrees for 45 minutes or until center is set. Yield: 4 servings.

Connie Tigue
Titus, Texas

EASY TUNA SOUFFLE

    1   7-oz. can tuna, flaked
    1/2 tsp. salt
    1/2 tsp. paprika
    1 tsp. lemon juice
    1 c. bread crumbs
    3/4 c. milk
    3 eggs, separated

Combine tuna, salt, paprika and lemon juice in bowl; mix well. Combine bread crumbs and milk in saucepan. Simmer for 5 minutes. Add milk mixture and beaten egg yolks to tuna mixture; mix well. Fold stiffly beaten egg whites gently into tuna mixture. Pour into greased baking dish. Place in pan of hot water. Bake at 350 degrees for 45 minutes or until set. Serve immediately. Yield: 4 servings.

Linda Bass
Baldwin, North Carolina

TUNA-RICE CASSEROLE

    1/4 c. chopped onion
    1 green pepper, chopped
    6 tbsp. butter
    1/4 c. flour
    1 c. milk
    2 c. cooked rice
    2   7-oz. cans tuna, drained
    1 can cream of chicken soup
    1 can cream of mushroom soup
    1   4-oz. can sliced mushrooms, drained
    1   2-oz. jar pimentos (opt.)

Combine onion, green pepper and butter in 10-inch glass baking dish. Microwave on High

for 5 minutes or until vegetables are tender. Blend in flour. Stir in milk. Microwave on High for 2 minutes or until slightly thickened, stirring once. Add remaining ingredients; mix well. Microwave for 10 minutes longer or until heated through, stirring once. Yield: 8 servings.

Kimberly Carol Wehrenberg
Kingfisher, Oklahoma

TUNA EXPRESS

    3/4 c. mayonnaise
    1 tbsp. lemon juice
    1 tsp. Worcestershire sauce
    1/2 tsp. dry mustard
    1/4 tsp. Tabasco sauce
    3   6-oz. cans tuna
    1 c. finely chopped celery
    1 c. small bread cubes
    1/2 c. chopped pecans
    2 tbsp. minced onion
    1/2 c. shredded Swiss cheese

Combine first 5 ingredients in bowl; mix well. Add tuna, celery, bread, pecans and onion; toss lightly. Spoon into greased shallow 1 1/2-quart casserole. Bake at 350 degrees for 20 to 25 minutes or until bubbly. Sprinkle cheese over top. Bake for several minutes longer or until cheese melts. Yield: 6 servings.

Jalene Corcoran
Follett, Texas

TOASTY TUNA CASSEROLE

    12 slices sandwich bread, crusts
        trimmed, toasted
    1   6-oz. can tuna, drained
    1/4 c. chopped onion
    1/4 c. mayonnaise
    6 slices American cheese
    1   10-oz. package frozen mixed
        vegetables, thawed
    1 can cream of celery soup
    1/4 c. milk

Arrange half the toast in ungreased 9 x 13-inch baking dish. Combine tuna, onion and mayonnaise in bowl; mix well. Spread over toast. Top with cheese and remaining toast. Combine vegetables, soup and milk in bowl; mix well. Spread over toast leaving 2-inch border. Bake at 350 degrees for 30 minutes. Yield: 6 servings.

Mary Frances Boyd
Stovall, North Carolina

Seafood

TUNA AU GRATIN

1 1/2 tbsp. flour
1 1/2 tbsp. melted butter
1 1/4 c. milk
3/4 tsp. salt
1/8 tsp. pepper
1/4 c. grated Cheddar cheese
1/2 pkg. medium noodles, cooked, drained
1 6-oz. can tuna, drained
3/4 c. grated Cheddar cheese

Blend flour and butter in saucepan. Add milk. Cook until thickened, stirring constantly. Remove from heat. Stir in seasonings and 1/4 cup cheese. Add noodles and tuna; mix well. Spoon into greased casserole. Sprinkle with 3/4 cup cheese. Bake at 375 degrees for 20 minutes or until cheese is melted. Yield: 4 servings.

Kathy Krejsek
Grant, Oklahoma

BAKED FISH MEDITERRANEAN

1 c. finely chopped onion
1 clove of garlic, minced
1/2 c. chopped celery
1 15-oz. can tomato sauce
1/8 tsp. ground cloves
1 bay leaf
1 1/2 c. shredded carrots
3/4 c. chicken broth
Salt and pepper to taste
2 lb. fish fillets

Saute onion, garlic and celery in skillet until tender. Add remaining ingredients except fish fillets. Simmer, covered, for 30 minutes, stirring occasionally. Roll up fillets; secure with toothpicks. Arrange in greased shallow baking dish. Cover with sauce. Bake at 350 degrees for 35 minutes or until fish flakes easily. Garnish with parsley. Yield: 8 servings.

Carol Lovett
Costa Mesa, California

BROILED FISH FILLETS

2 lb. fish fillets
2 tbsp. lime juice
3 tbsp. mayonnaise
1/2 c. Parmesan cheese
1/4 c. melted butter
3 tbsp. chopped green onion
Dash of Tabasco sauce

Arrange fillets in 10 x 15-inch broiler pan. Brush with lime juice. Broil for 6 to 8 minutes or until fish flakes easily. Combine remaining ingredients in bowl; mix well. Spread over fish. Broil for 2 to 3 minutes longer.
Yield: 6 servings.

Joann Ketterer
Shippensburg, Pennsylvania

CITRUS-MARINATED FISH FILLETS

1/2 c. dry vermouth
1 tbsp. grated orange rind
1 tsp. grated lemon rind
1/4 c. orange juice
2 tbsp. lemon juice
2 tbsp. oil
1 tbsp. sliced green onion
1 tbsp. minced parsley
1/4 tsp. salt
Pepper to taste
1 lb. fish fillets

Combine first 10 ingredients in jar; mix well. Pour over fillets in shallow dish. Marinate, covered, in refrigerator for 2 hours. Drain, reserving marinade. Bring strained marinade to a boil in large skillet. Add fillets. Simmer, covered, for 5 minutes or until fish flakes easily. Serve with hot cooked rice and thinly sliced lemon and orange.

Elizabeth Culbreth
Inman, South Carolina

FISH AND CHIPS

1 lb. fish fillets, cut into halves
3/4 c. flour
2 tsp. dill
1/2 tsp. salt
1/2 tsp. soda
1 tbsp. vinegar
Oil for deep frying
6 servings hot French-fried potatoes

Pat fish fillets dry with paper towels. Combine flour, dill and salt in bowl. Stir in mixture of soda and vinegar. Add 3/4 cup water; mix well. Dip fish into batter. Deep-fry in 3-inch deep 375-degree oil for 5 minutes or until brown. Serve with French-fried potatoes.
Yield: 6 servings.

Carolyn Frederick
Pinckney, Michigan

COOK'S CHOICE SEAFOOD

1/3 c. finely chopped celery
2 tbsp. butter

2 c. thick white sauce
1/2 c. cubed Cheddar cheese
1 4-oz. can mushrooms, drained
1 tbsp. onion flakes
2 tbsp. parsley
1/2 tsp. dry mustard
Dash of pepper
3 hard-boiled eggs, sliced
1 16-oz. package frozen fish fillets,
    thawed, chopped
1/2 c. cracker crumbs
2 tbsp. Parmesan cheese
2 tbsp. melted butter

Saute celery in 2 tablespoons butter in skillet. Combine white sauce and cheese in saucepan. Cook until cheese is melted, stirring constantly. Stir in sauteed celery, mushrooms and next 6 ingredients. Spoon into greased casserole. Toss cracker crumbs and Parmesan cheese with 2 tablespoons melted butter. Sprinkle over casserole. Bake at 350 degrees for 30 minutes. Yield: 4 servings.

Bertie Collins
Ellsinore, Missouri

FILLETS ELEGANTE

1 lb. frozen fish fillets, partially thawed
Pepper to taste
2 tbsp. butter
1 10-oz. can frozen cream of shrimp
    soup, thawed
1/4 c. Parmesan cheese
1/2 tsp. paprika

Arrange fillets in buttered 9-inch round baking dish. Season with pepper; dot with butter. Spread soup over top. Sprinkle with cheese and paprika. Bake at 400 degrees for 25 minutes or until fish flakes easily. Yield: 4 servings.

Lessie Oaks
Memphis, Tennessee

FLORENTINE FISH FILLETS

1 1/2 tbsp. melted butter
1 1/2 tbsp. flour
1/2 tsp. salt
1/8 tsp. pepper
1 c. milk
1/2 c. grated cheese
2 pkg. frozen chopped spinach,
    cooked, drained
2 lb. fish fillets

Blend butter, flour and seasonings in saucepan. Stir in milk gradually. Cook until thick, stirring constantly. Add cheese. Cook over very low heat until cheese is melted, stirring constantly. Spread spinach over bottom of greased 9 x 13-inch baking dish. Cover with sauce. Top with fillets. Bake at 375 degrees for 30 minutes.

Patricia Mixon
St. Louis, Oklahoma

FISHERMAN'S DELIGHT

1 sm. onion, chopped
1/4 c. margarine
1/4 c. flour
1 1/2 c. milk
1 tsp. parsley
Dash of pepper
1 sm. can mushrooms, drained
1 lb. whitefish, cut into cubes
1 sm. can shrimp, drained
3 potatoes, thinly sliced

Saute onion in margarine in saucepan. Stir in flour. Add milk gradually; mix well. Cook until thick, stirring constantly. Stir in parsley, pepper and mushrooms. Arrange whitefish and shrimp in buttered casserole. Layer half the sauce, potatoes and remaining sauce over seafood. Bake at 375 degrees for 1 hour or until potatoes are tender. Yield: 6 servings.

Coco Wilheim
Asheville, North Carolina

JAMBALAYA

1 lb. fish fillets
1/2 c. chopped onion
1/2 clove of garlic, minced
1/4 c. margarine
1 16-oz. can tomatoes
1 16-oz. can tomato sauce
1 tsp. sugar
1 tsp. Worcestershire sauce
1/2 tsp. salt
1/2 tsp. seafood seasoning
1/8 tsp. (about) hot pepper sauce
1 sm. can mushrooms
1 tsp. file powder

Microwave fish fillets using microwave instructions until fish flakes easily. Saute onion and garlic in margarine in large skillet until tender. Stir in tomatoes, next 6 ingredients and 1 1/2 cups water. Simmer, covered, for 3 minutes. Add fish and mushrooms. Simmer, uncovered, until heated through. Stir in file powder. Serve over rice. Yield: 8 servings.

Margaret Jordan
White Plains, New York

Seafood

MICROWAVE FISH FIESTA

1 lb. fish fillets
1 tsp. salt
1/4 tsp. pepper
1 sm. onion, thinly sliced
1 tomato, sliced
1 tbsp. lime juice
1 tbsp. oil
1 tbsp. minced parsley

Place fish in 8 x 8-inch glass baking dish. Sprinkle with salt and pepper. Microwave, covered, for 3 1/2 minutes. Top with onion and tomato slices. Sprinkle with remaining ingredients. Microwave, covered, for 2 minutes or until vegetables are tender-crisp and fish flakes easily. Yield: 4 servings.

Lula Smith
Sand Springs, Oklahoma

MICROWAVE ROSY FILLETS

1   16-oz. package frozen fish fillets,
     partially thawed
1/2 tsp. salt
1 can tomato soup
1/4 c. finely chopped celery
1/4 tsp. oregano
1 sm. onion, sliced
1 sm. lemon, sliced

Arrange fish in 8 x 8-inch glass baking dish. Sprinkle with salt. Microwave, covered, on High for 45 seconds. Combine soup, celery and oregano in bowl; mix well. Pour over fish. Top with onion and lemon slices. Microwave, covered, for 14 minutes or until fish flakes easily. Yield: 4 servings.

Mary Woodruff
Hotchkiss, Colorado

MICROWAVE FILLETS WITH LEMON SPINACH

2 tbsp. margarine
2 sm. onions, sliced
2 tbsp. flour
1 c. milk
1 tsp. instant chicken bouillon
1   16-oz. package frozen fish fillets,
     partially thawed
1/2 tsp. salt
2   10-oz. packages frozen chopped
     spinach, thawed, drained
3 tbsp. lemon juice
2 tbsp. Parmesan cheese
Paprika

Microwave margarine in 4-cup glass measure on High for 30 seconds or until melted. Add onions. Microwave, covered, for 1 minute or until tender. Stir in flour. Microwave, covered, for 45 seconds. Stir in milk and bouillon gradually. Microwave, covered, for 4 minutes or until thickened. Arrange fillets in 8 x 8-inch glass baking dish. Sprinkle with salt. Microwave, covered, on High for 4 minutes. Spoon spinach around fillets. Drizzle lemon juice over spinach. Cover with sauce. Microwave, covered, for 3 minutes or until fish flakes easily. Sprinkle cheese and paprika over top. Yield: 8 servings.

Janice Watson
Florence, Mississippi

EASY OVEN-FRIED FISH

1 lb. fish fillets
1/4 c. milk
1 1/2 tsp. salt
1/2 c. dry bread crumbs
2 tbsp. butter, melted

Dip fish in mixture of milk and salt. Coat with bread crumbs. Place in greased 9 x 13-inch baking pan. Drizzle with butter. Bake at 500 degrees for 10 minutes or until fish flakes easily. Yield: 4 servings.

Lois Springer
Oakboro, North Carolina

SUNSHINE OVEN-FRIED FISH

1 egg, beaten
6 tbsp. frozen orange juice
     concentrate, thawed
2 tbsp. soy sauce
1 lb. fish fillets
1/2 c. fine dry bread crumbs
2 tbsp. margarine, melted
1/2 tsp. lemon juice

Beat egg with orange juice concentrate and soy sauce. Dip fillets in egg mixture; coat with crumbs. Arrange in greased 7 x 12-inch baking dish. Drizzle mixture of margarine and lemon juice over top. Bake at 500 degrees for 10 minutes or until fish flakes easily. Yield: 4 servings.

Ruth Romesberg
Rockwood, Pennsylvania

PAN-FRIED FISH

2 lb. fish fillets
1 tsp. salt

1/8 tsp. pepper
1 egg
1/3 c. flour
1/3 c. cornmeal
1/3 c. Parmesan cheese
2 tbsp. shortening
2 tbsp. butter

Sprinkle fish with salt and pepper. Dip in mixture of egg and 1 tablespoon water. Coat with mixture of flour, cornmeal and cheese. Fry fish in mixture of shortening and butter in skillet over medium heat for 5 minutes on each side or until browned. Yield: 10 servings.

Mary Burns
Lake Norden, South Dakota

FISH FILLETS PARMESAN

1 1/2 lb. fish fillets
2 tbsp. lemon juice
1/3 c. olive oil
1/2 c. fine dry bread crumbs
1/2 c. Parmesan cheese
1 tbsp. minced parsley
1/2 tsp. rosemary (opt.)

Dip fillets in mixture of lemon juice and olive oil. Coat with mixture of remaining ingredients. Arrange in greased 9 x 13-inch baking dish. Bake at 500 degrees for 12 minutes or until fish flakes easily. Yield: 6 servings.

Jane Parnell
Fort Sumner, New Mexico

PASTA WITH SEAFOOD SAUCE

1/2 c. chopped onion
1/2 c. chopped green pepper
1 clove of garlic, minced
1 tbsp. olive oil
1 tbsp. butter
1 28-oz. can tomatoes, cut up
1/2 c. dry wine
1/4 c. minced parsley
1/2 tsp. salt
1/2 tsp. basil
1/4 tsp. oregano
1 lb. fish fillets
12 oz. hot cooked pasta

Saute onion, green pepper and garlic in mixture of olive oil and butter in skillet until tender. Add tomatoes with juice, wine, parsley and seasonings. Simmer for 35 minutes, stirring occasionally. Cut fillets into 1-inch pieces; drain on paper towel. Add to tomato mixture. Simmer for 5 minutes or until fish flakes easily. Serve over pasta. Yield: 6 servings.

June Barnett
Onekama, Michigan

FISH PLAKI

1 med. onion, sliced
1 clove of garlic, minced
2 med. tomatoes, sliced
1 c. chopped parsley
1/4 c. corn oil margarine
2 lb. fish fillets
1/2 tsp. salt
1/2 tsp. oregano
1/4 tsp. pepper
1/2 c. bread crumbs
1/4 c. corn oil margarine

Saute onion, garlic, tomatoes and parsley in 1/4 cup margarine in large skillet. Arrange fillets in greased 9 x 13-inch baking dish. Sprinkle with seasonings. Spread sauteed mixture over the top. Sprinkle with crumbs; dot with 1/4 cup margarine. Bake, covered, at 350 degrees for 35 minutes or until fillets flake easily.
Yield: 6-8 servings.

Photograph for this recipe below.

Seafood

POACHED FISH

1 med. onion, sliced
3 slices lemon
3 sprigs of parsley
1 bay leaf
1 tsp. salt
2 peppercorns
1 lb. fish fillets

Combine onion, lemon, parsley, bay leaf, salt and peppercorns in 1 1/2 inches water in 10-inch skillet. Bring to a boil. Arrange fillets in skillet. Simmer for 4 to 6 minutes or until fish flakes easily. Yield: 4 servings.

Barbara Fifer
Dover, Delaware

SEAFOOD CREOLE

1/3 c. chopped onion
1/3 c. chopped green pepper
1 clove of garlic, minced
3 tbsp. butter
1   16-oz. can tomatoes, chopped
2 tbsp. minced parsley
1 tbsp. instant chicken bouillon granules
Dash of Tabasco sauce
1 tbsp. cornstarch
16 oz. fish fillets, cubed

Saute onion, green pepper and garlic in butter in skillet until tender. Add tomatoes, next 3 ingredients and 1/2 cup water; mix well. Simmer, covered, for 10 minutes. Blend cornstarch with 3 tablespoons cold water. Stir into tomato mixture. Cook until thickened, stirring constantly. Add fish. Simmer, covered, for 5 minutes or until fish flakes easily. Serve over hot cooked rice. Yield: 6 servings.

Lavelle Eckout
Ansley, Nebraska

SEAFOOD ENCHILADAS

1 tbsp. butter, melted
1   6-oz. can tomato paste
1/2 c. chopped fresh parsley
1/2 tsp. oregano
1/2 tsp. salt
1/8 tsp. pepper
1 clove of garlic, crushed
1 pt. sour cream
1   8-oz. can tomato sauce
1 tbsp. grated lemon rind
2 tbsp. fresh lemon juice
1 lb. fish fillets, cooked, flaked
1   7 1/2-oz. can crab meat, drained

1 tbsp. grated lemon rind
2 tbsp. fresh lemon juice
2 tbsp. instant minced onion
10 tortillas
3 tbsp. butter
2 or 3 California lemons, sliced

Combine first 7 ingredients in skillet. Simmer for 5 minutes, stirring frequently. Add sour cream, tomato sauce, lemon rind, lemon juice and 1/2 cup water; mix well. Combine fish and crab meat in bowl. Add 1 tablespoon lemon rind, 2 tablespoons lemon juice and onion; mix well. Fry tortillas in butter in skillet for several seconds until soft. Spoon seafood mixture onto tortillas; roll to enclose filling. Pour half the sauce into greased baking pan. Arrange tortillas in dish. Top with remaining sauce. Top with lemon slices. Bake at 350 degrees for 30 minutes. Yield: 5 servings.

Photograph for this recipe on opposite page

QUICK FISH-VEGETABLE MEDLEY

1 lb. fish fillets
1 tsp. salt
1/4 tsp. pepper
1   10-oz. package frozen green peas
1 med. cucumber, chopped
1/2 c. diagonally sliced celery
1 sm. onion, sliced
1/2 tsp. salt
1 tbsp. lemon juice
1/4 c. margarine

Arrange fish in 2-quart round glass casserole. Sprinkle with 1 teaspoon salt and pepper. Microwave, covered, on High for 3 1/2 minutes. Sprinkle peas, cucumber, celery and onion over fish. Sprinkle with 1/2 teaspoon salt and lemon juice. Dot with margarine. Microwave, covered, for 6 minutes or until vegetables are tender-crisp and fish flakes easily. Yield: 4 servings.

Vivian Hallet
Tower Hill, Illinois

Shellfish

NEW ENGLAND CLAM FRITTERS

2 eggs, lightly beaten
1 c. chopped clams
1 tsp. salt

96

1/8 tsp. pepper
1/2 c. milk
1/2 c. clam juice
2 c. flour
1 tbsp. baking powder
Oil for deep frying

Combine first 8 ingredients in order given in bowl; mix well after each addition. Drop by spoonfuls into deep 375-degree oil. Fry until dark brown. Drain on paper towels.

Lorna Thorne
Waycross, Georgia

SPECIAL CLAM LINGUINE

2 onions, chopped
1 lb. mushrooms, sliced
6 to 8 cloves of garlic, minced
4 tsp. olive oil
2   10-oz. cans baby clams
2   6-oz. cans minced clams
1 can clam juice
Salt and pepper to taste
1/2 tsp. oregano
1 pkg. linguine, cooked
Parmesan cheese

Saute onions, mushrooms and garlic in olive oil in skillet until golden. Stir in clams, clam juice and seasonings. Simmer, covered, for 20 minutes. Serve over linguine. Top with Parmesan cheese. Yield: 6-8 servings.
Note: Thicken with mixture of cornstarch and a small amount of water, if desired.

Dorothy Richards
Maysville, California

LITTLE NECK CLAMS
WITH LINGUINE

5 cloves of garlic, chopped
1/2 c. olive oil
20 fresh little neck clams in shells
8 med. tomatoes, chopped
1 tsp. fresh basil
Pinch each of salt and pepper
1 lb. linguine
2 tbsp. Parmesan cheese
1 tbsp. finely chopped parsley

Combine garlic, olive oil and clams in 16-inch skillet. Cook for 5 minutes. Stir in tomatoes and seasonings. Cook, covered, for 10 to 15 minutes or until clams open. Cook linguine in boiling water in saucepan for 7 minutes; drain. Add to clam sauce. Garnish with Parmesan cheese and parsley.

Angela Black
Woonsocket, Rhode Island

SHELLS IN RED CLAM SAUCE

1/2 c. chopped onion
1/2 c. chopped celery
1/2 c. chopped carrot
2 tbsp. bacon drippings
1   16-oz. can tomatoes, chopped
2 tbsp. tomato paste
1/2 tsp. sugar
1/4 tsp. thyme
1/2 tsp. salt
8 sm. clams in shells
1/3 c. dry white wine
4 slices crisp-fried bacon, crumbled
1 egg, beaten
1   7-oz. can minced clams, drained
1/2 c. finely chopped cooked chicken
1/4 c. Parmesan cheese
6 to 8 lg. pasta shells, cooked

Saute onion, celery and carrot in bacon drippings in skillet for 10 minutes. Add next 5 ingredients; mix well. Simmer for 30 minutes, stirring occasionally. Add clams in shells, wine and bacon. Simmer for 15 minutes. Combine egg, minced clams, chicken and Parmesan cheese in bowl. Stuff into hot shells. Arrange shells in shallow greased baking dish. Arrange clams around stuffed shells. Pour sauce over all. Bake at 350 degrees until heated through. Yield: 4-6 servings.

Pam Truhelt
Woodland, Mississippi

Seafood

CLAM SOUFFLE

1 c. milk
12 saltine crackers, crumbled
2 tbsp. melted butter
1   7-oz. can minced clams
Salt, pepper and onion powder to taste
2 eggs, well beaten

Combine milk and cracker crumbs in bowl. Let stand for 10 minutes. Add butter, clams, seasonings and eggs; mix well. Pour into greased baking dish. Bake at 325 degrees for 30 to 40 minutes or until set and lightly browned.

Christy Campbell
Sweetwater, Georgia

SPAGHETTI WITH MUSHROOM-CLAM SAUCE

2 1/2 c. sliced mushrooms
1/3 c. chopped onion
3/4 tsp. minced garlic
1/2 c. olive oil
1 doz. cherrystone clams, chopped
1   6-oz. can tomato paste
1 tomato, chopped
2 tbsp. parsley flakes
2 tbsp. green pepper flakes
1/2 tsp. salt
1/8 tsp. pepper
1/8 tsp. thyme
8 oz. spaghetti, cooked

Saute mushrooms, onion and garlic in olive oil in skillet until mushrooms are lightly browned. Add 1 1/2 cups water, clams, tomato paste, tomato and seasonings. Bring to a boil. Simmer for 1 hour, stirring occasionally. Serve over hot spaghetti. Yield: 6 servings.

Photograph for this recipe below.

SPAGHETTI WITH CLAM-TOMATO SAUCE

1 clove of garlic, chopped
1/2 c. chopped green pepper
2 tbsp. margarine, melted
1/2 c. clam juice
2   7 1/2-oz. cans minced clams, drained
2   8-oz. cans tomato sauce
1/8 tsp pepper
3/4 tsp. celery salt
Italian seasoning to taste
1 lb. spaghetti, cooked

Saute garlic and green pepper in margarine in skillet until tender. Add clam juice, clams, tomato sauce and seasonings. Cook over low heat for 10 minutes, stirring frequently. Serve over hot spaghetti. Yield: 8 servings.

Mattie Maudlin
Harrisburg, Pennsylvania

STUFFED CLAMS OREGANO

2   7-oz. cans minced clams, drained
3/4 c. butter, melted
1 c. dry bread crumbs
Dash of garlic powder
2 tbsp. chopped parsley
2 tbsp. Parmesan cheese
4 tsp. lemon juice
1/8 tsp. hot pepper sauce
1 tsp. oregano

Combine all ingredients in bowl; mix well. Spoon into 8 seafood baking shells. Bake at 425 degrees for 10 minutes. Yield: 8 servings.

June Sherwin
Kansas City, Missouri

CLAMS IN WINE

60 clams in shells
1 c. salt
1 1/2 c. chicken broth
1 1/2 c. dry white wine
1/2 c. sliced green onions
1/3 c. chopped parsley
1 clove of garlic, minced
1 tbsp. minced fresh mint, crushed (opt.)
1 tsp. basil
1/2 tsp. oregano

Soak clams in mixture of 1/3 cup salt and 1 gallon water. Let stand for 15 minutes; rinse. Repeat process 2 times. Combine remaining ingredients in large saucepan. Bring to a boil. Add clams. Simmer, covered, for 10 to 15 minutes or until shells open. Remove clams; discard unopened shells. Strain pan juices. Serve clams with strained juices for dipping.

Judy Meek
Wichita, Kansas

BAKED STUFFED QUAHOGS

1 c. seasoned bread crumbs
Juice of 1 lemon
1 tsp. garlic powder
1 tbsp. parsley flakes
1/4 tsp. cayenne pepper
1/3 c. olive oil
Salt and pepper to taste
12 quahogs
1/4 c. bread crumbs
Butter

Mix first 6 ingredients and salt and pepper in bowl. Put quahogs through food grinder; reserve liquid. Add reserved liquid and a small amount of water to seasoned bread crumb mixture; stir until crumbly. Stir in quahogs and 1/4 cup bread crumbs. Spoon into quahog shells. Dot with butter. Bake at 400 degrees for 30 minutes. Yield: 6-8 servings.

Carol Waters
Rye, New York

BOILED DUNGENESS CRABS

3 Dungeness crabs, dressed
1/2 c. salt
Melted butter

Wash crabs inside and out. Place in mixture of 8 quarts boiling water and salt. Simmer, covered, for 15 minutes; drain. Crack claws and legs. Serve with butter. Yield: 6 servings.
Note: May serve cold with mayonnaise.

Bonnie Franklin
Oakland, California

SHERRIED CRAB AND ARTICHOKES

2 c. crab meat
1/4 lb. mushrooms, sliced
1 tsp. parsley
2 tsp. lemon juice
1 tsp. grated onion
1 c. mayonnaise
3 tbsp. Sherry
1/2 tsp. Worcestershire sauce
1/2 tsp. prepared mustard
1/2 green pepper, finely chopped
1 pkg. frozen artichoke bottoms, thawed
Parmesan cheese to taste
Paprika

Combine first 10 ingredients in bowl; mix well. Place artichoke bottoms in greased casserole. Cover with crab mixture. Sprinkle with Parmesan cheese. Garnish with paprika. Bake at 375 degrees for 30 minutes.

Anne Hill
Butte, Montana

DEVILED CRAB

1 tbsp. finely chopped green pepper
2 tsp. finely chopped onion
6 tbsp. melted butter
6 tbsp. flour
1 tsp. salt
1/2 tsp. mustard
1 1/2 c. milk
1 tsp. Worcestershire sauce
2 egg yolks, slightly beaten
1 lb. crab meat, drained, flaked
2 tsp. chopped pimento
2 tbsp. olive oil
1 tsp. catsup
2 tbsp. mustard
2 tbsp. Sherry
1 c. fine bread crumbs
Paprika to taste
2 tbsp. melted butter

Saute green pepper and onion in 6 tablespoons butter in saucepan until onion is lightly browned. Add flour, salt and 1/2 teaspoon mustard. Heat until bubbly; remove from heat. Add milk gradually, stirring until smooth. Stir in 1 teaspoon Worcestershire sauce. Bring to a boil, stirring constantly. Cook for 1 to 2 minutes; remove from heat. Stir a small amount of hot mixture into egg yolks; stir egg yolks into hot mixture. Cook for 3 to 5 minutes longer, stirring constantly. Add crab meat and pimento; mix gently. Simmer until heated through; remove from heat. Blend olive oil, catsup, 2 tablespoons mustard and 2 tablespoons water in bowl. Add to crab mixture with Sherry; mix well. Spoon into 6 buttered baking shells. Top with crumbs and paprika. Drizzle with 2 tablespoons melted butter. Bake at 450 degrees for 6 to 7 minutes or until lightly browned.
Yield: 6 servings.

Linda Johnson
Charlotte, Michigan

Seafood

INDIVIDUAL CRAB MEAT CASSEROLES

2 tbsp. finely chopped onion
1/2 c. finely chopped celery
1/4 c. butter
3 tbsp. flour
3/4 tsp. salt
2 c. half and half
1/4 c. Sherry
1 egg, beaten
1/4 tsp. Tabasco sauce
3 c. cooked crab meat
2 tbsp. chopped parsley
2 tbsp. butter, melted
1 1/2 c. fine fresh bread cubes

Saute onion and celery in 1/4 cup butter in saucepan. Do not brown. Blend in flour and salt. Add half and half and Sherry gradually. Cook until thickened, stirring constantly. Remove from heat. Stir a small amount of hot mixture into egg; stir egg mixture into hot mixture. Add Tabasco sauce, crab meat and parsley. Spoon into 6 individual baking shells. Combine 2 tablespoons butter and bread cubes. Sprinkle over crab mixture. Bake at 350 degrees for 20 minutes. Garnish each serving with lemon twist and sprig of parsley.
Yield: 6 servings.

Photograph for this recipe above.

DELICIOUS CRAB CASSEROLE

1 c. cooked rice
1 6-oz. can crab meat
5 hard-boiled eggs, sliced
1 1/2 c. mayonnaise
1/2 tsp. salt
1/4 tsp. cayenne pepper
Dash of pepper
1/8 tsp. crushed tarragon
1 tbsp. minced parsley

2 tbsp. chopped onion
1 6-oz. can evaporated milk
1 c. shredded cheese

Combine rice, crab meat, eggs and mayonnaise in bowl; mix well. Add remaining ingredients except cheese; mix well. Spoon into greased baking dish. Sprinkle cheese over top. Bake at 350 degrees for 20 minutes.

Eleanor M. Jones
Prince George, Maryland

BOILED HARD-SHELL BLUE CRABS

24 hard-shell blue crabs
1/3 c. salt

Place crabs in mixture of salt and 6 quarts boiling water. Simmer, covered, for 15 minutes; drain. Remove top shell and discard spongy material. Crack claws and legs. Serve hot or cold with favorite cocktail sauce.

Sylvia Sutton
Miami, Florida

CRAB-RICE CASSEROLE

2 c. cooked rice
1 7-oz. can crab meat
1 4-oz. can chopped mushrooms
3/4 c. mayonnaise
1/2 c. chopped green pepper
1 med. onion, chopped
1 c. tomato juice
1/2 c. milk
1/8 tsp. chili powder
1/2 c. bread crumbs
1 tbsp. butter, melted

Combine first 9 ingredients in bowl; mix well. Spoon into greased baking dish. Toss crumbs with butter. Sprinkle over top. Bake at 350 degrees for 45 minutes. Yield: 6 servings.

Cathy Joplin
Alameda, California

EASY CRAB IMPERIAL

1 7-oz. can crab meat, flaked
1 c. mayonnaise
4 egg whites, stiffly beaten
1/4 tsp. salt
Dash of pepper
1/4 c. bread crumbs

Combine crab meat and mayonnaise in bowl; mix well. Fold in egg whites, salt and pepper. Pour into greased baking dish. Sprinkle with crumbs. Bake at 350 degrees for 45 minutes.

Annabel D. Osbourn
Jefferson, West Virginia

SHERRIED CRAB IMPERIAL

1 lb. back fin crab meat
1/4 c. melted margarine
2 tbsp. flour
1 c. cream
2 egg yolks, beaten
1/4 tsp. each salt and cayenne pepper
1 tsp. horseradish
2 tbsp. Sherry
Paprika

Place crab meat in greased shallow baking dish. Blend margarine and flour in saucepan. Stir in cream. Bring to a boil over low heat, stirring constantly. Simmer for 2 minutes, stirring constantly. Stir a small amount of hot mixture into egg yolks; stir egg yolks into hot mixture. Add salt, cayenne pepper and horseradish. Cook for 3 minutes, stirring constantly. Remove from heat; stir in Sherry. Spoon over crab meat. Sprinkle with paprika. Bake at 350 degrees for 15 minutes. Yield: 6-8 servings.

Erla Click
Bluefield, West Virginia

TIPSY CRAB CASSEROLE

1/4 c. melted butter
2 tbsp. flour
1/2 c. cream
1/2 tsp. each salt and pepper
Dash of red pepper
1/2 tsp. dry mustard
Dash each of Tabasco sauce,
   Worcestershire sauce
2 tbsp. Sherry
2 tbsp. Bourbon
1 lb. back fin crab meat
1/2 c. bread crumbs
2 tbsp. melted butter

Blend 1/4 cup butter and flour in saucepan. Stir in cream. Cook until thickened, stirring constantly. Stir in seasonings, Sherry and Bourbon. Add crab meat; mix well. Spoon into buttered baking dish. Toss bread crumbs with 2 tablespoons butter. Sprinkle over casserole. Bake at 350 degrees until browned.

Diedre Somer
Kanab, Utah

CRAB JAMBALAYA

1 med. onion, chopped
1 clove of garlic, minced
2 tbsp. butter
1/2 chili pepper, chopped
1/8 tsp. white pepper
Dash of cayenne pepper
2 med. tomatoes, chopped
2 c. broth
2 c. crab meat
1 c. rice
Salt to taste

Saute onion and garlic in butter in skillet until lightly browned. Stir in remaining ingredients. Simmer, covered, for 20 minutes. Let stand until liquid is absorbed. Yield: 6 servings.

Allison Martin
Preston, California

FROG LEGS GRUYERE

18 sm. frog legs
1/4 c. lemon juice
1/4 c. light cream
Salt and white pepper to taste
1/2 c. butter
2 tsp. minced shallots
1 tbsp. minced onion
1 c. dry white wine
1/4 c. Marsala
3 lg. oysters, minced
1/2 c. sliced sauteed mushrooms (opt.)
1/4 c. Marsala
Dash of cayenne pepper
1/2 c. grated Gruyere cheese

Soak frog legs in very cold water for 3 hours; drain on paper towel. Dip in mixture of lemon juice and cream. Sprinkle with salt and pepper. Melt butter in medium skillet; stir in shallots and onion. Add frog legs. Saute over low heat for 3 minutes on each side. Add white wine and 1/4 cup Marsala. Poach gently for 15 minutes or until tender, turning once. Remove frog legs to ovenproof platter; strain pan juices into small saucepan. Add oysters, mushrooms and 1/4 cup Marsala. Simmer for 10 minutes. Season with cayenne pepper and salt to taste. Pour sauce over frog legs; sprinkle with cheese. Bake at 400 degrees for 3 to 5 minutes until cheese is bubbly and lightly browned. Garnish with lemon wedges. Serve immediately.
Yield: 6 servings.

Tracy Regis
Forest City, Arkansas

Seafood

BROILED LOBSTER TAILS

1   24-oz. package frozen rock
      lobster tails
2 tbsp. salt
1/3 c. melted butter
1 tbsp. lemon juice
1/2 c. butter
1 tbsp. minced parsley
1/4 tsp. red pepper sauce

Add lobster tails to mixture of salt and 2 quarts boiling water. Simmer, covered, for 15 minutes; drain. Remove thin under shell. Thread on skewer. Place meat side up on rack in broiler pan; brush with 1/3 cup butter. Broil 3 inches from heat source for 2 minutes. Combine remaining ingredients in saucepan. Heat until butter melts, stirring constantly. Serve with lobster. Yield: 4 servings.

Barbara Smoot
Selma, Indiana

LOBSTER CANTONESE

2 tbsp. preserved black beans,
      washed, drained
2 cloves of garlic, finely chopped
1 tbsp. soy sauce
1 c. ground pork
1/2 tsp. salt
1/2 tsp. sugar
1 tsp. soy sauce
2 tbsp. oil
1 tsp. salt
1/8 tsp. pepper
2 lb. large lobster tails, cut into
      1/2-in. slices
2 green onions, cut into 1-in. pieces
1 c. chicken broth
2 tbsp. cornstarch
2 eggs, beaten

Mash black beans and garlic together in bowl; add 1 tablespoon soy sauce. Combine pork with 1/2 teaspoon salt, sugar and 1 teaspoon soy sauce in bowl; marinate for 15 minutes. Heat oil in skillet. Add 1 teaspoon salt and pepper; add pork. Stir-fry for 4 minutes. Add lobster. Stir-fry for 2 minutes or until heated through. Add green onions and black bean mixture; mix well. Add broth. Cook, covered, for 10 minutes. Add cornstarch blended with 2 tablespoons water Cook until thickened, stirring constantly. Remove from heat. Stir in eggs. Yield: 6-8 servings.

Florence Polter
Middlesburg, Pennsylvania

LOBSTER-MUSHROOM CASSEROLE

24 oz. rock lobster tails
1 lb. mushrooms, sliced
1 c. chopped onion
1 bay leaf
1 tsp. dried tarragon
2 tbsp. cornstarch
2 c. yogurt
4 oz. water chestnuts, sliced
Salt and pepper to taste

Drop rock lobster tails into boiling salted water in saucepan. Cook for 2 minutes after water returns to a boil. Drain and rinse with cold water. Cut away underside membrane; remove and slice meat. Combine mushrooms, onion, bay leaf and tarragon with 1/4 cup water in small saucepan. Simmer until mushrooms are tender. Remove bay leaf. Mix cornstarch with a small amount of water to make a paste. Combine cornstarch paste and yogurt in large saucepan. Simmer until thickened, stirring constantly. Add vegetables, lobster, water chestnuts and seasonings; mix lightly. Pour into greased casserole. Bake at 350 degrees for 20 minutes. Yield: 6 servings.

Wilma Davis
Watertown, Tennessee

ROCK LOBSTER CHOP SUEY

1 clove of garlic, chopped
2 tbsp. peanut oil
1 lb. frozen rock lobster tails, thawed
1 bunch scallions, sliced into 1-in. pieces
1 1/2 c. sliced celery
1   16-oz. can Chinese vegetables, drained
2 tbsp. soy sauce
3 tbsp. cornstarch
1 c. chicken broth
Salt to taste

Saute garlic in oil in skillet for 5 minutes. Remove underside membrane of rock lobster tails; pull out meat in 1 piece. Cut meat into 1-inch crosswise slices. Add lobster, scallions, celery and Chinese vegetables to skillet. Stir-fry over medium heat for 5 to 7 minutes or until lobster meat is opaque and vegetables are tender-crisp. Combine soy sauce, cornstarch and chicken broth in bowl; mix well. Pour evenly over lobster in skillet. Cook over low heat until thickened, stirring constantly. Season with salt. Serve over hot cooked rice. Garnish with Chinese noodles. Yield: 6 servings.

Photograph for this recipe on opposite page.

CORAL BAY LOBSTER

1 1/2 lb. lobster meat, cut into pieces
3 tbsp. butter
3 tbsp. Brandy, heated
1 tsp. flour
1 c. sour cream
1   10-oz. package frozen spinach,
      cooked, drained
1/2 c. cooked peas
1/4 c. chopped cooked carrots
1 c. Hollandaise sauce
1 tbsp. Parmesan cheese

Saute lobster in butter in skillet. Add Brandy; ignite. Add flour and sour cream; mix well. Add vegetables. Simmer for 10 minutes, stirring occasionally. Remove from heat. Stir in Hollandaise sauce. Pour into greased 1 1/2-quart casserole. Sprinkle with cheese. Bake at 450 degrees for 10 minutes. Serve with hot cooked rice. Yield: 4 servings.

June A. Terry
Yanceyville, North Carolina

LOBSTER CREPES

3 eggs
1/4 tsp. salt
3/4 c. flour
3/4 c. milk
1/4 c. melted butter
6   4-oz. frozen rock lobster tails
1/2 lb. mushrooms, sliced
1 clove of garlic, crushed
1/4 c. butter
1/4 c. minced fresh parsley
1/4 c. minced fresh spinach
1/3 c. flour
1 can chicken broth
1 c. light cream
Salt and pepper to taste

Beat eggs and 1/4 teaspoon salt together in medium bowl. Add 3/4 cup flour gradually; beat until smooth. Add milk and 1/4 cup melted butter; beat well. Chill, covered, for 1 hour or longer. Place lightly oiled 8-inch crepe pan over medium heat. Pour in enough batter to cover bottom of pan with very thin layer. Cook until batter is set and edges turn golden brown. Turn over gently with spatula. Cook for several seconds longer. Repeat with remaining batter. Stack crepes between waxed paper. Cook rock lobster tails in boiling salted water in large saucepan for 2 minutes. Drain; rinse with cold water. Remove shells and chop meat. Saute mushrooms and garlic in 1/4 cup butter in skillet for 5 minutes; stir in parsley, spinach and 1/3 cup flour. Add broth and cream gradually. Cook over low heat until sauce is thickened, stirring constantly. Stir in lobster. Season with salt and pepper to taste. Heat until bubbly. Heat crepes in 250-degree oven for 5 minutes. Spoon sauce onto each crepe; roll up. Place on ovenproof platter; keep warm. Garnish with chopped parsley. Yield: 6 servings.

Ella Post
Red Oak, Iowa

FRIED LOBSTER WITH FONDUE

2 lb. frozen lobster tails
Sliced zucchini, mushrooms, green peppers
Cauliflowerets
1 c. butter
3 c. oil
1 tsp. aromatic bitters
Salt and pepper to taste
1 lb. Swiss cheese, grated
3 tbsp. flour
2 c. dry white wine
3 tbsp. Brandy

Place lobster tails in boiling salted water in saucepan. Boil for 2 to 3 minutes. Do not overcook. Remove lobster from shells; chop into bite-sized pieces. Place lobster in center of serving dish; arrange vegetables around edge. Chill in refrigerator. Combine butter, oil, bitters, salt and pepper in chafing dish over flame. Mix cheese and flour in bowl. Heat wine in fondue pot over flame. Add cheese gradually, mixing well after each addition. Stir in Brandy. Cook vegetables and heat lobster on fondue forks in oil mixture. Dip into fondue. Yield: 4 servings.

Millie Wroy
Scotts Bluff, Nebraska

103

Seafood

LOBSTER NEWBURG SUPREME

1 1/2 lb. cooked lobster
2 tbsp. butter
1/4 c. Brandy
1 c. heavy cream
3 egg yolks
Seasonings to taste

Cut lobster into bite-sized pieces. Saute in butter in skillet for 5 minutes. Add Brandy; ignite. Combine cream and egg yolks in double boiler. Cook until mixture coats spoon, stirring constantly. Add lobster and seasonings. Serve in patty shells, toast cups or over rice.

Lucy Calhoun
Kelso, Washington

LOBSTER NUGGETS

6 to 8 lobster tails
Lime juice
2 eggs, beaten
2 c. cracker meal
Oil for deep frying

Remove lobster meat from shells; split lengthwise. Cut each piece into thirds. Marinate lobster in lime juice in glass bowl in refrigerator for 1 hour. Drain. Dip lobster in egg. Coat with cracker meal. Deep-fry in hot oil for 1 to 2 minutes until golden. Do not overcook.
Yield: 4 servings.

Marilyn Frisbee
Cabool, Missouri

ROCK LOBSTER IN PASTA SHELLS

1   5-oz. package giant pasta shells
3   8-oz. packages South African rock
    lobster tails
1/2 c. chopped celery
1/2 c. chopped onion
1 clove of garlic, chopped
1/4 c. butter

1 egg
1 1/2 c. cottage cheese
1/4 c. Parmesan cheese
Salt and pepper to taste
2 c. spaghetti sauce
1/4 c. melted butter
1/2 c. dry bread crumbs

Cook pasta shells in boiling salted water until just tender. Drain; cover with cold water. Remove underside membrane from lobster tails. Remove and chop meat. Saute celery, onion and garlic in 1/4 cup butter in skillet until golden. Add lobster meat. Saute until opaque. Cool. Stir in egg, cottage cheese and Parmesan cheese. Season with salt and pepper. Stuff well drained and dried pasta shells. Pour spaghetti sauce into greased shallow casserole. Place shells in single layer in sauce. Combine 1/4 cup butter and crumbs; sprinkle over shells. Bake at 350 degrees for 30 minutes or until lightly browned. Yield: 6 servings.

Photograph for this recipe on this page.

ROCK LOBSTER AND POTATOES NORMANDE

3   6-oz. frozen rock lobster tails
3 c. sliced cooked potatoes
2 tbsp. butter, melted
2 tbsp. flour
2 c. milk
1 tsp. salt
1/2 tsp. pepper
1/4 c. drained capers
1/2 lb. Cheddar cheese, grated

Parboil rock lobster tails in boiling salted water for 5 minutes. Drain immediately; rinse with cold water. Cut away underside membrane with kitchen shears. Remove lobster meat; slice. Combine potato slices and lobster meat in greased 2-quart casserole. Blend butter and flour in saucepan. Stir in milk gradually. Cook over low heat until thickened, stirring constantly. Add salt, pepper, capers and cheese. Cook until cheese is melted. Pour into greased casserole. Bake at 375 degrees for 20 minutes. Yield: 6 servings.

Cecilia Neal
Medina, Ohio

LOBSTER THERMIDOR

6   1-lb. frozen lobster tails, cooked
1 c. sliced fresh mushrooms
1/4 c. melted butter
1/4 c. flour

1 tsp. dry mustard
Dash of nutmeg
Dash of cayenne pepper
1 tsp. salt
1 c. milk
1 c. half and half
2 egg yolks, slightly beaten
1 tsp. lemon juice
2 tbsp. Sherry
1/2 c. fine bread crumbs
2 tbsp. Parmesan cheese
6 tbsp. melted butter

Remove lobster from shells; chop meat and reserve shells. Saute mushrooms in 1/4 cup butter in saucepan. Add flour, mustard, nutmeg, cayenne pepper and salt; mix well. Add milk and half and half gradually. Cook until thickened stirring constantly. Stir a small amount of hot mixture into egg yolks. Stir egg yolks into hot mixture. Cook until thickened, stirring constantly. Stir in lemon juice, Sherry and lobster meat. Spoon into reserved shells. Sprinkle mixture of bread crumbs, cheese and 6 tablespoons butter over lobster. Place on baking sheet. Bake at 400 degrees for 15 minutes.

Nora Westman
Eugene, Oregon

MUSSELS DELIGHT

1 sm. onion, sliced
4 cloves of garlic, pressed
4 stalks celery, chopped
3 tbsp. olive oil
2 qt. mussels, scrubbed
8 oz. Chablis
Pinch of thyme

Saute onion, garlic and celery in oil in skillet until onion is tender. Stir in mussels, Chablis and thyme. Cook, tightly covered, over medium heat for 3 to 4 minutes or until shells open. Shake skillet briskly; remove from heat. Let stand, covered, for 2 minutes. Drain, reserving broth. Serve with cups of melted butter and reserved broth. Yield: 4 servings.

Lynn Bell
Portsmouth, Rhode Island

BOTANY BAY OYSTERS

4 doz. oysters
1/4 c. dry Sherry
6 tbsp. butter
1 clove of garlic, crushed
1 1/3 c. fresh white bread crumbs
1 1/2 tbsp. freshly chopped parsley

2 tsp. finely grated lemon rind
Salt and freshly ground pepper to taste

Arrange oysters on 4 oyster plates; drizzle with Sherry. Heat butter in skillet until bubbly; add garlic. Saute until golden. Add remaining ingredients. Saute until bread crumbs are golden. Spoon over oysters. Bake at 400 degrees for 5 minutes or until heated through. Garnish with lemon slices. Serve immediately.

Carol Winter
Bountiful, Utah

OYSTERS CASINO

3 slices bacon, chopped
1/4 c. chopped onion
2 tbsp. chopped green pepper
2 tbsp. chopped celery
Salt and pepper to taste
1/2 tsp. Worcestershire sauce
2 drops of hot sauce
1 tsp. lemon juice
1 pt. oysters, drained

Saute first 4 ingredients in skillet. Add seasonings; mix well. Arrange oysters in buttered baking dish. Top with sauce. Bake at 350 degrees for 20 minutes or until brown.
Yield: 4 servings.

Regina Smith
Yakushka Bay, Oregon

DEVILED OYSTERS

2 tbsp. melted butter
2 tbsp. (heaping) flour
3/4 c. milk
1/2 tsp. salt
Pepper to taste
1 tsp. Worcestershire sauce
1 egg yolk, beaten
1 pt. fresh oysters
Paprika
Buttered bread crumbs

Blend butter and flour in double boiler. Add milk and seasonings. Cook until thickened, stirring constantly. Stir a small amount of hot mixture into egg yolk; stir egg yolk into hot mixture. Parboil oysters in oyster liquor until curled. Drain; cut into bite-sized pieces. Add to sauce. Spoon into buttered casserole. Sprinkle with paprika; top with bread crumbs. Bake at 350 degrees until brown. Yield: 4 servings.

Shirley Chandler
Clayton, Missouri

Seafood

OYSTERS BIENVILLE

3 tbsp. butter, melted
3 tbsp. flour
2 c. milk
Salt and white pepper to taste
1 1/2 c. minced green peppers
1 c. minced green onions
2 cloves of garlic, minced
1/4 c. butter
1/2 c. white wine
1/2 c. chopped pimento
2/3 c. shredded American cheese
1/2 c. bread crumbs
3 doz. oysters on the half shell
Rock salt

Blend 3 tablespoons butter and flour in sauce-pan. Stir in milk, salt and pepper. Cook until thickened, stirring constantly. Saute green peppers, green onions and garlic in 1/4 cup butter in saucepan. Add wine. Bring to a boil. Add pimento, white sauce, cheese and bread crumbs. Adjust seasonings. Simmer for 20 minutes. Place 6 oysters in each of 6 pie plates filled with rock salt. Spoon sauce over oysters. Bake at 400 degrees for 10 minutes or until lightly browned. Serve immediately.

Pru Bryson
Tifton, Georgia

EGGPLANT-OYSTER CASSEROLE

2 med. eggplant
2   10-oz. cans oysters
1/4 c. butter
1/2 lb. fresh mushrooms, sliced
2 tbsp. chopped shallots
1/2 c. seasoned bread crumbs
Tabasco sauce to taste
2 tbsp. chopped shallots
1/4 c. butter
1/4 c. chopped parsley
3 cloves of garlic, minced
1 tsp. basil
1/2 tsp. thyme
Salt to taste
1/2 c. seasoned bread crumbs
1 c. grated Cheddar cheese
1/2 c. evaporated milk
1/4 c. melted butter

Prick eggplant with fork. Place in baking dish. Bake at 350 degrees for 30 minutes or until very tender; cool. Peel and cut into 1/4-inch slices. Cook oysters in oyster liquid in saucepan until edges curl. Remove oysters; chop finely. Add 1/4 cup butter, mushrooms and 2 table-spoons shallots to oyster liquid in saucepan.

Simmer for 10 minutes. Add oysters, 1/2 cup crumbs and Tabasco sauce; mix well. Saute 2 tablespoons shallots in 1/4 cup butter in skillet for 5 minutes. Add parsley, garlic, basil, thyme, salt and 1/2 cup crumbs; mix well. Alternate layers of eggplant, crumb mixture and oyster mixture in greased shallow 6 x 10-inch baking dish. Sprinkle cheese over top. Drizzle with evaporated milk and 1/4 cup butter. Bake at 350 degrees for 30 minutes. Yield: 4-6 servings

Christy Flynn
Pinehurst, North Carolina

OYSTER PIE

1/4 c. butter, melted
1/4 c. flour
Salt and pepper to taste
2 c. milk
30 saltines, crushed
1 qt. oysters
3 hard-boiled eggs, sliced
1 recipe 1-crust pie pastry

Blend butter and flour in saucepan. Cook until lightly browned. Season with salt and pepper. Stir in milk gradually. Cook until thickened, stirring constantly. Layer cracker crumbs, oysters seasoned with salt and pepper and hard-boiled eggs in 6 x 10-inch baking dish. Pour sauce over layers. Top with pie pastry; cut vents. Bake at 350 degrees for 30 minutes or until brown. Yield: 4 servings.

Pat Wallace
Jacksonville, Florida

OYSTERS ROCKEFELLER

5 tbsp. butter, melted
1/2 c. strained spinach
2 tbsp. minced onion
2 tsp. minced celery
3 tbsp. fine dry crumbs
1/4 tsp. herb blend for fish
1/4 tsp. anchovy paste
1/4 tsp. salt
Pepper to taste
2 doz. oysters on the half shell
Rock salt

Combine all ingredients except oysters and rock salt in bowl; mix well. Arrange oysters in 4 pie plates filled with rock salt. Broil for 5 minutes. Spoon spinach mixture onto oysters. Broil until bubbly. Serve immediately. Yield: 4 servings.

Gwen Schofield
Enid, Oklahoma

EASY SCALLOPED OYSTERS

1 c. bread crumbs
1 c. cracker crumbs
3/4 c. melted butter
2 pt. oysters
6 tbsp. oyster liquid
1/4 c. cream
1/4 tsp. salt
Pepper to taste

Combine bread, cracker crumbs and butter in bowl; mix well. Alternate layers of crumb mixture, oysters, oyster liquid, cream and seasonings in buttered baking dish, ending with crumb mixture. Bake at 450 degrees for 30 minutes. Let stand for 10 minutes before serving. Yield: 10 servings.

Alice S. Burgess
Fayette, West Virginia

SCALLOPED OYSTERS AND MUSHROOMS

1 pt. medium oysters
1/4 lb. mushrooms, sliced
6 tbsp. margarine
3 tbsp. flour
Milk
3 tbsp. chopped parsley
Salt and pepper to taste
1/4 tsp. oregano
1 8-oz. package noodles, cooked
4 hard-boiled eggs, chopped
1 c. bread crumbs

Drain oysters, reserving liquid. Saute mushrooms in margarine in skillet; remove mushrooms. Blend flour into pan drippings. Stir in oyster liquid mixed with enough milk to measure 1 3/4 cups. Add parsley and seasonings. Cook until thickened, stirring constantly. Alternate layers of noodles, chopped eggs, oysters and mushrooms in 9 x 13-inch baking dish. Pour sauce over layers. Top with bread crumbs. Bake at 400 degrees for 15 minutes. Yield: 4-6 servings.

Connie Townswick
Barron, Wisconsin

SCALLOPS AMANDINE

3/4 lb. fresh scallops, thickly sliced
1/3 c. flour
1/4 tsp. salt
2 tbsp. butter
3 tbsp. slivered almonds
2 tbsp. butter
1 tbsp. lemon juice
1 tbsp. minced parsley

Coat scallops with mixture of flour and salt. Saute in 2 tablespoons butter in skillet until golden brown. Remove to warm platter. Saute almonds in 2 tablespoons butter until golden brown. Stir in lemon juice and parsley. Serve over scallops. Yield: 4 servings.

Beth Dawkins
Cheboygan, Michigan

CRUMB-TOPPED SCALLOPS

12 oz. scallops
3/4 c. half and half
1 c. dry bread crumbs
1/2 c. melted butter
2 tsp. celery seed
1 tsp. salt
1/4 tsp. pepper
Paprika

Arrange scallops in greased 9-inch square baking dish. Alternate layers of half and half, bread crumbs mixed with butter, celery seed, salt and pepper over scallops. Sprinkle with paprika. Bake at 375 degrees for 25 minutes or until bubbly. Yield: 4 servings.

Angela Buxton
Poplar Bluff, Missouri

SCALLOPS IN MUSHROOM SAUCE

2 c. sliced mushrooms
1 tbsp. butter
2 10-oz. packages scallops
1 can cream of mushroom soup
1/2 c. sour cream
1 tsp. lemon juice
1 tsp. paprika
1/4 tsp. salt
1/8 tsp. pepper
1/2 c. shredded Cheddar cheese

Saute mushrooms in butter in skillet until tender. Stir in scallops. Cook for 10 minutes; drain. Place scallops and mushrooms in buttered 6 x 10-inch baking dish. Blend remaining ingredients except cheese in bowl. Pour over scallop mixture. Top with cheese. Bake at 400 degrees for 15 to 20 minutes or until bubbly. Yield: 4 servings.

Geraldine Cannon
Shreveport, Louisiana

Seafood

EASY SCALLOP CASSEROLE

1/2 lb. scallops
1/2 lb. haddock, cut into bite-sized pieces
1 can cream of shrimp soup
Buttered bread crumbs

Simmer scallops in a small amount of water in saucepan for 5 minutes; drain. Place with haddock in buttered 2-quart casserole. Pour soup over top. Sprinkle with bread crumbs. Bake at 350 degrees for 30 minutes. Yield: 4-6 servings.

Meredith G. Flemming
East Providence, Rhode Island

FLORIDA GRAPEFRUIT SCALLOPS

1/2 c. oil
1/2 c. Florida grapefruit juice
1/4 c. finely chopped parsley
1 clove of garlic, crushed
1 1/2 tsp. chervil
1/2 tsp. pepper
1 lb. scallops
1/2 c. bread crumbs
1 1/2 c. Florida grapefruit
   sections, chopped
2 tbsp. dry bread crumbs
1 tsp. paprika

Combine oil, grapefruit juice, parsley, garlic, chervil and pepper in bowl; mix well. Add scallops. Marinate in refrigerator for 1 hour or longer. Drain scallops, reserving marinade. Combine scallops and 1/2 cup crumbs; toss to mix. Add grapefruit sections; mix well. Spoon into 4 scallop shells. Sprinkle mixture of 2 tablespoons bread crumbs and paprika over each serving. Drizzle 1 tablespoon reserved marinade over each. Broil 6 inches from heat source for 10 to 12 minutes or until golden brown. Yield: 4 servings.

Photograph for this recipe on this page.

MICROWAVE SCALLOPS AND MUSHROOMS

12 oz. frozen scallops
1/4 lb. fresh mushrooms, sliced
1 sm. onion, sliced
1/2 green pepper, sliced
Salt and pepper to taste

Microwave scallops in covered casserole on High for 3 minutes. Add vegetables. Microwave on High for 8 to 10 minutes. Season with salt and pepper. Yield: 2 servings.

Gillian Edwards
Cairo, Illinois

SCALLOPS VERMICELLI

1 lb. mushrooms, quartered
6 tbsp. unsalted butter
Salt and pepper to taste
6 tbsp. butter
4 shallots, minced
2 cloves of garlic, minced
6 scallions, minced
1 lb. bay scallops
6 tbsp. vermouth
1 tbsp. minced parsley
1 lb. vermicelli
Parmesan cheese

Saute mushrooms in 6 tablespoons butter in skillet. Season with salt and pepper; remove mushrooms. Add 6 tablespoons butter to skillet. Add shallots, garlic and scallions. Saute lightly. Add scallops and vermouth. Cook until heated through. Add parsley and mushrooms. Cook vermicelli in boiling salted water in saucepan for about 5 minutes; drain. Add to scallop mixture. Cook for 3 to 4 minutes or until liquid is absorbed, stirring constantly. Serve with Parmesan cheese. Yield: 4 servings.

Calene Patterson
Casper, Wyoming

SHRIMP AND ARTICHOKE SKILLET

12 oz. shrimp, cooked
1 9-oz. package frozen artichoke hearts
1 7 1/2-oz. can tomatoes, cut up
1/3 c. chopped green onions
2 tbsp. minced parsley
2 tbsp. lemon juice
2 tbsp. dry Sherry (opt.)
1 tbsp. wine vinegar
1/2 tsp. basil
1/2 tsp. marjoram
1/2 tsp. salt

Seafood

Dash of pepper
1/2 c. shredded fontina cheese
1/4 c. Parmesan cheese

Combine first 12 ingredients in skillet. Simmer for 10 minutes or until liquid is reduced. Sprinkle cheeses over top. Serve over hot cooked rice. Yield: 4 servings.

Susie Mills
Durham, North Carolina

ASPARAGUS AND SHRIMP CASSEROLE

2 lg. cans asparagus
2 hard-boiled eggs, sliced
1 sm. can sliced water chestnuts
1 sm. can mushroom pieces
1 sm. can sliced ripe olives
1 lg. can shrimp
1 c. grated cheese
1 can mushroom soup
12 crackers, crushed
1 sm. can onion rings

Layer first 7 ingredients in order listed in buttered 1 1/2-quart casserole. Pour soup blended with 1/2 soup can water over layers. Spread cracker crumbs over top. Bake at 350 degrees for 30 minutes. Arrange onion rings over top. Bake for several minutes longer until onion rings are browned.

Martha Eames
Montclair, New Jersey

SHRIMP CACCIATORE

1/2 c. each minced onion, green pepper
2 cloves of garlic, minced
1/3 c. olive oil
1   20-oz. can tomatoes
1   8-oz. can tomato sauce
1/2 c. red wine
2 tsp. salt
1/4 tsp. pepper
1/2 tsp. allspice
1 bay leaf, crumbled
1/4 tsp. thyme
Dash of cayenne pepper
2 lb. shrimp, cooked

Saute onion, green pepper and garlic in olive oil in skillet until onion is tender. Add remaining ingredients except shrimp. Simmer for 20 minutes. Add shrimp. Heat to serving temperature.

Nelda Emerson
Oakley, Kansas

SHRIMP CURRY

4 c. sliced mushrooms
1 c. finely chopped onions
2 cloves of garlic, crushed
1/4 c. oil
4 med. tomatoes, peeled, chopped
1 tbsp. curry powder
1 tsp. chili powder
Salt and pepper to taste
2 lb. shrimp
2 tbsp. cornstarch
1 c. yogurt
2 c. cooked rice

Saute first 3 ingredients in oil in large skillet for 3 to 5 minutes or until tender. Stir in tomatoes and seasonings. Simmer for 10 to 12 minutes, stirring occasionally. Add shrimp. Cook, covered, for 7 minutes or until shrimp are pink. Dissolve cornstarch in 1 tablespoon water in small bowl. Stir into shrimp mixture. Cook until thickened, stirring constantly; remove from heat. Add yogurt; mix well. Heat to serving temperature. Do not boil. Serve with rice.

Loretta Wilson
Goshen, Indiana

SHRIMP EGG FOO YUNG

2 c. fresh bean sprouts
6 eggs, beaten
3 scallions, finely chopped
1 c. chopped cooked shrimp

Combine all ingredients in bowl; mix well. Pour 1/2 cup at a time into small hot oiled skillet. Brown on both sides. Serve with soy sauce. Yield: 6 servings.

Jodie Harrow
Blankston, Texas

FRENCH-FRIED SHRIMP

1/2 c. flour, sifted
1 tsp. sugar
1/4 tsp. salt
1 egg, beaten
2 lb. shrimp
Oil for deep frying

Sift flour, sugar and salt into bowl. Combine egg and 1/4 cup water in small bowl; beat well. Add to flour mixture; mix until smooth. Dip shrimp into batter. Deep-fry at 375 degrees until golden brown. Drain on paper towels. Serve with soy sauce or tartar sauce.

Tipley Herndon
Salem, Oregon

Seafood

SHRIMP CUSTARD TARTS

1 lb. cooked shrimp, chopped
8 unbaked 4-in. tart shells
4 slices crisp-fried bacon, crumbled
1/2 c. Parmesan cheese
4 eggs, slightly beaten
1 c. instant nonfat dry milk powder
1/2 tsp. thyme
1/2 tsp. hot pepper sauce
3/4 tsp. salt
Paprika

Place shrimp in tart shells. Sprinkle with bacon and cheese. Combine eggs, milk powder, 2 cups water and remaining ingredients except paprika in bowl; mix well. Spoon into tart shells. Sprinkle with paprika. Place shells on baking sheet. Bake, lightly covered with foil, at 450 degrees for 10 minutes. Reduce temperature to 350 degrees. Bake for 10 minutes. Remove foil. Bake for 15 minutes longer or until set.
Yield: 8 servings.

Photograph for this recipe above.

PHOENIX-TAIL SHRIMP

1 tsp. salt
1/8 tsp. pepper
1 tsp. dry Sherry
1 lb. fresh shrimp with tails,
    shelled, butterflied
3/4 c. flour
1/4 c. cornstarch
2 tsp. baking powder
1/2 tsp. salt
Oil for deep frying

Combine salt, pepper and Sherry in bowl. Add shrimp; mix well. Marinate in refrigerator. Combine next 4 ingredients and 3/4 cup cold water in bowl; mix until smooth. Heat oil to 350 de-grees. Add 1 tablespoon hot oil to batter; mix well. Dip shrimp by tail into batter, leaving tail uncovered. Deep-fry 6 or 8 at a time for 2 min-utes or until golden brown; drain. Serve hot with roasted salt and Szechwan peppercorn dip or sweet and sour sauce.

Connie Taylor
Pine Bluff, Arkansas

SHRIMP IN GARLIC SAUCE

2 lb. shrimp
2 tbsp. oil
2 sm. cloves of garlic, minced
1 6-oz. can tomato paste
2 tsp. salt
1/2 tsp. each pepper, basil
1/2 c. chopped onion

Saute shrimp in oil in skillet for 5 minutes or until pink. Add remaining ingredients with 1 cup water; mix well. Simmer until heated through. Yield: 6 servings.

Jobeth Bellows
Joplin, Missouri

SHRIMP A LA GRECQUE

2 onions, chopped
1 clove of garlic, minced
3 tbsp. olive oil
2 2-lb. cans Italian tomatoes
1 can tomato paste
3 doz. shrimp
1 stick butter
3/4 c. ouzo
Chopped parsley
Feta cheese
4 c. hot cooked rice

Saute onions and garlic in olive oil in skillet until tender. Stir in tomatoes and tomato paste. Cook until thickened. Saute shrimp in butter in skillet until pink. Pour ouzo over shrimp; ignite. Add shrimp to tomato sauce. Cook for 5 min-utes. Pour into serving dish. Top with parsley and feta cheese. Serve with rice.
Yield: 4-6 servings.

Tiffany Scholes
Corpus Christi, Texas

ELEGANT SHRIMP WITH PASTA

1/4 c. heavy cream
1 1/2 c. sour cream
1 tbsp. soy sauce
1/2 tsp. Worcestershire sauce

1/2 tsp. dry mustard
1 tsp. dillweed
1/4 tsp. white pepper
1/2 lb. small shrimp
1 lb. fresh pasta, cooked

Combine cream, sour cream and seasonings in saucepan. Heat until very warm. Add shrimp. Cook until shrimp turn pink. Serve over hot pasta. Yield: 4 servings.

Glenda Charles
Wilmington, Delaware

PASTA WITH SHRIMP AND WINE

1 c. chopped onion
2 tbsp. butter
1 tbsp. olive oil
1 c. dry white wine
1 tbsp. instant chicken bouillon
1 tsp. basil
1/2 tsp. salt
1/8 tsp. pepper
12 oz. shrimp
1 c. chopped peeled tomato
10 oz. pasta, cooked
1/4 c. butter, melted
1/2 c. Parmesan cheese
1/2 c. minced parsley

Saute onion in mixture of butter and olive oil in skillet until tender. Do not brown. Add wine, bouillon and seasonings. Simmer until liquid is reduced to 1/3 cup. Add shrimp. Simmer, covered, for 5 minutes. Add tomato. Heat to serving temperature. Toss hot pasta with melted butter, cheese and parsley. Serve shrimp mixture over pasta mixture.

Georgette Clark
Clayton, Missouri

FRIED SHRIMP WITH CURRIED CONCORD DIP

1 c. yogurt
1/2 c. Concord grape jam
2 tsp. lemon juice
1 tsp. horseradish
1/2 tsp. curry powder
1 sm. clove of garlic, minced
1/8 tsp. ginger
1 c. flour
1 tsp. baking powder
1 tsp. salt
1 egg
1 c. milk

1/4 c. oil
1 1/2 lb. fresh shrimp with tails
Flour
Oil for deep frying

Combine yogurt, jam, lemon juice, horseradish, curry powder, garlic and ginger in bowl; mix well. Chill until serving time. Combine flour, baking powder, salt, egg, milk and 1/4 cup oil. Beat until smooth. Dry shrimp thoroughly. Dust lightly with flour. Dip 1 at a time into batter; shake off excess batter. Deep-fry at 375 degrees for 4 minutes or until golden brown. Drain on paper towels. Serve with sauce.

Photograph for this recipe on page 3.

GOLDEN SHRIMP PUFF

10 slices white bread, crusts trimmed, cubed
6 eggs, beaten
3 c. milk
3 tbsp. minced parsley
3/4 tsp. dry mustard
1/2 tsp. salt
2 c. shredded American cheese
2 c. chopped shrimp

Spread bread cubes in greased 9 x 13-inch baking dish. Combine eggs with next 4 ingredients; beat well. Stir in cheese and shrimp. Pour over bread cubes. Bake at 325 degrees for 1 hour or until knive inserted in center comes out clean.

Janet Scott
Andover, Maryland

SHRIMP WITH SPAGHETTI AND MUSHROOMS

2 cloves of garlic, minced
6 lg. mushrooms, chopped
1 lb. shrimp, chopped
1/2 c. butter
1 tsp. salt
1/4 tsp. pepper
1 8-oz. package spaghetti, cooked
1/4 c. Parmesan cheese

Saute garlic, mushrooms and shrimp in butter in large skillet over low heat for 5 minutes or until shrimp turn pink. Sprinkle with seasonings. Add spaghetti and cheese; toss gently. Cook until heated through. Garnish with chopped parsley. Serve with additional cheese.

Shari Godwin
DeGraff, Ohio

Seafood

ORIENTAL SHRIMP AND RICE CASSEROLE

1 lb. shrimp
2 tbsp. butter
2 c. chopped celery
2 c. chopped onion
6 stalks bok choy, chopped
1 pkg. frozen Chinese vegetables
1 1/2 c. chicken broth
1/4 c. soy sauce
2 tbsp. cornstarch
3 c. cooked rice

Saute shrimp in butter in skillet until pink. Add next 3 ingredients. Cook for 3 minutes. Stir in Chinese vegetables. Simmer, covered, for several minutes. Combine broth, soy sauce and cornstarch in small bowl. Pour over vegetable mixture. Cook until thickened, stirring constantly. Place rice in casserole. Pour shrimp mixture over top. Bake at 350 degrees for 30 minutes.

Vesta Deal
White Plains, New York

QUICK SHRIMP AND RICE

3 c. cooked shrimp
1/4 c. butter
1 can cream of shrimp soup
1 c. milk
2 tbsp. lemon juice

Saute shrimp in 1/4 cup butter in skillet until heated through. Add remaining ingredients; mix well. Heat to serving temperature. Serve over hot cooked rice. Yield: 4 servings.

Debbie Hobough
Braman, Oklahoma

SHRIMP ROCKEFELLER

1 1/3 c. cooked spinach, chopped
6 slices crisp-fried bacon, crumbled
1 c. minced onion
3 tbsp. minced parsley
2 bay leaves, crumbled
1/2 tsp. celery salt
1/2 c. butter
1/2 c. fine dry bread crumbs
1 lb. shrimp, cooked

Combine spinach, bacon, onion, parsley, bay leaves and celery salt in bowl; mix well. Saute in butter in skillet until heated through, stirring constantly. Stir in bread crumbs. Cook for 1 minute. Place 2/3 of the shrimp in greased 1-cup ramekins. Spoon spinach mixture over shrimp. Arrange remaining shrimp on top. Bake at 400 degrees for 5 minutes or until heated through. Yield: 4 servings.

Photograph for this recipe below.

SKEWERED SHRIMP AND MUSHROOMS

1/3 c. olive oil
1/3 c. oil
3 tbsp. lemon juice
1 tbsp. minced parsley
1 clove of garlic, minced
1/4 tsp. salt
Dash of cayenne pepper
1 lb. shrimp
16 lg. fresh mushroom caps

Combine first 7 ingredients in bowl; mix well. Add shrimp and mushrooms. Marinate in refrigerator for 2 hours or longer, stirring occasionally. Drain, reserving marinade. Thread shrimp and mushrooms alternately onto skewers. Place on rack in broiler pan. Broil 5 inches from heat source for 6 minutes or until shrimp turn pink, turning once and basting with reserved marinade several times. Brush with marinade just before serving. Yield: 4 servings.

Susan Prinsen
Atlanta, Georgia

Seafood

SHRIMP TEMPURA

1 egg, beaten
1 c. sifted flour
1 tsp. salt
1 lb. fresh shrimp with tails, butterflied
1 sm. sweet potato, peeled, thinly sliced
Oil for deep frying
1/4 lb. fresh green beans,
    sliced lengthwise
3 carrots, cut into thin 2-in. long strips
1 c. beef bouillon
3 tbsp. soy sauce
1 tbsp. sugar
1 tbsp. Sherry

Combine egg and 2/3 cup water. Add flour and salt gradually, beating until smooth. Dip shrimp and sweet potato into batter to coat lightly. Deep-fry for 2 to 3 minutes or until golden brown. Dip green beans, several at a time, into batter; repeat with carrot strips. Fry vegetable clusters in deep hot oil until golden brown. Combine remaining ingredients in small saucepan. Bring to a boil. Serve with fried shrimp and vegetables.

Cecilia Holcomb
Garber, Oklahoma

BREADED SQUID

2 lb. squid
1 egg, beaten
1/4 c. milk
1 c. fine dry bread crumbs
1/2 tsp. salt
1/4 tsp. pepper
1/4 to 1/3 c. flour
1/4 c. butter
Tomato sauce

Remove and discard head and tentacles from squid; rinse well inside and out. Slice into 1/2-inch rings. Rinse and pat dry. Beat egg with milk. Combine crumbs, salt and pepper. Coat rings with flour. Dip in egg mixture and roll in crumb mixture to coat. Cook in butter in skillet for 2 minutes on each side. Serve with tomato sauce.

Octavia Lyons
Daytona Beach, Florida

COQUILLE ST. JACQUES

1/4 c. melted butter
3 tbsp. flour
1 tsp. salt
1/8 tsp. white pepper
2 c. light cream
1/4 c. finely chopped onion
2 tbsp. butter
1/2 lb. scallops, sliced
1/2 c. sliced mushrooms
3/4 lb. cooked shrimp
1/2 lb. crab meat
2 tbsp. Sherry
5 tbsp. bread crumbs

Blend 1/4 cup butter with flour, salt and white pepper in skillet. Stir in cream gradually. Simmer until smooth and thickened, stirring constantly. Saute onion in 2 tablespoons butter in small skillet. Add scallops. Saute for 5 minutes; remove onion and scallops. Add mushrooms. Saute for 3 minutes. Combine onion, scallops, mushrooms, shrimp, crab meat, Sherry and sauce; mix lightly Spoon into buttered baking shells; sprinkle with bread crumbs. Bake at 400 degrees for 15 minutes or until heated through. Yield: 4 servings.

Ruby Gentry
Pleasant Hill, California

FETTUCINI WITH SEAFOOD SAUCE

1 lb. fettucini
A small amount of oil
12 oysters
1/2 lb. scallops
1/2 lb. shelled shrimp
1 pt. heavy cream
1/2 c. grated cheese
1/2 stick butter
2 egg yolks, beaten
1/2 tsp. chopped garlic
Salt and white pepper to taste
Nutmeg to taste
2 tomatoes, peeled, chopped, cooked
1/4 lb. snow peas, steamed

Cook fettucini in boiling salted water in large saucepan until just tender; drain. Rinse with cold water. Mix in oil. Cook oysters, scallops and shrimp in skillet over low heat for 3 minutes; drain. Bring cream to a boil in large saucepan. Simmer for 3 minutes; remove from heat. Stir in cheese and butter. Stir a small amount of hot mixture into egg yolks; stir egg yolks into hot mixture. Add garlic, salt, white pepper, nutmeg, tomatoes and snow peas; mix well. Combine fettucini with oysters, scallops and shrimp on large serving platter. Cover with hot sauce. Serve immediately. Yield: 4 servings.

Betty Rowe
Santa Fe, New Mexico

Seafood

HOT SEAFOOD SALAD

1 lb. crab meat
1 lb. cooked shrimp
1 lb. lobster
2 c. mayonnaise
1/4 c. chopped onion
1/2 c. chopped green pepper
1 1/2 c. chopped celery
1/2 tsp. salt
1 tbsp. Worcestershire sauce
2 c. crushed potato chips
Paprika

Combine seafood, mayonnaise, vegetables and seasonings in bowl; mix well. Spoon into buttered 3-quart casserole. Top with potato chips. Sprinkle with paprika. Bake at 400 degrees for 20 to 25 minutes or until bubbly. Serve over hot cooked rice. Yield: 12 servings.

Virginia Lamore
Warren, Michigan

MEDITERRANEAN SEAFOOD

4 cloves of garlic, chopped
1/2 c. olive oil
12 shrimp in shells
3 lobster tails, cut into 1-in. pieces
1 c. white vermouth
2 c. Italian tomatoes, drained
2 bay leaves
1/2 tsp. oregano
Salt and pepper to taste
12 clams, scrubbed
4 c. cooked rice

Saute garlic in olive oil in skillet over medium-high heat for 1 minute. Add shrimp and lobster. Saute for 1 minute. Add vermouth. Simmer for 2 to 3 minutes. Remove lobster and shrimp; set aside. Add tomatoes, bay leaves, oregano, salt, pepper and clams. Simmer for 2 to 4 minutes or until clams open. Discard bay leaves. Add lobster and shrimp. Heat to serving temperature. Spoon over hot rice in serving bowl. Garnish with parsley. Yield: 6 servings.

Marilyn McCoy
Bennington, Vermont

SEAFOOD BELMONT

6 tbsp. butter, melted
1/2 c. flour
2 c. milk
1 c. heavy cream
1/2 tsp. salt
1/4 tsp. cayenne pepper
3 tbsp. catsup
1 tbsp. Worcestershire sauce
1 1/2 tbsp. lemon juice
1/4 c. dry Sherry
1 c. grated sharp Cheddar cheese
10 artichoke hearts, sliced
1 lb. crab meat
2 lb. large shrimp, cooked
1 c. buttered bread crumbs

Blend butter and flour in saucepan. Add milk and cream gradually. Cook until thickened, stirring constantly; remove from heat. Add seasonings, Sherry and cheese; mix well. Layer sauce, artichokes, crab and shrimp in greased baking shells, beginning and ending with sauce. Top with crumbs. Bake at 350 degrees for 20 minutes or until bubbly. Broil until browned. Yield: 8-10 servings.

Dianne Havertine
Wheaton, Illinois

SEAFOOD LASAGNA

1 can cream of shrimp soup
1 can crab meat
1 can tiny shrimp
1 c. cream-style cottage cheese
1 8-oz. package cream cheese, softened
1 c. shredded Cheddar cheese
1 onion, finely chopped
1 egg
1 tsp. basil
Salt and pepper to taste
8 oz. lasagna noodles, cooked
2 tomatoes, sliced
1/2 c. Parmesan cheese

Combine soup, crab meat and shrimp in saucepan. Heat until bubbly. Combine cottage cheese, cream cheese, Cheddar cheese, onion, egg and seasonings in bowl; mix well. Layer 1/3 of the noodles and half the cheese mixture in greased 9 x 13-inch baking dish. Layer half the remaining noodles and all the soup mixture on top. Layer remaining noodles, cheese mixture and tomato slices on top. Bake at 350 degrees for 45 minutes. Sprinkle with Parmesan cheese. Bake for 15 minutes longer.

Myrna Johnson
Ashland, Kentucky

SHRIMP AND SCALLOPS GRUYERE

1 lb. fresh scallops
1 tsp. lemon juice
1/2 lb. mushrooms, sliced
2 tbsp. chopped green pepper

Seafood

2 tbsp. butter
3/4 c. flour
3/4 c. melted butter
3 c. milk
12 oz. Gruyere cheese, cubed
1/2 c. dry white wine
1/4 tsp. garlic powder
1/4 tsp. white pepper
1/4 tsp. dry mustard
2 tsp. lemon juice
2 tsp. tomato paste
1 lb. cooked shrimp

Poach scallops in salted water with 1 teaspoon lemon juice in saucepan for 10 minutes; drain. Saute mushrooms and green pepper in 2 tablespoons butter in skillet until tender; set aside. Combine flour and 3/4 cup melted butter in double boiler. Stir in milk gradually. Cook until thickened, stirring constantly. Add cheese. Cook until cheese is melted, stirring constantly. Stir in wine. Add seasonings, 2 teaspoons lemon juice, tomato paste and sauteed vegetables; mix well. Add scallops and shrimp; mix well. Cook over low heat for 10 to 15 minutes. Serve over hot cooked rice. Yield: 6-8 servings.

Nora Broome
Steamboat Springs, Colorado

GULF SHRIMP AND CRAB AU GRATIN

6 tbsp. melted butter
6 tbsp. flour
3 c. milk
1 lb. lump crab meat
1 lb. shrimp, cooked
3 tbsp. butter
3 oz. sharp cheese, shredded
Salt and pepper to taste
1/2 c. cracker crumbs
1/2 c. Romano cheese
1 tbsp. paprika
3 tbsp. butter

Blend 6 tablespoons melted butter and flour in medium saucepan. Cook for 1 minute. Stir in milk. Cook until thickened, stirring constantly. Saute crab meat and shrimp in 3 tablespoons butter in saucepan. Add white sauce, sharp cheese, salt and pepper. Cook until heated through, stirring constantly. Spoon into greased casserole. Top with cracker crumbs, Romano cheese and paprika. Dot with 3 tablespoons butter. Bake at 350 degrees until golden brown. Yield 6 servings.

Laurena Dole
Clarksburg, West Virginia

SHRIMP AND LOBSTER FIESTA

1/2 c. chopped onion
1 clove of garlic, minced
1 tbsp. butter
1 can cream of mushroom soup
2 tbsp. dry white wine
1 c. chopped cooked shrimp
1/2 c. tomatoes, drained
3 tbsp. chopped parsley
1/8 tsp. marjoram
2 c. cooked noodles
2 lobster tails, cooked, sliced
1 tbsp. melted butter

Saute onion and garlic in butter in skillet until tender. Combine with 1/2 cup water and remaining ingredients except lobster and melted butter in greased 1 1/2-quart casserole; mix well. Arrange lobster on top. Brush with melted butter. Bake at 350 degrees for 30 minutes or until bubbly. Yield: 4 servings.

Doreen Kirk
Doniphan, Missouri

MOBY DICK'S DELIGHT

1 1/2 lb. cooked shrimp
1 c. crab meat
1 can sliced water chestnuts, drained
1/2 c. chopped pimento
3 tbsp. chopped onion
3 tbsp. chopped green pepper
1   4-oz. can sliced mushrooms, drained
3 tbsp. butter
2 tbsp. flour
1 tsp. each salt and pepper
2 tbsp. melted butter
1/2 c. dry Sherry
3 c. light cream
1   8-oz. package egg noodles,
    cooked, drained

Combine shrimp, crab meat, water chestnuts and pimento in bowl; mix well. Saute onion, green pepper and mushrooms in 3 tablespoons butter in skillet for 5 minutes. Add to shrimp mixture; mix well. Blend flour, salt and pepper with melted butter in saucepan. Cook for 1 minute; remove from heat. Add Sherry and cream; mix well. Cook over medium heat until thickened, stirring constantly. Add seafood mixture; mix well. Fold in noodles. Spoon into greased baking dish. Bake at 400 degrees for 20 minutes or until bubbly. Yield: 6-8 servings.

Linda Dobbins Laumann
Chesapeake, Maryland

Herb and Spice Chart

Allspice, a pungent, aromatic spice, comes in whole or powdered form. It is excellent in marinades, particularly in game marinade, or curries.

Basil can be chopped and added to cold poultry salads. If your recipe calls for tomatoes or tomato sauce, add a touch of basil to bring out a rich flavor.

Bay leaf, the basis of many French seasonings, is nice added to soups, stews, marinades and stuffings.

Bouquet garni, a must in many Creole cuisine recipes, is a bundle of herbs, spices and bay leaf tied together and added to soups, stews or sauces.

Celery seed, from wild celery rather than our domestic celery, adds pleasant flavor to bouillon or stock.

Chervil is one of the traditional *fines herbes* used in French-derived cooking. (The others are tarragon, parsley and chive.) It is particularly good in omelets or soups.

Chives, available fresh, dried or frozen, can be substituted for raw onion in any poultry recipe.

Cinnamon, ground from the bark of the cinnamon tree, is important in preparing desserts as well as savory dishes.

Coriander adds an unusual flavor to soups, stews, chili dishes, curries and some desserts.

Cumin is a staple spice in Mexican cooking. To use, rub seeds together and let them fall into the dish just before serving. Cumin also comes in powdered form.

Garlic, one of the oldest herbs in the world, must be carefully handled. When cooking, do not simmer until black or it will create an offensive odor. For best results, press or crush garlic clove against the kitchen table; then cook. If your recipe calls for sliced garlic, substitute grated or pressed garlic. The flavor will improve noticeably.

Marjoram is an aromatic herb of the mint family. It is good in soups, sauces, stuffings and stews.

Mustard (dry) brings a sharp bite to sauces. Sprinkle just a touch over roast chicken for a delightful flavor treat.

Oregano is a staple herb in Italian, Spanish and Mexican cuisines. It is very good in dishes with a tomato foundation; it adds an excellent savory taste.

Paprika, a mild pepper, adds color to many dishes, and it is especially attractive with poultry. The very best paprika is imported from Hungary — there is a world of difference between it and the supermarket variety.

Rosemary, a tasty herb, is an important seasoning in stuffing for duck, partridge and capon.

Sage, the perennial favorite with all kinds of poultry, adds flavor to stuffings. It is particularly good with goose.

Tarragon, one of the *fines herbes,* has wonderful flavor and goes well with all poultry dishes except one; it is too pungent for poultry soups.

Thyme is used in combination with bay leaf in soups and stews.

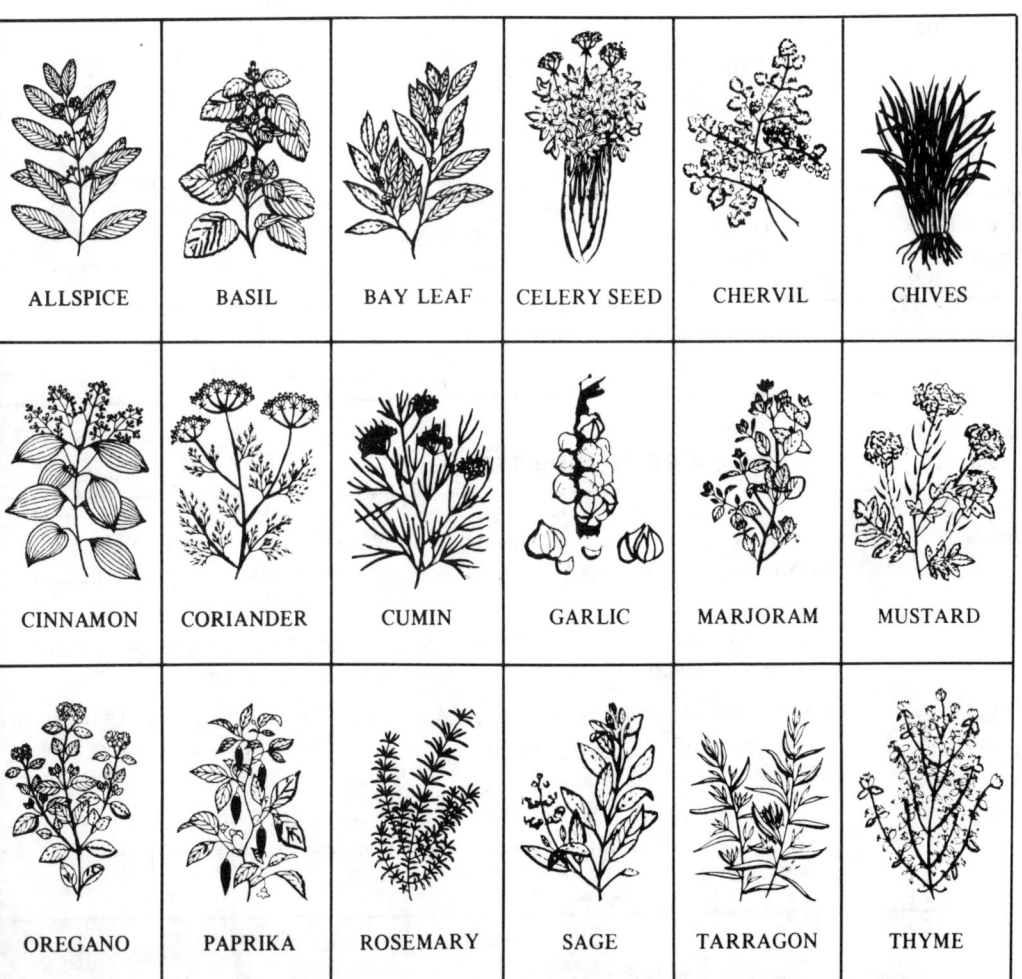

ALLSPICE	BASIL	BAY LEAF	CELERY SEED	CHERVIL	CHIVES
CINNAMON	CORIANDER	CUMIN	GARLIC	MARJORAM	MUSTARD
OREGANO	PAPRIKA	ROSEMARY	SAGE	TARRAGON	THYME

Charts

Cheese Chart

HOW MUCH TO BUY

If a recipe calls for 2 1/2 cups of Cheddar cheese, how much do you buy? If the recipe calls for 3 cups of cottage cheese, will one carton be enough? Use this table when buying cheese for cooking.

BUY:	IF YOU NEED:			
	Cottage Cheese	Shredded	Grated	Crumbled
3/4 ounce			1/4 cup	
1 ounce		1/4 cup	1/3 cup	1/4 cup
1 1/2 ounces			1/2 cup	
2 ounces	1/4 cup	1/2 cup	2/3 cup	1/2 cup
2 1/4 ounces			3/4 cup	
3 ounces		3/4 cup	1 cup	3/4 cup
4 ounces	1/2 cup	1 cup	1 1/3 cups	1 cup
8 ounces	1 cup	2 cups	2 2/3 cups	2 cups
12 ounces	1 1/2 cups	3 cups	4 cups	3 cups
1 pound	2 cups	4 cups		4 cups

CHEESE CHART

NATURAL CHEESE	CHARACTERISTICS AND USES
Bel Paese	A soft cheese often used in cooking to replace mozzarella. Although it is an Italian cheese, there is a very good American version bearing the same name that is made in Wisconsin.
Blue	A crumbly and sharp-flavored soft dessert cheese that is white and contains blue mold. French blue cheese is referred to as "bleu cheese."
Brie	A soft, creamy dessert cheese ranked as one of the world's great cheeses. It should be served at room temperature. At room temperature, good Brie is almost always runny.
Camembert	A soft, creamy, rich dessert cheese that is another of the world's great cheeses. Camembert that is shrunken in appearance or smells like ammonia is past its prime.

NATURAL CHEESE	CHARACTERISTICS AND USES
Cheddar	A variety of hard cheese that is the most popular American cheese. Cheddar is sold as mild, mellow, or sharp cheese. Mild has aged 2-3 months; mellow from 6-9 months; and sharp, from 12-15 months. Excellent for eating or cooking.
Cottage	The large or small drained curd of soured whole or skim milk. One of the few soft cheeses suitable for cooking.
Cream	An unripened American soft cheese that is popular for desserts. Like cottage cheese, cream cheese is a soft cheese suitable for cooking.
Edam	A mild, semihard cheese. It was originally Dutch cheese that now has several American versions. It has a bright red exterior rind and pale gold interior. Edam is primarily an eating cheese.
Feta	The most popular of Greek cheeses. White and crumbly, it has a unique flavor that is perfect for Hellenic cuisine.
Gorgonzola	A white and blue-veined Italian pressed cheese that may range from soft (very young) to semihard (aged). It is used in cooking, for desserts, or in sandwiches. An American gorgonzola is made in Wisconsin.
Gouda	Like gorgonzola, the mild-flavored gouda cheese becomes firmer with age. It was originally a Dutch cheese, that now has several American versions. Gouda is a popular dessert cheese.
Monterey	Also known as Monterey Jack, this California cheese is of two types: a semihard cheese and a hard cheese. Both are good cooking cheeses.
Mozzarella	A semisoft white cheese popular in Italian dishes. There are American versions but they lack the flavor of the Italian varieties.
Parmesan	A staple hard cheese of Italian cookery. American Parmesans, sold already grated, have only a fraction of the flavor of the original, ungrated cheese.
Provolone	An Italian hard cheese that has a smoky flavor and is used primarily for appetizers or sandwiches. The American version has little of the flavor of the Italian cheese.
Ricotta	An Italian cottage-type cheese. American cottage cheese can be sutstituted in almost every recipe calling for ricotta.
Romano	A very hard Italian cheese grated like Parmesan and used for cooking. There is also an American Romano.
Roquefort	A soft dessert cheese that is white with a characteristic blue veining. The veining comes from the penicillin mold that gives this cheese its sharp flavor.
Swiss	The common United States term for any of the Emmentaler or Gruyere cheeses. Used in cooking. (Not to be confused with the process cheese of the same name.)
Touloumisso	A spicy Greek cheese that is very good.

Charts

Equivalent Chart

	WHEN RECIPE CALLS FOR:	YOU NEED:
Cereal & Bread	1 c. soft bread crumbs	2 slices
	1 c. fine dry bread crumbs	4-5 slices
	1 c. small bread cubes	2 slices
	1 c. fine cracker crumbs	24 saltines
	1 c. crushed cornflakes	3 c. uncrushed
	4 c. cooked macaroni	1 8-oz. package
	3 1/2 c. cooked rice	1 c. uncooked
Dairy	1 c. freshly grated cheese	1/4 lb.
	1 c. cottage cheese or sour cream	1 8-oz. carton
	2/3 c. evaporated milk	1 sm. can
	1 2/3 c. evaporated milk	1 tall can
Vegetables & Meat	4 c. diced cooked chicken	1 5-lb. chicken
	4 c. sliced or diced raw potatoes	4 medium
	1 c. chopped onion	1 large
	2 c. canned tomatoes	1 16-oz. can
	1 c. grated carrot	1 large
	1 4-oz. can mushrooms	1/2 lb. fresh
Fruit	4 c. sliced or chopped apples	4 medium
	2 c. pitted cherries	4 c. unpitted
	3 to 4 tbsp. lemon juice plus 1 tsp. grated rind	1 lemon
	1/3 c. orange juice plus 2 tsp. grated rind	1 orange
	4 c. cranberries	1 lb.
	3 c. shredded coconut	1/2 lb.
	4 c. sliced peaches	8 medium
	2 c. pitted prunes	1 12-oz. package
	3 c. raisins	1 15-oz. package

COMMON EQUIVALENTS

1 tbsp. = 3 tsp.	4 qt. = 1 gal.
2 tbsp. = 1 oz.	6 1/2 to 8-oz. can = 1 c.
4 tbsp. = 1/4 c.	10 1/2 to 12-oz. can = 1 1/4 c.
5 tbsp. + 1 tsp. = 1/3 c.	14 to 16-oz. can (No. 300) = 1 3/4 c.
8 tbsp = 1/2 c.	16 to 17-oz. can (No. 303) = 2 c.
12 tbsp. = 3/4 c.	1-lb. 4-oz. can or 1-pt. 2-oz. can (No. 2) = 2 1/2 c.
16 tbsp. = 1 c.	1-lb. 13-oz can (No. 2 1/2) = 3 1/2 c.
1 c. = 8 oz. or 1/2 pt.	3-lb. 3-oz. can or 46-oz. can or 1-qt. 14-oz. can = 5 3/4 c.
4 c. = 1 qt.	6 1/2-lb. or 7-lb. 5-oz. can (No. 10) = 12 to 13 c.

Index

CHICKEN

almond
 casserole 41
  overnight 43
amandine, crusty 38
and biscuits casserole 39
and dressing with giblet gravy 47
and garden vegetables casserole 26
arroz con pollo 29
artichoke casserole 38
asparagus dinner 38
baked
 crunchy 27
 Parmesan, easy 28
barbecued
 blue ribbon 30
 oven-barbecued 26
 sauce 30
breasts
 a la Russe 16
 and artichoke hearts 16
 and crab duet 40
 and peppers, skillet 25
 apple-spiced 21
 barbecued 21
 Bombay chicken 19
 cashew 24
 chalupas 16
 cheesy 22
 chow mein 25
 company chicken 17
 cordon bleu
  sour cream 20
  supreme 20
 crab-stuffed 21
 curried 19
 divan, easy 39
 elegante 18
 enchiladas verde 47
 ginger 25
 island-style 22
 Kiev 21
 lemonade 18
 little fingers 17
 Milano 17
 mozzarella 17
 paella 22
 patio chicken 23
 peanut butter chicken, grilled 31
 piccata 23

plum-glazed, and rice 23
quick-step 17
Reuben, baked 18
rolled, with country ham and rice . . . 20
saltimbocca 18
Sunday chicken 19
super chicken 18
sweet and sour, stir fry 24
taco chicken 44
Tahitian chicken 19
Waikiki Beach 20
with almond-olive sauce 22
with spaghetti 24
with wild rice 19
broccoli casserole, favorite 43
cacciatore 31
cheesy casserole 38
chicken livers
 and mushrooms 37
 casserole 37
 party 38
chicken wiggly 48
chili, walnut 46
chingalingas 46
chow mein 32
confetti 31
coq au vin 25
country chicken, one-pot 34
creamed, with baked rice squares 42
crepes 46
Crock·Pot 32
croquettes 47
curried chicken casserole 39
curry, easy 32
easy casserole 30
enchilada casserole, layered 44
fried
 curried 33
 different 32
 oven-fried
  sour cream 27
  spicy 28
 saucy 32
 sesame-fried 28
golden peachy 27
gourmet 26
grilled
 chicken breasts, barbecued 21
 Hawaiian chicken 30

Index

lemon-grilled 31
peanut butter chicken 31
ruby-glazed 31
jambalaya 28
macaroni overnight casserole 40
Marengo 33
Mexican casserole, cheesy 44
microwave
Parmesan chicken 34
moist and crispy 27
Monterey 44
mosaic 34
orange chicken 29
delight 26
Parmesan, microwave 34
Pepsi chicken 34
pie
chicken dinner pie 45
potpie, quick 27
with vegetables 45
prune saute 33
quick and easy casserole 43
rice casseroles
brown rice 43
dilled 42
oriental 41
wild rice 42
roll, Greek 30
rose 23
salad, see Salads
sauce for barbecue chicken 30
saucy chicken 24
savory casserole 40
Singapore chicken 34
soup, see Soups
sour cream squares 40
Spanish chicken 29
stack-up dinner, Japanese 48
stew, see Stews
tarragon chicken 34
tarts 41
tetrazzini
almond 46
creamy 46
thighs
pilaf, saffron 28
with apricot sauce, golden 29
three-cheese bake 41
whole chickens
Bengali chicken with
black-eyed peas 37

roast
cherry-glazed 36
with butternut squash 36
with dilled stuffing 36
with herbs 35
slow and easy 35
spicy baked 35
stuffed with spinach dressing 36
with cashews, casserole 39
with eggplant casserole 43

Chowder see Soups

CORNISH GAME HENS
a la Bourbon 56
baked 54
glazed 54
mandarin 56
roast
Spanish-roasted 56
with orange stuffing 55
with blueberries 56
with herbed rice 55
with honeyed rice stuffing 55
with sesame rice 56

DOVE
breasts
and wild rice dressing 54
braised 54
smothered 54

DUCK
baked
honey-baked, with
mushroom sauce 60
in sweet and sour sauce 61
breasts, charcoal-broiled 58
cajun duck 58
duckling
canard Concorde 57
fruit-stuffed, with lemon glaze 58
quarters with
pineapple-orange sauce 59
Sherried spiced 60
with old-fashioned apricot sauce 57
plum good duck 59
roast, with citrus garnish 59
stroganoff 60
wine-spiced 60
with avocado-orange sauce 58
with Brandied peaches 57
with orange stuffing 61
with wine sauce 60

Index

FISH
albacore
  broiled 76
  fresh albacore with tomato sauce ... 76
bass
  sea bass, spiced 76
  striped bass, easy bake 76
catfish
  barbecued 77
  fried 77
  in beer batter 77
cod
  baked, with vegetable sauce 78
  cutlets Kiev 77
fish fillets
  and chips..................... 92
  broiled 92
  citrus-marinated 92
  cook's choice seafood 92
  elegante 93
  fiesta, microwave 94
  fisherman's delight 93
  fish plaki 95
  Florentine 93
  jambalaya 93
  Mediterranean, baked 92
  oven-fried
    easy 94
    sunshine 94
  pan-fried 94
  Parmesan 95
  pasta with seafood sauce 95
  poached 96
  rosy fillets, microwave 94
  seafood creole 96
  seafood enchiladas 96
  vegetable medley, quick 96
  with lemon spinach, microwave 94
flounder
  fillets
    and asparagus rolls 78
    baked, in wine sauce 78
    creole 78
    rosemary, microwave 78
    saucy 78
    steamed 79
    vegetable casserole 79
    with spinach-ricotta filling 79
grouper
  fillets, baked 80

haddock
  fillets
    baked, with
      lemon-mushroom sauce 80
    creamy baked 80
    saucy baked 80
    seafood teriyaki 80
halibut
  foil-baked 81
  with wine-mushroom sauce 81
herring
  smoked 81
microwave
  fish fillets
    fiesta 94
    rosy fillets 94
    vegetable medley 96
    with lemon spinach 94
  flounder rosemary 78
pompano
  grilled 81
red snapper
  grilled 86
  Key lime 86
  stuffed 86
salmon
  crepes, party 82
  croquettes 82
  Florentine 83
  macaroni casserole 82
  puff 83
  quiche 83
  Romanoff 84
  salad loaf 83
  steaks, poached 84
  whole salmon
    baked, lemony 82
    stuffed
      baked 84
      seafood-stuffed 84
    with sour cream, baked 82
sardines
  omelets, Spanish 85
sole
  fillets
    Florentine 87
    San Francisco sole 86
    Spanish 87
    with dill sauce 87
Spanish mackerel
  fillets, broiled 81

Index

torsk
   parsley-buttered 88
trout
   baked 85
   barbecued 85
   crispy fried rainbow trout 85
   fillets, crisp 86
   meuniere 86
   southern-grilled 85
tuna
   Aegean casserole 88
   au gratin 92
   cheesy tuna and rice muffinettes 88
   creamy casserole 88
   crepes 89
   divan 89
   gourmet casserole 89
   loaf 90
   macaroni casserole 90
   noodle
      crispy 90
      Newburg 90
   quiche 90
   quick casserole 89
   rice casserole 91
   see albacore
   souffle, easy 91
   toasty casserole 91
   tuna express 91
turbot
   spicy broiled 88

GOOSE
baked 61
breasts
   cacciatore 62
   Stillwater goose breast 61
Christmas goose 62
stuffed, golden 62

Grouse
roasted, with wine sauce 62

JAMBALAYA
chicken 28
company 71
crab 101
creole 71
fish fillet 93
shrimp, microwave 71

Partridge
huntsman-style 63
with artichoke hearts 63

PHEASANT
and vegetables 6
baked, with oyster dressing 6
barley casserole 6
in wine and cream 6
roast, with wild rice 6
spit-roasted 6
supreme 6
with nutted rice 6

Quail
baked in mushroom sauce 6
Sherried 6
sour cream 6

SALADS
chicken
   crunchy 1
   curry 1
   flying farmer chicken salad 1
   hot salads
      crunchy 4
      favorite 4
      with walnuts 4
   luncheon salad 1
   royale 1
crab
   macaroni 7
   northwest crab salad bowl 74
lobster
   salad of the states 74
seafood
   hot 114
   supreme 74
shrimp, New Orleans 7
tuna
   Coronado tuna salad 7
   green pea 7
   macaroni 7
   tasty 7

SANDWICHES
clam rolls, toasted 7
crab
   baked 7
   cheesy crab buns 7
   muffins 7
shrimp 7
tuna
   bunwiches 7
   cheesies 7

Index

SHELLFISH

clams
    fritters, New England 96
    in wine 98
    linguine
        special 97
        with little neck clams 97
    Mediterranean seafood 114
    quahogs, baked stuffed 99
    shells in red clam sauce 97
    souffle 98
    spaghetti
        with clam-tomato sauce 98
        with mushroom-clam sauce 98
    stuffed clams oregano 98
crab
    and gulf shrimp au gratin 115
    blue crabs
        hard-shell, boiled 100
    coquille St. Jacques 113
    delicious casserole 100
    deviled 99
    Dungeness crabs, boiled 99
    imperial
        easy 100
        Sherried .101
    individual casseroles 100
    jambalaya .101
    Moby Dick's delight 115
    rice casserole 100
    seafood Belmont 114
    seafood lasagna 114
    Sherried crab and artichokes 99
    tipsy casserole 101
frog legs Gruyere 101
lobster
    and shrimp fiesta 115
    lobster tails
        and potatoes Normande 104
        broiled .102
        Cantonese lobster 102
        chop suey 102
        Coral Bay lobster 103
        crepes 103
        fried, with fondue 103
        in pasta shells 104
        Mediterranean seafood 114
        mushroom casserole 102
        nuggets .104
        thermidor 104
    Newburg supreme 104

microwave
    scallops and mushrooms 108
    shrimp creole, easy 69
mussels delight 105
oysters
    Bienville 106
    Botany Bay oysters 105
    casino 105
    deviled 105
    eggplant casserole 106
    pie 106
    Rockefeller .106
    scalloped
        and mushrooms 107
        easy 107
    seafood sauce with fettucini 113
scallops
    amandine .107
    and mushrooms, microwave 108
    and shrimp Gruyere 114
    coquille St. Jacques 113
    crumb-topped 107
    easy casserole 108
    Florida grapefruit scallops 108
    in mushroom sauce 107
    seafood sauce with fettucini 113
    vermicelli .108
shrimp
    a la Grecque 110
    and artichoke skillet 108
    and asparagus casserole 109
    and crab au gratin 115
    and lobster fiesta 115
    and mushrooms, skewered 112
    and rice
        oriental .112
        quick 112
    and scallops Gruyere 114
    and wine with pasta 111
    cacciatore .109
    coquille St. Jacques 113
    creole
        Louisianne 69
        microwave, easy 69
    curry 109
    custard tarts 110
    egg foo yung 109
    fried
        French-fried 109
        Phoenix-tail shrimp 110
        with curried Concard dip 111

Index

in garlic sauce 110
Mediterranean seafood 114
Moby Dick's delight 115
puff, golden 111
Rockefeller 112
seafood Belmont 114
seafood lasagna 114
seafood sauce with fettucini 113
tempura 113
with pasta, elegant 110
with spaghetti and mushrooms 111
squid, breaded 113

SOUPS
chicken
chicken gizzard, chunky 14
chili, southwestern 14
corn, Dutch 14
Indonesian soup 14
chowder
clam
creamy 68
Crock·Pot 68
Manhattan 68
New England 68
codfish 68
fish
and vegetable, New England 69
easy 69
salmon, Puget Sound 69
gumbo
seafood, easy 70
shrimp 70
lobster 73
Russian solianka 73

Squab
roast, with wild rice 65

STEWS
chicken
Brunswick stew 14
quick 15

chowder, see Soups
cioppino 71
crawfish etouffee 72
jambalaya, see Jambalaya
oyster
easy 72
holiday 72
paella, California 70
shrimp etouffee 72

TURKEY
and spinach lasagna with white sauce . . . 51
breasts
cacciatore 48
piccata 48
plantation turkey 49
cheese casserole 51
curry 48
cutlet Pacifica 49
gobble-it-up casserole 49
ratatouille 51
whole turkeys
harvest turkey dinner 50
roast, with giblet gravy 50
rotisserie-barbecued 50
smoked, with apricot glaze 50

Library of Congress Cataloging in Publication Data
Main entry under title:
Potpourri of poultry & seafood favorites of home
    economics teachers.
    Includes index.
    1. Cookery (Poultry)   2. Cookery (Seafood)
I. Favorite Recipes Press.   II. Title: Potpourri of
poultry and seafood favorites.
TX750.P66 1985   641.6'65   85-6904
ISBN 0-87197-196-8

PHOTOGRAPHY CREDITS

Concord Grape; Spanish Green Olive Commission; National Pasta Association; The J. M. Smucker Company; Idaho Potato Commission; Fleischmann's Margarine; National Macaroni Institute; California Prune Advisory Board; Spice Islands; The Rice Council; United Dairy Industry Association; Louisiana Yam Commission; California Avocado Advisory Board; National Duckling Council; Charcoal Briquet Institute; National Fisheries Institute; Olive Advisory Board; Ocean Spray Cranberries, Inc.; American Dairy Association; Norway Sardine Industry; Tuna Research Foundation; Sunkist Growers; The American Mushroom Institute; The McIlhenney Co.; Ruth Lundgren, Ltd., South African Rock Lobster Service Corp.; American Dry Milk Institute, Inc.; International Shrimp Council.
    Cover photograph compliments of Florida Citrus Commission.

Cookbooks available from Favorite Recipes Press are chock-full of mouth-watering, home-tested recipes that earn you the best compliment of all... "More Please!"

Every Favorite Recipe Press Cookbook is fully indexed and includes: • 128 to 232 pages • 300 to 500 delicious family-pleasing recipes • lie-flat spiral binding • wipe-clean color covers • color or black-and-white photos

TITLE	Item #	Price
1985 COOKBOOK COLLECTIBLES — Set includes: • THE JUST-FOR-TWO COOKBOOK, including menus for special occasions • THE COMPLETE VEGETABLE COOKBOOK, including nutritious main dishes • POTPOURRI OF POULTRY AND SEAFOOD FAVORITES • THE COMPLETE CAKE COOKBOOK, including fancy cakes and frostings	60399	$19.95
OTHER BEST SELLERS FROM FAVORITE RECIPES PRESS		
MICROWAVE MAGIC — work magic with your microwave!	60380	8.95
FAVORITE RECIPES OF HOME ECONOMISTS — over 500 recipes with nutritional analysis	37508	7.95
THE PIES AND PASTRIES COOKBOOK — time-honored secrets of pastry making	37516	4.95
THE NORTH-OF-THE-BORDER COOKBOOK — recipes in Spanish and English	37540	5.25
GREAT AMERICAN HERITAGE COOKBOOK — regional favorites from across the land	37524	6.95
TODAY'S ALL-PURPOSE COOKBOOK — use every day for complete meal plans	36412	6.95
GROUND BEEF COOKBOOK — recipes for fancy fare, foreign favorites, casseroles, etc.	34770	6.95
HOLIDAY SEASONS — including special occasion menus	14974	6.95
COOK LITE & EAT RIGHT — the be-good-to-yourself cookbook	34789	4.95
COOKING WITH CONVENIENCE FOODS — creative budget-wise recipes	47562	4.95
ENTERTAINING MADE EASY — for simple elegance	47570	4.95
NEW DESSERTS COOKBOOK — perfect for any occasion	60402	7.95
BREADS — bread-baking expertise at your fingertips	14915	4.95
CASSEROLES — the perfect casseroles for family suppers or celebrations	60410	4.95
HOLIDAY COOKBOOK — holiday specialties for all seasons	38857	6.95
BETTY'S BEST RECIPES! From THE TENNESSEAN ... Reduced!	29254	5.95
MEATS — over 475 recipes for every kind of meat, poultry and seafood	14923	4.95
OUTDOOR COOKBOOK — the total plan for outdoor cooking	34762	4.95
HONEY COOKBOOK, Nature's Golden Treasure ... Reduced!	01619	6.95

FAVORITE RECIPES PRESS COOKBOOK ORDER FORM

TITLE	Item #	Qty.	Price	Total
Postage & Handling	99929		$ 1.95	$ 1.95

Subtotal	
Add state & local tax	
Total Payment	

PS

To place your charge card orders,
call our toll-free number
1-800-251-1542
or clip and mail convenient order form.

Name _____

Address _____

City _____ State _____ Zip _____

Daytime Phone ( ) _____

☐ Payment enclosed.

☐ Please Charge My: ☐ MasterCard ☐ Visa

Expiration Date _____

Account Number _____

Signature _____

- No COD orders please.
- Prices subject to change without notice.
- Books offered subject to availability.
- Make checks payable to Great American Opportunities.

Please mail completed
order form to:
Great American Opportunities, Inc.
P. O. Box 77, Nashville, TN 37202